FRANCA HELG HOUSE
GALLIATE LOMBARDO, 2018

PHOTOS BY
HEINZ PETER KNES

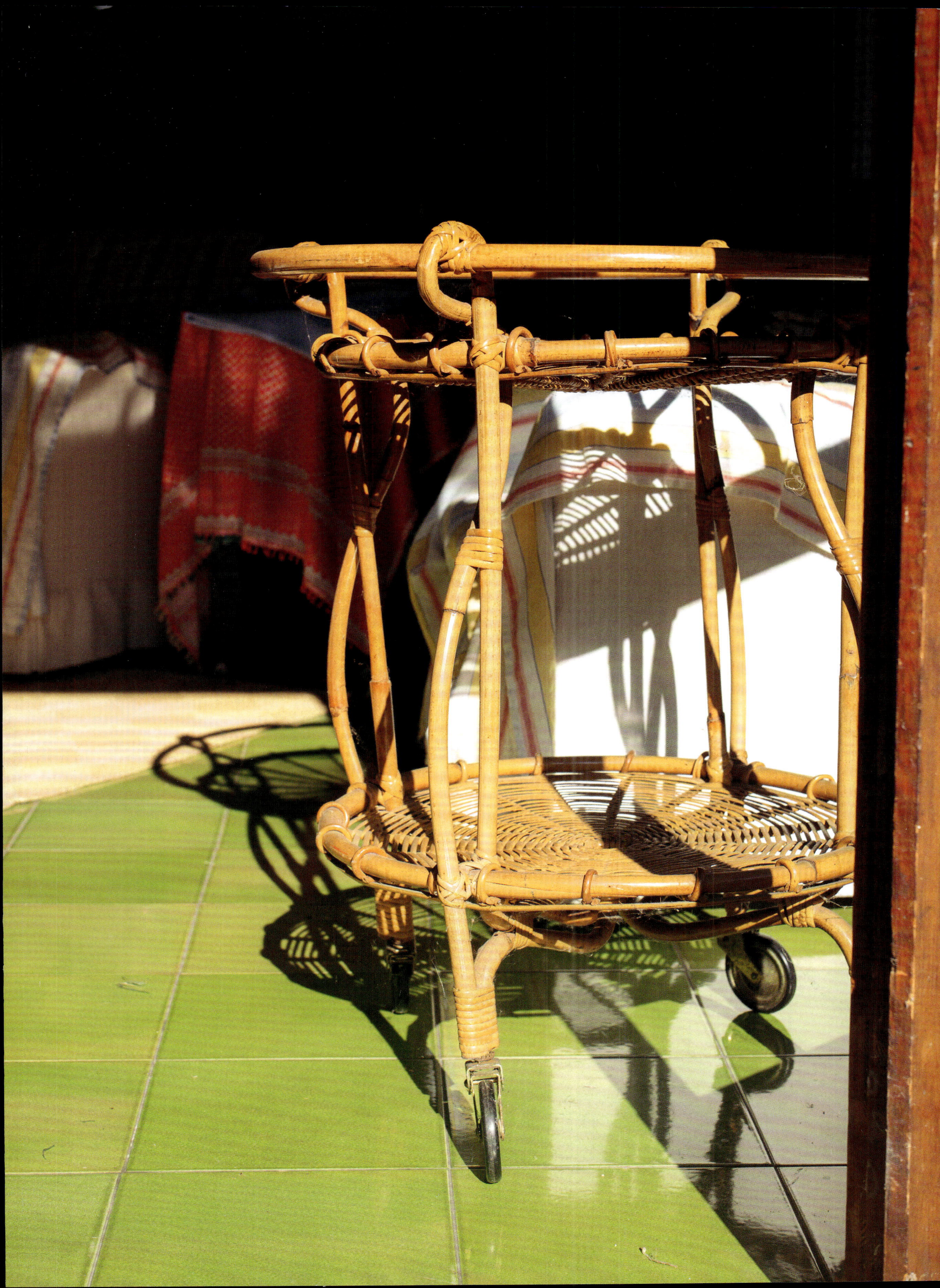

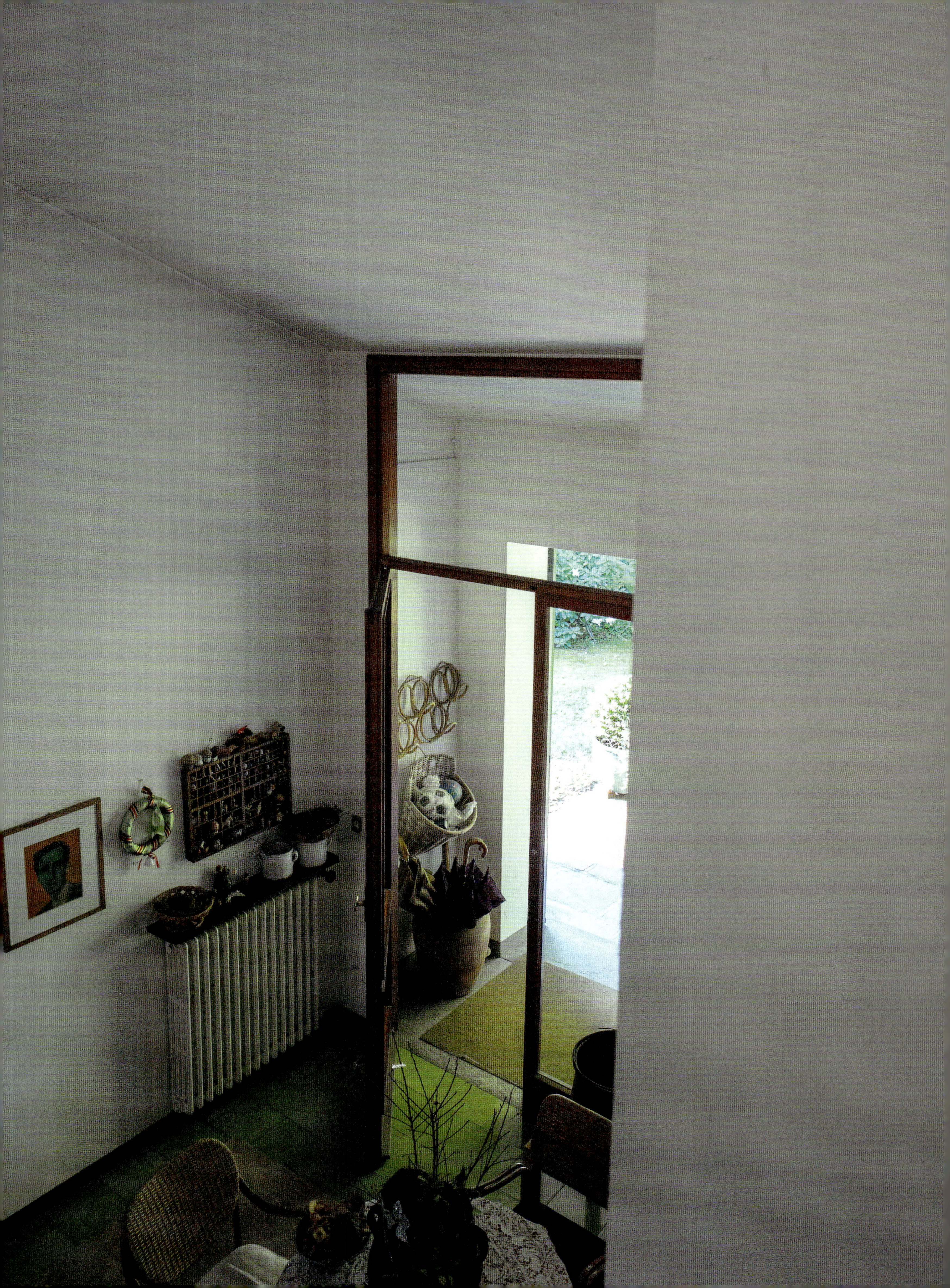

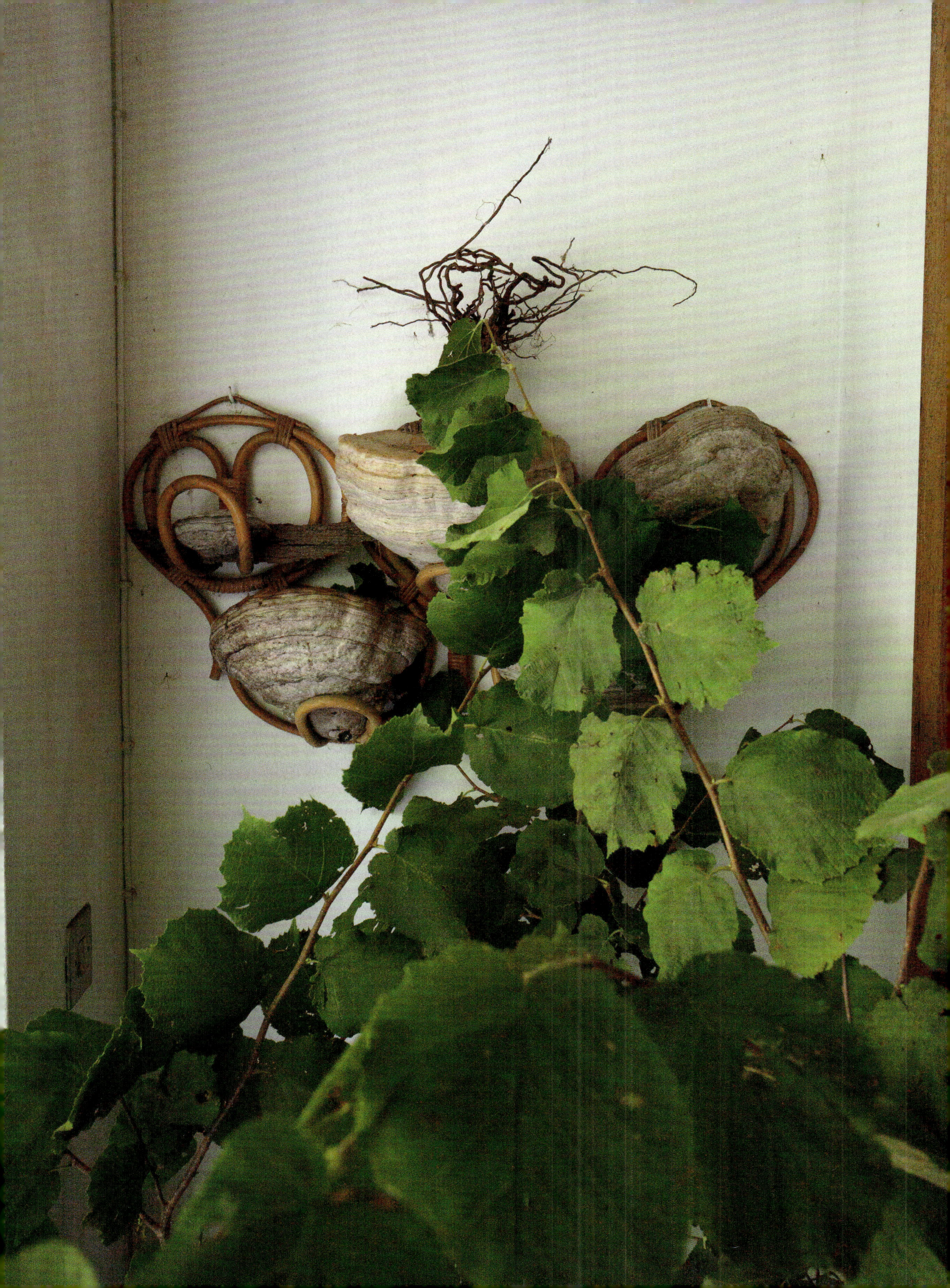

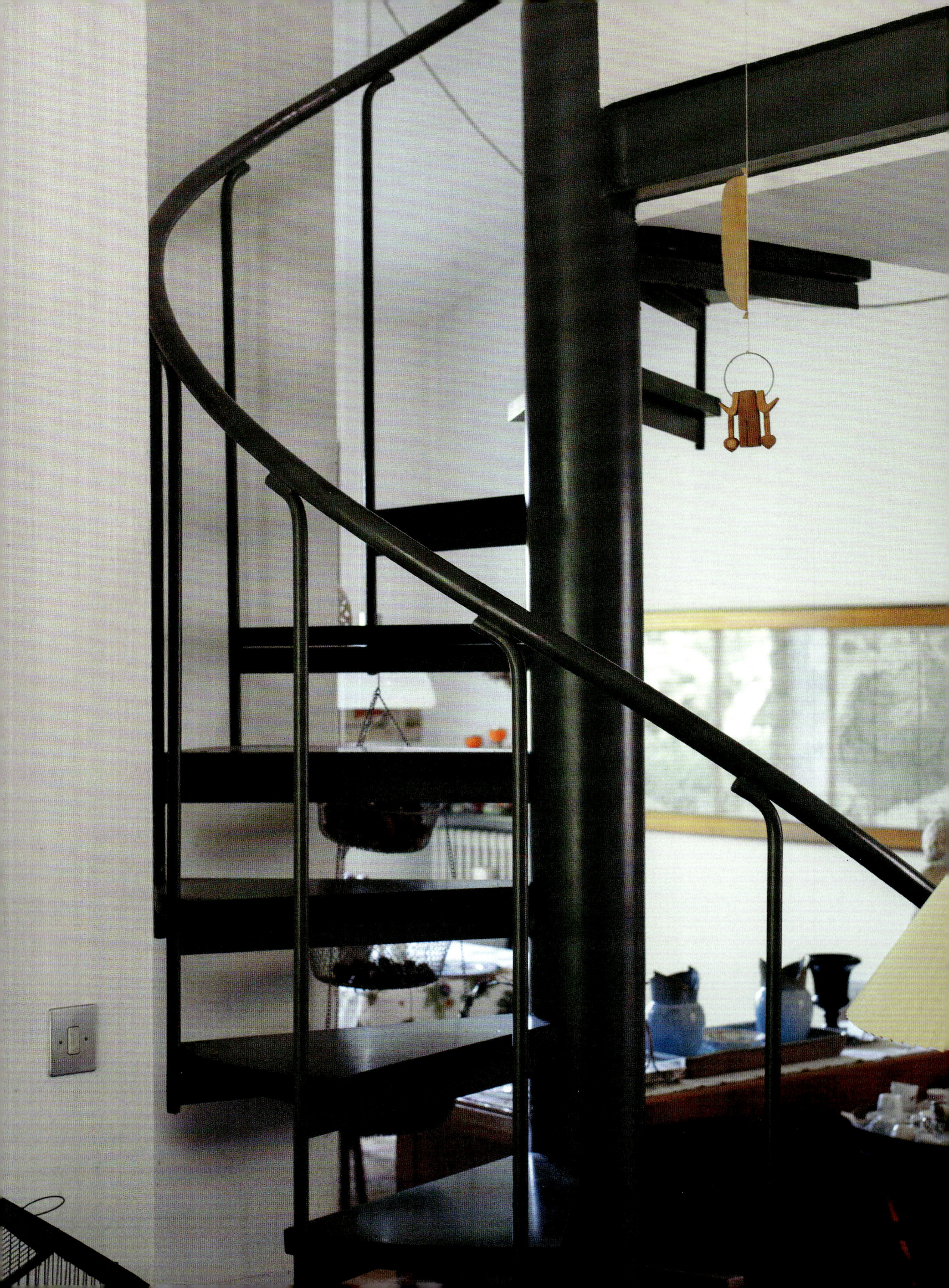

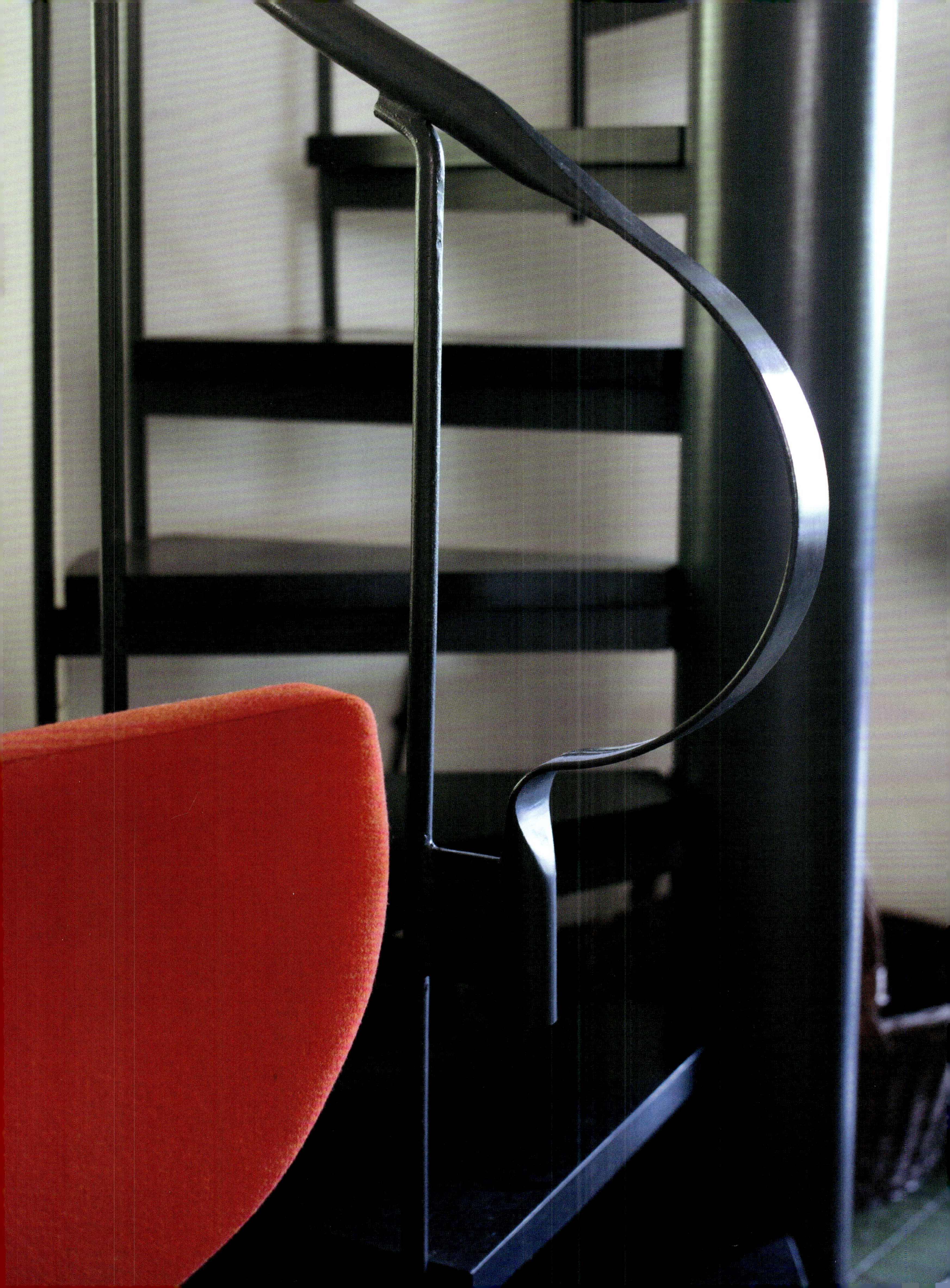

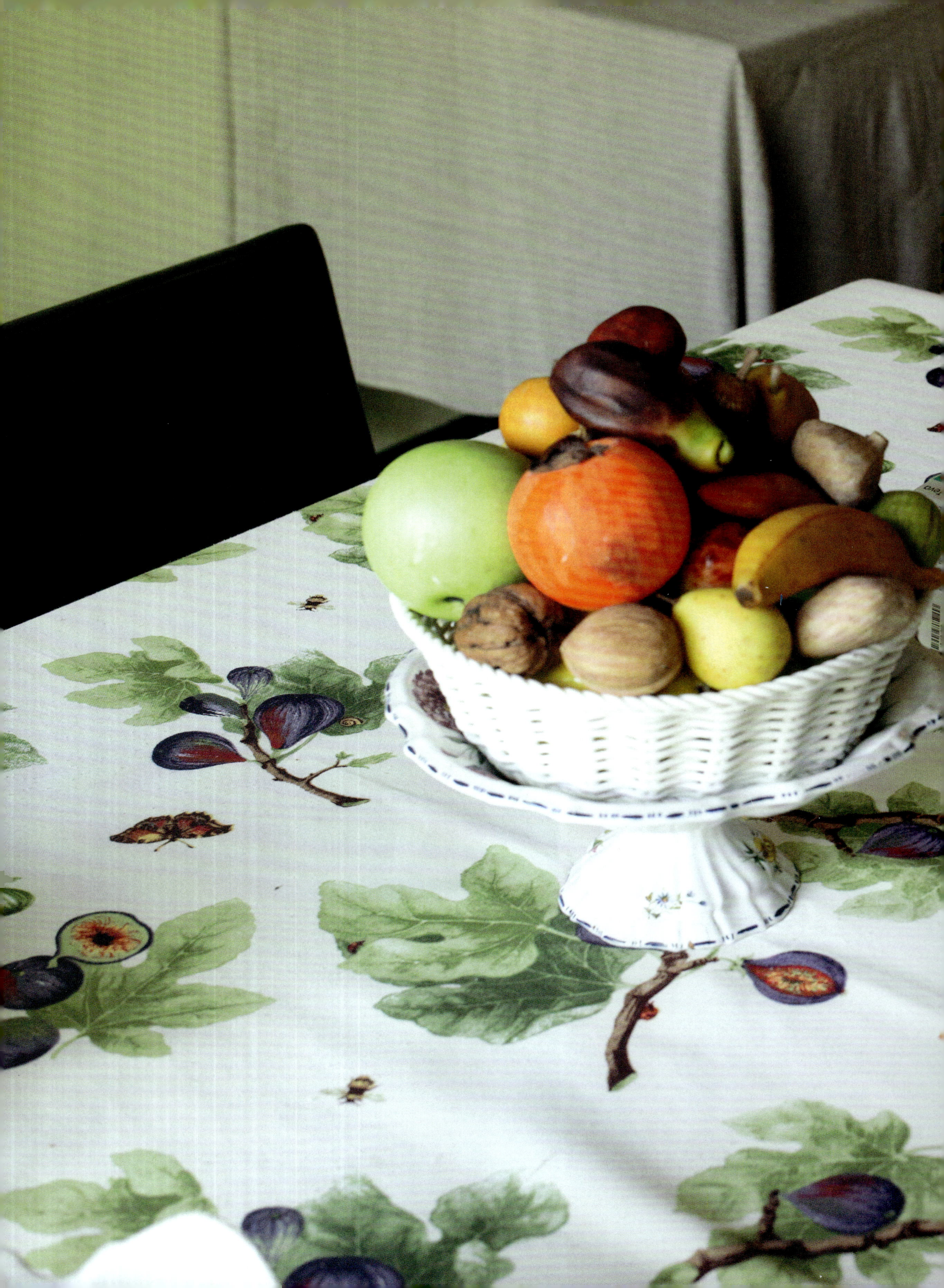

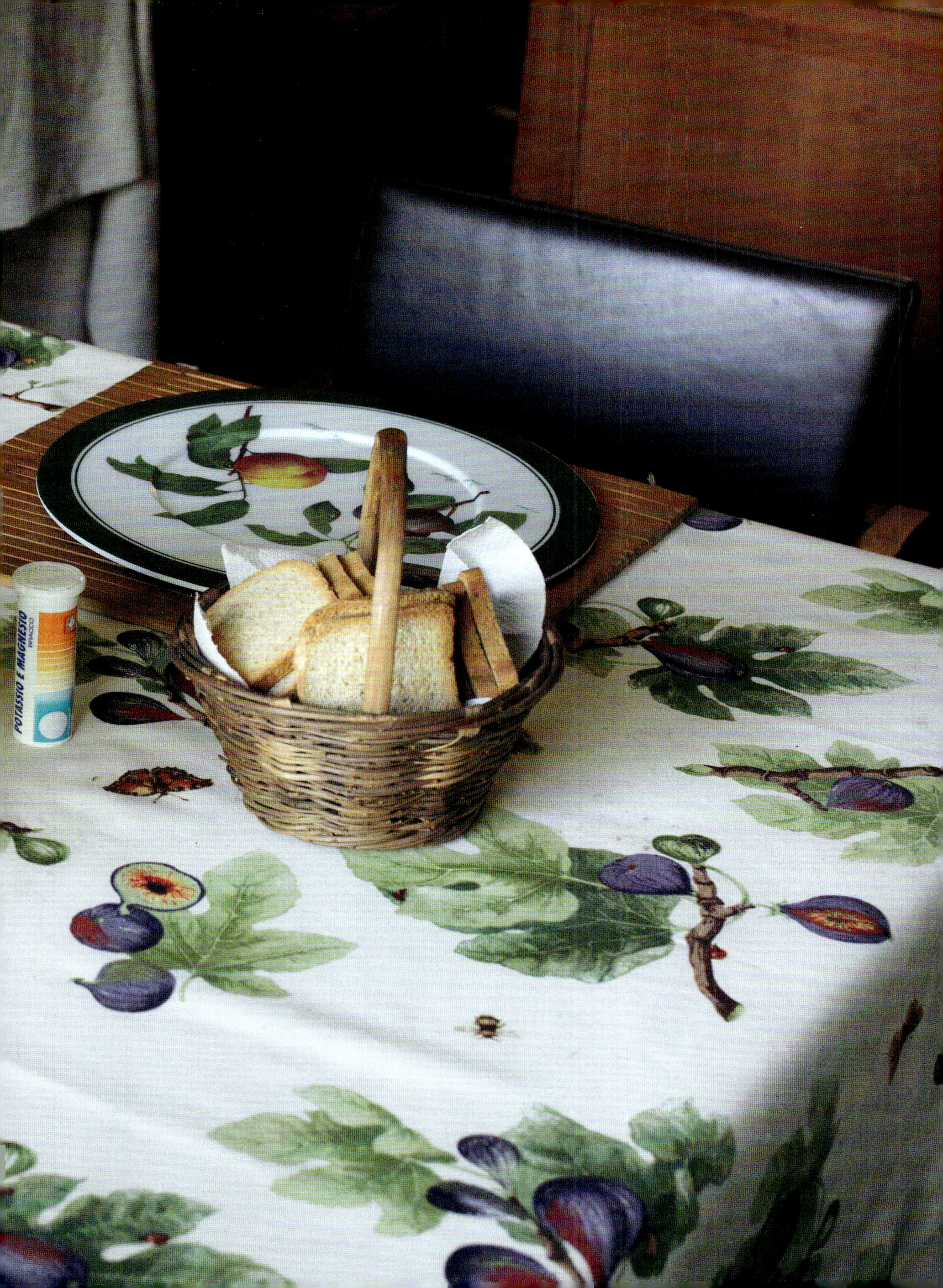
POTASSIO E MAGNESIO

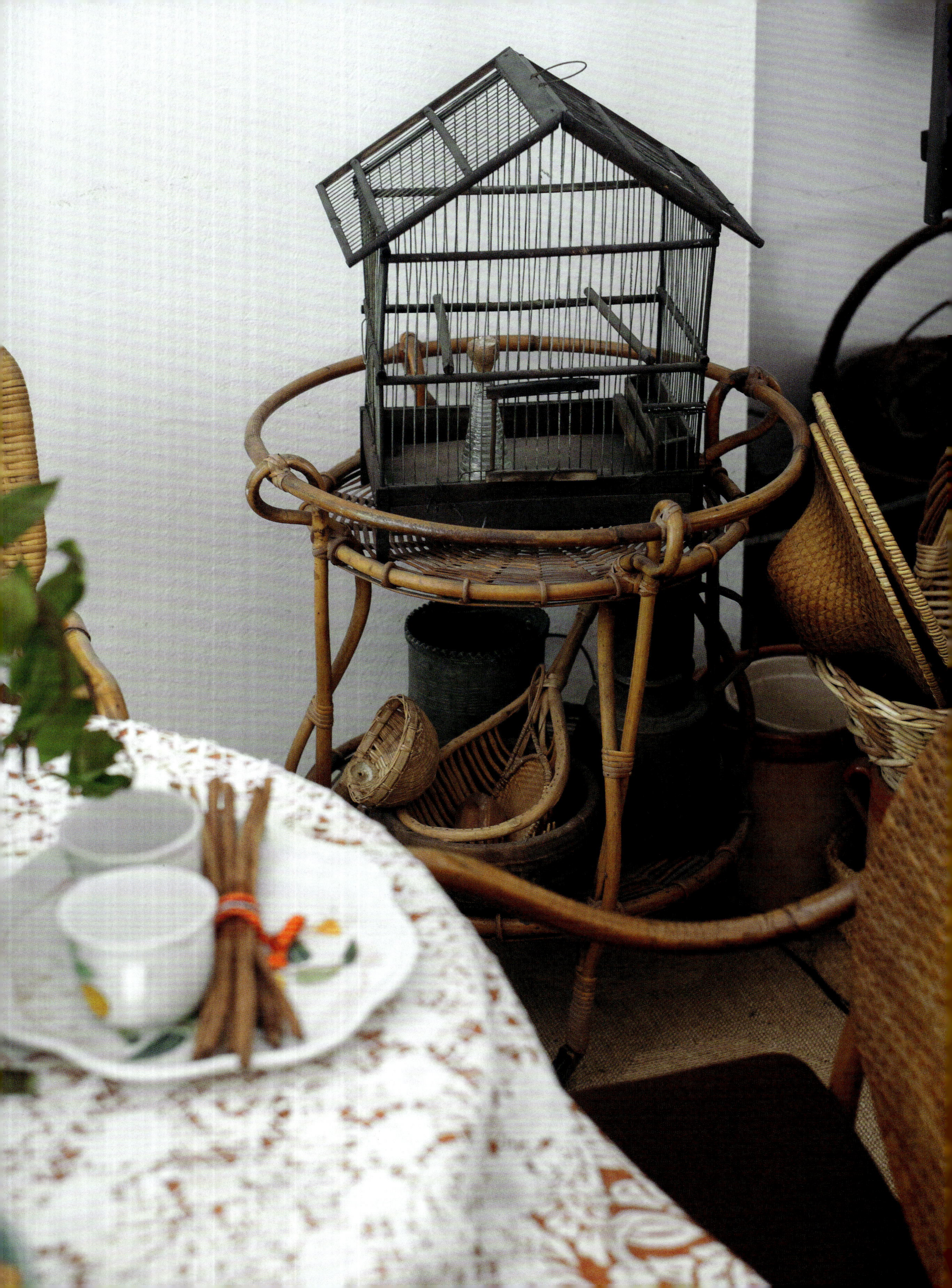

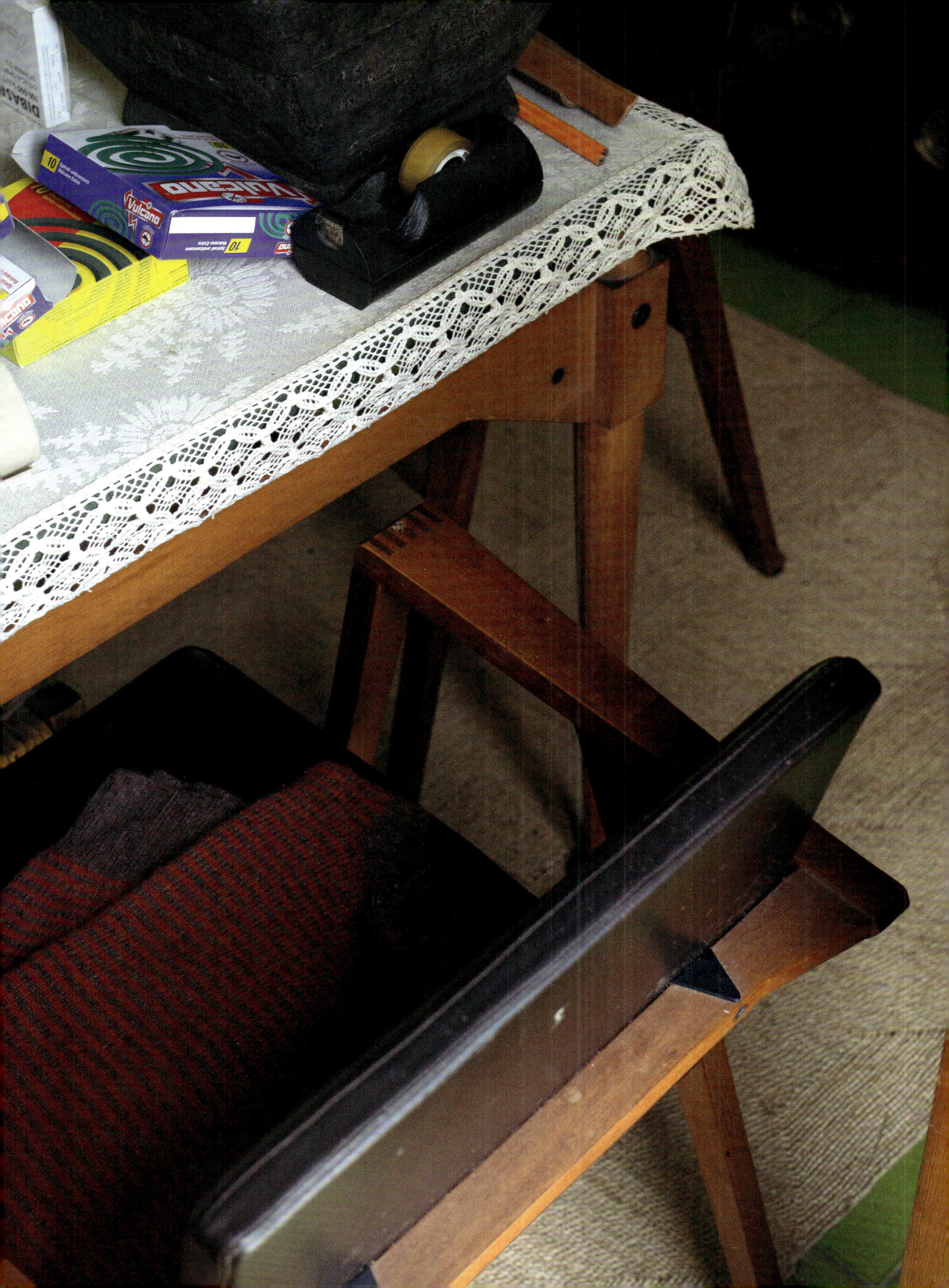

Vulcano
10

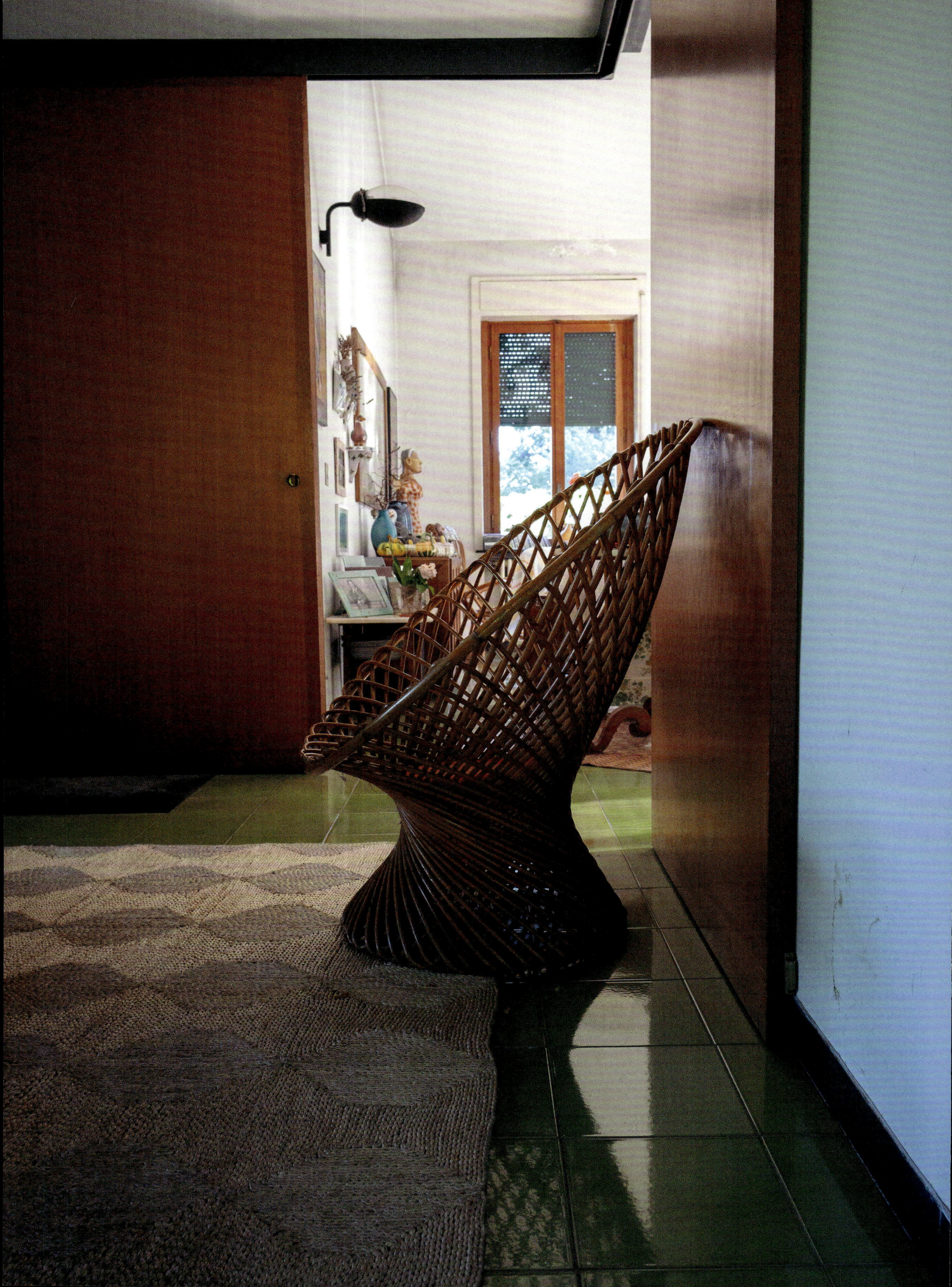

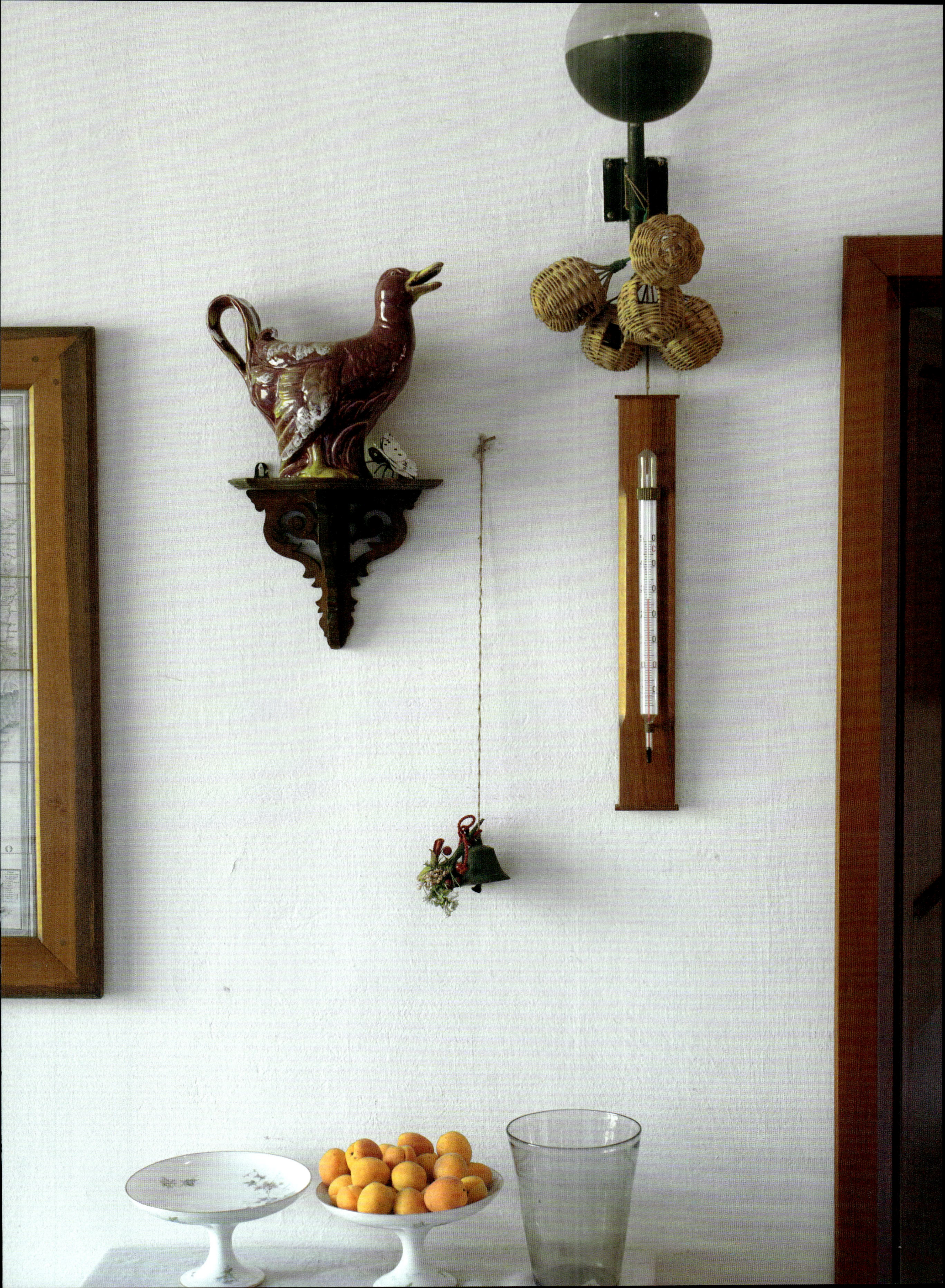

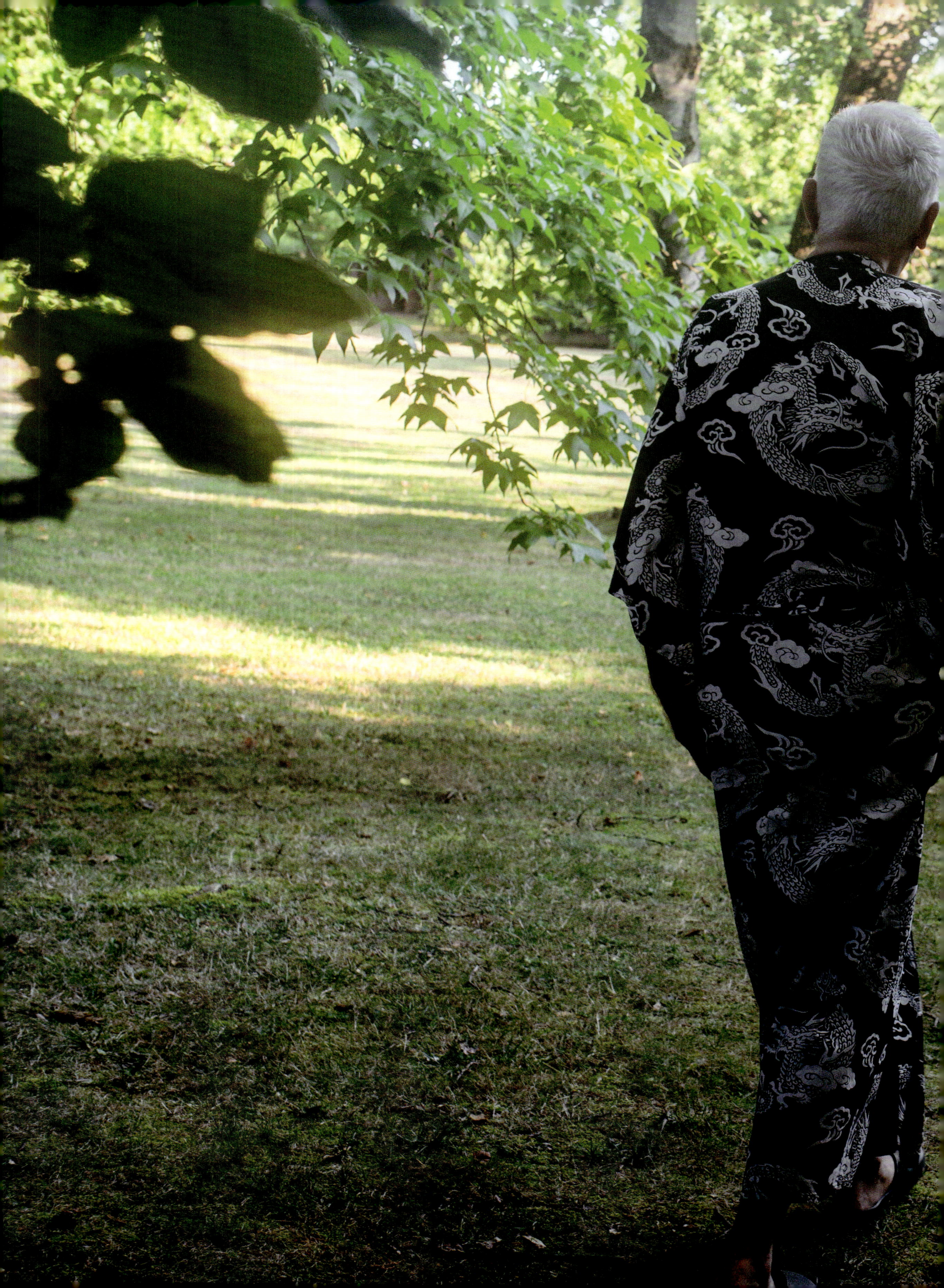

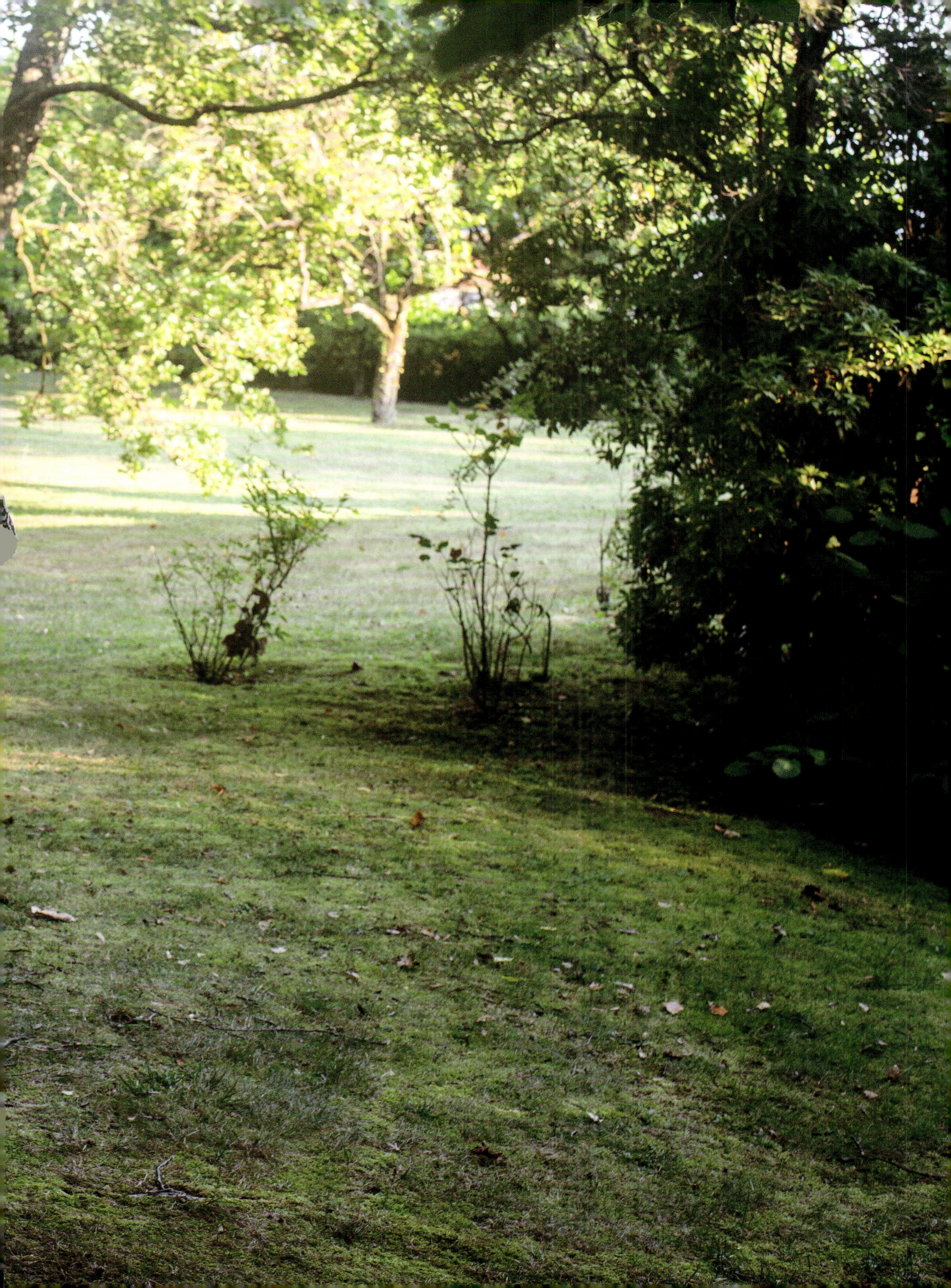

THE LAST DAYS IN GALLIATE

LEONOR ANTUNES

SKIRA

Pirelli HangarBicocca

FOREWORD

The exhibition by Leonor Antunes, a prominent artist who in 2019 is representing Portugal at the Venice Biennale, is a project that has arisen out of a prolonged period of research into the history of Milan and its cultural scene, closely linked above all with the architecture and design of the 1950s and 1960s.

As such, it was inevitable that she would engage sooner rather than later with the history of Pirelli, which was a central player on that scene. Indeed, the first, and most extensive, work in the show—the large linoleum floor that covers the entire exhibition space—draws its inspiration from the floor of the Pirelli Tower, created by Gio Ponti.

Taking this as her starting point, Antunes has focused on the work of two great architects, Franco Albini and Franca Helg, highlighting in particular the latter, who was one of Italy's first female architects.

This exhibition thus affords an opportunity to also rediscover the history of the local area and the history of the company itself, highlighting the continuity between Pirelli's corporate culture and the identity of Pirelli HangarBicocca, which is the latest high-profile manifestation of this culture.

MARCO TRONCHETTI PROVERA
CHAIRMAN,
PIRELLI HANGARBICOCCA

PREFAZIONE

La mostra di Leonor Antunes, artista che nel 2019 rappresenta il Portogallo alla Biennale di Venezia, è un progetto che nasce da un lungo periodo di ricerca sulla storia di Milano e della sua scena culturale, strettamente legata all'architettura e al design degli anni cinquanta e sessanta.

Inevitabile è stato perciò, ben presto, l'incontro con la storia di Pirelli, che di quella scena è stato attore centrale: la prima e più ampia opera in mostra, il grande pavimento di linoleum che copre tutto lo spazio espositivo, è infatti ispirata al pavimento del grattacielo Pirelli realizzato da Gio Ponti.

A partire da questa base Antunes ha ricostruito la figura di due grandi architetti, Franco Albini e Franca Helg, mettendo in luce in particolare la personalità di quest'ultima, una delle prime donne architetto in Italia.

Questa mostra diventa quindi anche un'occasione per riscoprire la storia del territorio e la storia stessa dell'azienda, sottolineando la continuità tra la cultura d'impresa di Pirelli e l'identità di Pirelli HangarBicocca, che di questa cultura è l'ultima rilevante manifestazione.

MARCO TRONCHETTI PROVERA
PRESIDENTE,
PIRELLI HANGARBICOCCA

THE LAST DAYS IN GALLIATE

Leonor Antunes's sculptures are bound up with her scrupulous research into the place, space, and time in which they are exhibited, and they take as their starting point a sophisticated investigation into crafts and into the international modernist movement. While, at first glance, the works may appear to be abstract or imaginary forms, a more in-depth reading allows us to grasp that their output is based on memory and on complex processes of stratification, fully justifying Adam Szymczyk's definition of Antunes's pieces as "thinking objects."[1] Neither readymades nor mere citations of elements of the past, the works arise out of the selection and appropriation of details and fragments of objects, furnishings, works of art, or architecture that are admired by Antunes. Beginning with their simple measurement—an act that underpins her creative process and that becomes a bona fide tool for understanding and study—the selected elements are isolated and transformed into forms that are entirely new in terms of their scale, volume, and material. As the artist herself states: "I do not think in terms of creating something new, but rather of using the past as a source for linking things together."[2]

Classifiable as devices for knowledge and reflection, the works continually engage with the place in which they come to life, taking into account both of the institution that hosts them, its history, its architecture, and the visitors that animate it, and in a wider sense of the city and the surrounding cultural milieu. Milan and its rich modernist tradition—embodied in particular by the work of the architects Franca Helg (1920–1989), Franco Albini (1905–1977), and Gio Ponti (1891–1979)—thus becomes the thematic core of the exhibition titled *the last days in Galliate* and especially of research that sees the appearance of new figures in the panorama of references and citations most beloved by the artist. Building on a number of studies of Carlo Scarpa (1906–1978) initiated by Antunes during her participation in the 57. Venice Biennale for her majestic work *...then we raised the terrain so that I could see out* (2017), *the last days in Galliate* is inextricably linked to stories discovered and places visited during the months of preparation for the exhibition project, including the home of Franca Helg in Galliate Lombardo (in the province of Varese), the residential building she designed on Milan's Via Cimarosa, the Albini Foundation, the Pirelli Tower, the Gio Ponti Archive, the Pirelli Foundation, the Pirelli factories in Milan, Bollate, and Settimo Torinese, and the rattan furniture workshop of the Bonacina1889 company at Lurago d'Erba, near Como.[3]

The title of the exhibition *the last days in Galliate* is a reference to Franca Helg, citing as it does the name of the place located around one hour from Milan, facing Lake Varese and the Alpine foothills, where Helg designed and constructed in 1961–1962 a family home for her parents—one of the few examples of buildings designed by her not under the auspices of the Albini-Helg studio—and in which she herself then lived for the last years of her life. A key figure in the Milanese modernist tradition, Helg joined the Albini studio as a partner in 1951, and her story enables Antunes to explore the part played by female artists, architects, and designers who, during the years in which they practiced their professions, were very often isolated or forced into secondary positions in what was a working environment very much *dominated* by men. Despite the full recognition of her role by Franco Albini—who openly declared "the fact that the practice was in both of our names is proof positive of our equal participation and our relationship of reciprocal trust"[4]—and despite her renown in Italy, Helg is undoubtedly lesser known on the international architecture scene.

The title *the last days in Galliate* also alludes to another pioneer, the Cuban designer Clara Porset (1895–1981), whose cutting-edge approach to interior design had been at the heart of an Antunes exhibition at the Museo Tamayo in Mexico City (2018) and in a previous solo show at the Kunsthalle in Basel in 2013. Similarly titled *the last days in chimalistac*, after the name of the district of Mexico City where Porset had spent the last years of her life, the exhibition in Basel was the first project in which Leonor Antunes investigated and reflected upon the figure and the work of Anni Albers (1899–1994), a designer of German origins who was forced to flee to the United States in the wake of the Nazi-ordered closure of the Bauhaus school and who is today considered one of the most important names of the twentieth century thanks to her avant-garde research into graphic design and textiles.

The Milanese exhibition brings together for the first time these three figures—Franca Helg, Clara Porset, and Anni Albers—who belong to different geographical, cultural, and temporal contexts, but who share both a marked, innovative sensibility towards the integration of traditional arts on the one side and modernist design and architecture on the other, and a fundamental awareness of working towards emancipation and cultural renewal.

One of the first works that we come across on the itinerary, and the title of which is the same as that of the entire exhibition, *the last days in Galliate* (2018) faithfully reproduces a detail of the Franca Helg house in Galliate Lombardo, encapsulated starting from its spatial and temporal co-ordinates.[5] Composed of a long aluminum pipe covered in black leather, the work reflects the shape and dimensions (almost six meters long) of the handrail designed by Helg for the staircase in Galliate, but the black line of its volume, shorn of its support function, traverses the space, collapsing down from the ceiling before coming to rest on the floor. Antunes selects a characteristic architectural element of many of Albini and Helg's designs—recalling the iconic handrail made in 1961 for the stations of the Milan underground—and interprets its form by subjecting it to invisible internal and external forces such as weight and gravity, which go beyond the precise measurements and initial observations made by the artist, introducing instead a random element that certainly echoes Marcel Duchamp's experiments with the idea of a unit of measurement that would not be purely rational or standardized.[6]

The same free approach vis-à-vis a presumed "original" is to be found in the sculptures *Clara 2* and *Clara 4* (2018). Part of a larger series, these wood-and-rope works are sited directly on the floor and pay homage to Clara Porset. A student of Josef Albers (1888–1976) at Black Mountain College in North Carolina, and then a close friend of his and of his wife Anni, Porset had fled Cuba in the 1930s in opposition to the reactionary military regime of Fulgencio Batista; having taken refuge in Mexico, she began an enthusiastic research into the local folklore. It is specifically Porset's study of the traditional shape of the lowered Mexican *butaques* chair that underpins the series of Leonor Antunes's sculptures, themselves made by hand from wood and rope, albeit without practical function.

A unifying element tying together such diverse works and apparently distant histories is the major intervention on the floor, titled *modified double impression* (2018). This site-specific work covers the entire 1,400 m^2 of the exhibition space of the Shed and is the outcome of the union of different elements and sources: it is, in fact, a giant inlay of yellow, black, and gray linoleum tiles, composed on the basis of the 1978 print by Anni Albers titled *Double Impression I*, here duplicated and re-proportioned to match the space. At previous exhibitions, including the installation for the 57. Venice Biennale in 2017, Leonor Antunes had created large floor works, but it is in Milan that for the first time cork is not being used as the main covering material—often used as an inlay or incision in other materials, including brass—but linoleum. The work takes its cue from the iconic floor designed by Gio Ponti for the Pirelli Tower in 1960, for which a standardized industrial material of the period—linoleum—was deployed, but with an innovative touch through the daring use of black and white, combined with the so-called "fantastic yellow," mixed in accordance with the principle of dripping to produce a marble-like effect. For the floor of the Shed, Antunes adopts a similar color scheme (yellow, black, and gray), and thanks to the intersection between Gio Ponti's unconventional colors and the dynamism and movement that result from the amplifying of the scale of the Albers design, it achieves a new sense of volume, creating what is a new environment. The use of yellow introduces a new note into the palette habitually employed by the artist, who only rarely has recourse to primary colors, preferring instead the natural shades of her materials, such as rope, wood, leather, brass, rubber, or cork.[7]

It is not just the cultural and historical context in which the artist operates that drives her research, but also the architectural setting. Antunes engages in a systematic, carefully thought-out way with the exhibition space, creating site-specific works in which every element of the existing architecture is taken into consideration and contributes to the arrangement and final composition of the sculptural elements. Every exhibition is, then, at once a tribute to a given context and a uniquely immersive environment, as well as a total work of art in and of itself. An essential and integral part of the creative process is the positioning of the works in the space, in an operation that sees the artist devoting a great deal of time to the matter of arranging the individual pieces, personally tying ropes and elements to the ceiling until she achieves a sense of harmony and an extremely precise, calculated set-up, which completely transforms the space without the requirement to erect dividers or artificial walls. In this context, all of the works co-exist and it is almost impossible to see one work as separate from the others, in a play of overlapping levels and transparencies.

The environment generated at Pirelli HangarBicocca by the aforementioned *modified double impression*—and the use of the space in accordance with an unconventional scheme—becomes even more immersive thanks to the creation, next to a space that has an entirely horizontal thrust, of a complex system formed by works that also operate on the vertical axis, between the floor and the ceiling. With *enlarged rods* (2018)—a work composed of twenty-four slender pieces of wood with brass bases and tops, grouped into clusters of three or four and united by means of a weave of cotton-fiber rope—the artist creates a modular system of screens scattered around the Shed. Inspired by the mahogany uprights designed in 1956 by the Albini-Helg studio as flexible and modular structures for the fit-out of the Olivetti showroom in Paris—but without their characteristic triangular shelves on which, at various heights, were displayed the Olivetti typewriters and calculators, symbols of the Italian post-war economic boom—the vertical elements designed by Antunes are expanded to match the height of the exhibition space and become tools for looking through, lenses, or diaphragms that, in their repetition, break the symmetry of the environment, recalling central themes in minimalist sculpture, such as the idea of modularity and the concept of seriality.

The triangular relationship that is established between the object, the space, and the viewer is also central to *shed* (2018), a work named after the place where it was created—the gallery at Pirelli HangarBicocca known as the Shed. Like enlarged rods, *shed* uses as its launch pad an element designed by the Albini-Helg studio: the LB7 bookcase, renowned for its infinite assembly options, used a pre-defined system of vertical elements and horizontal shelves without the need for anchoring to the wall, allowing it to be freely positioned, simply standing in place thanks to the pressure between the floor and ceiling. *Shed*'s thirty-two pieces of white aluminum and brass, enlarged with respect to the original proportion so as to fit perfectly into the space between the floor and the metal beams of the ceiling, are divided into two symmetrical, mirrored groups, distributed one next to the other, in line with the gantry crane that crosses the space longitudinally. In the intersection with the existing architecture, they create sub-divisions and more intimate spaces, perfect for moments of reflection.

Alongside the works, and naturally the viewer engaging with them, it is light that helps to create the volumes; indeed, light is used as a sculptural, rhythmic element, with an effect that is very different from any traditional museum lighting system. The exhibition is illuminated by the artist using *lamps* (2018), a series of twenty-three tubular-brass lamps each unfolding in a single uninterrupted line from the base to the summit, where the bulb is attached, the height of which corresponds to that of a hypothetical human figure. With their environmental illumination, these sculptures delineate intimate spaces with a human-scale, domestic feel, in contrast to the immensity of the surrounding setting. In parallel, and in addition to the intervention on the existing floor, the space is totally transformed by the opening of eight skylights that bring, for the first time, natural overhead light into the Shed. The rays of light—or the darkness in the evening—penetrate through the openings in the ceiling, modifying at once the perception of, and the atmosphere within, the space, depending on their intensity and on the time of day, or the month, in which the visit takes place.

Fascinated by the uniqueness and by the specific technical skills and manual processes that are intrinsic to craft production, and which are necessarily divergent from rapid, massive industrial manufacturing, for *the last days in Galliate* Antunes is experimenting for the first time with two new materials: cane, the strands of which can be curved by hand using heat, and rattan, which is thinner and more ductile, its strands being woven around the cane. Building on the collaboration that was developed in the 1950s and 1960s between the Albini-Helg studio and the Vittorio Bonacina company—one of the last manufacturers in Europe still producing furniture from natural fibers—the artist created the series of six hanging sculptures titled *Franca* (2018). For Antunes, it was important to work with the same company that Albini and Helg had collaborated with, as was the idea of having the same people make the new objects. The business, today renamed Bonacina1889, is indeed run by the third generation of the family and the current owner, Mario Bonacina, had worked directly with Franca Helg. To make the new sculptures, which enlarge—until they reach a length of almost four meters—the detail of a table leg and the hooks of a coat hanger designed by Helg in 1955 and 1959, respectively, Antunes proceeded deliberately in the footsteps of Franca Helg, making life-sized copies on paper of the two-dimensional design of the object (the sculpture in this case) and then using it as a guide for the bending of the canes. Working closely with the craftspeople at Bonacina, and just as had happened to Franca Helg, it became necessary for Antunes to adjust the original design to match the characteristics and limits imposed by the materials and to put her trust in the skills of the talented artisans. In the exhibition, the *Franca* sculptures are accompanied by a further series of works that duplicate the forms but differ in the material used (in this case, brass), and consequently in the method of processing. These divergences are made clear in the title, *discrepancies with F.H.* (2018).

In the exhibition at Pirelli HangarBicocca, the catalogue may be to all intents and purposes seen not as a separate publication documenting it, but rather as an integral part of the exhibition itself, thus underlining its conceptual nature. First of all, the format of the catalogue, and the choice of paper stock and binding are the same as those of the *Rivista Pirelli*, the iconic periodical published by Pirelli from 1948 to 1972, in which technical and scientific information appeared alongside up-to-the-minute social and cultural discussion. The magazine, distributed via newsstands and as such intended for a mass-market (non-elitist) readership, benefited from the input of intellectuals such as Italo Calvino, Umberto Eco, and Eugenio Montale, and it was not unusual to find within it advertising campaigns and projects created by artists and designers such as Bruno Munari in response to commissions from Pirelli itself. Leonor Antunes was immediately captivated by the history contained in the periodical and the idea of referencing it through the exhibition catalogue seemed like a natural choice to make.

As a testament to some of the experiences and the places encountered during the genesis of the exhibition, and in addition to the images of the show itself taken by Nick Ash, the catalogue also contains photographs by Heinz Peter Knes at Galliate Lombardo, Milan, Settimo Torinese, and Lurago d'Erba. Like the works of Antunes, these images are never explanatory references; rather, they aim to capture something of the atmosphere through details and fragments. They amount to a sequence of close-ups that are echoed in the works in the exhibition: the catalogue opens with shots of the house and garden designed by Franca Helg at Galliate Lombardo and today entrusted to the architect Antonio Piva, her student at the Politecnico and subsequently a partner in the Albini-Helg studio. It then continues with photographs of the interior of the Pirelli plants at Bollate, Milan, and Settimo Torinese, in which the focus is on the materials used, such as natural rubber and copper wire, which albeit captured in the industrial process of manufacturing tires, still recall manual, customized processes. Later on in the catalogue we find snapshots of rattan crafting at the Bonacina1889 factory at Lurago d'Erba.

The spirit of the magazine and the catalogue that documents *the last days in Galliate* thus merges with the figures at the forefront and the works themselves, contributing to the exhibition's reflection on the passage of time. In an article published in 1952 in the *Rivista Pirelli* titled "Tutto al mondo deve essere coloratissimo" [Everything in the world must be colorful], Gio Ponti expresses his love for the use of color, as well as the idea that what is deemed "traditional" is actually the result of bold experiments: "Everyone who mostly 'wears gray,' the 'darker,' the more distinguished (the people whom I detest) is always speaking of 'tradition.' Yet these poor souls are unaware that tradition has always been the exception (or rather the masterpiece that proves the rule). Tradition has always been health, strength, life, and therefore color and it has never worn gray trousers, gray jackets, or gray overcoats, which are all things that make gray faces, gray spirits, and gray lives. True tradition, the kind I adore, the kind safeguarded by innovators, has always been colorful and sanguine."[8] In the same way, the works of Leonor Antunes attribute the same value to the concept of tradition, rediscovering in certain artisanal and vernacular techniques a radical idea of innovation and understanding.

1 Adam Szymczyk, "Thinking Objects," in Adam Szymczyk (ed.), *Leonor Antunes: the last days in chimalistac*, exhibition catalogue, Kunsthalle Basel, Basel (Berlin: BOM DIA BOA TARDE BOA NOITE, 2016).

2 Leonor Antunes in Jennifer Higgie, "Sculptors discuss Sculpture," *Frieze*, 147, May 2012, pp. 204–206.

3 Other places visited by Leonor Antunes included the Piero Portaluppi Foundation, the Achille Castiglioni studio, Casa Boschi di Stefano, Villa Necchi Campiglio, the private apartment at one time inhabited by the architect Piero Portaluppi at the Casa degli Atellani, which still houses his marble collection, the Vico Magistretti Foundation Studio Museum, and the exhibitions of Amalia Del Ponte at the Museo del Novecento, *Lucio Fontana. Ambienti/Environments* at Pirelli HangarBicocca, and *Ettore Sottsass. There is a Planet* at the Milan Triennale. I think it is important to keep track of these places and stories as an index of the process of assimilation and subsequent synthesis enacted by the artist during the definition of the exhibition project.

4 Franco Albini, *Introduction* to the thesis by Franca Helg for the qualification to teach Architectural Composition at the Politecnico di Milano. Document dated July 13, 1966, held at the Franco Albini Foundation, Milan and published in Vittorio Prina, *Franca Helg a Galliate Lombardo* (Florence: Alinea, 2006), pp. 21–22.

5 In terms of the relationship and methods with which Leonor Antunes approached existing elements in order to transport them into entirely new works, it is interesting to re-read her words: "I often refer to specific communal buildings or houses in my work; however, I never document these places, I only measure them. This process helps me to delineate the work I then make in terms of size, weight, mass and gravity." Cf. Jennifer Higgie, "Sculptors discuss Sculpture," Op. cit.

6 See in particular the Marcel Duchamp work *3 Standard Stoppages* dating from 1913–1914 with which the artist proposes a personal version of the unit of measurement of the meter. The work involves dropping three meter-long threads on a canvas set horizontally, which is then cut into three strips based on the random curves assumed by the threads during their fall, thus suggesting a new idea of length.

7 It is, however, noteworthy that in the same exhibition, the series of four hanging and modular sculptures, *altereted climbing form I, II, III* (2017) and *IV* (2018), made of painted brass, feature the use of green alongside ochre, white, gold, and black. Inspired by an abstract relief by Mary Martin, a British constructivist artist, the work appears as a floating screen composed of various rectangular tiles suspended and united by very thin metal cables, in a homage to the minimalist tradition and its patterns of geometric forms and surfaces. I also like to think that the choice of such a bright, vivid color as yellow was more or less unconsciously influenced by her having seen the exhibition of Lucio Fontana's *Ambienti/Environments* during her first visit to Pirelli HangarBicocca.

8 Published in *Rivista Pirelli*, no. 5, 1952. Available online: http://search.fondazionepirelli.org/bookreader/riviste/RivistaPirelli/1952_5.html#page/26/mode/2up.

Le sculture di Leonor Antunes si legano a un'accurata ricerca sul luogo, lo spazio e il tempo in cui vengono esposte e nella loro genesi partono da una sofisticata indagine su pratiche di artigianato, le cosiddette *crafts*, e sul movimento modernista internazionale. Se a un primo sguardo le opere appaiono come forme astratte e di immaginazione, una lettura più approfondita rende conto di un lavoro che si basa sulla memoria e su complessi processi di stratificazione e che giustifica a pieno titolo la definizione data da Adam Szymczyk di "oggetti pensanti"[1]. Né ready-made né mere citazioni di elementi del passato, le opere nascono dalla selezione e appropriazione di dettagli e frammenti di manufatti, arredi, opere d'arte o architetture oggetto dell'ammirazione di Antunes e a partire dalla loro semplice misurazione — azione che sta alla base del processo creativo e che diventa vero e proprio strumento di comprensione e studio — gli elementi selezionati vengono isolati e trasformati in forme del tutto nuove per scala, volume e materiale. "Non miro a creare qualcosa di nuovo", dichiara l'artista, "bensì uso il passato come fonte per collegare le cose."[2]

Classificabili come dispositivi di conoscenza e riflessione, le opere si relazionano continuamente col luogo in cui prendono vita, sia rispetto all'istituzione che le ospita, alla sua storia, all'architettura e ai visitatori che la animano, sia, in senso più ampio, rispetto alla città e all'ambiente culturale circostante. Milano e la sua ricca tradizione modernista, e in particolare l'opera degli architetti Franca Helg (1920-1989), Franco Albini (1905-1977) e Gio Ponti (1891-1979), diventa così nucleo tematico per la mostra "the last days in Galliate" e specialmente per ricerche che vedono la comparsa di nuove figure nel panorama di riferimenti e citazioni più cari all'artista. Proseguendo alcuni studi su Carlo Scarpa (1906-1978) avviati da Antunes in occasione della sua partecipazione alla 57ma Biennale di Venezia per la maestosa opera *... then we raised the terrain so that I could see out* [poi abbiamo alzato il terreno affinché potessi vedere fuori, 2017], la mostra "the last days in Galliate" si lega intrinsecamente a storie scoperte e luoghi visitati durante i mesi di preparazione del progetto espositivo — tra cui la casa dell'architetto Franca Helg a Galliate Lombardo, in provincia di Varese, l'edificio residenziale da lei progettato a Milano in via Cimarosa, la Fondazione Albini, il grattacielo Pirelli, l'Archivio Gio Ponti, la Fondazione Pirelli, gli stabilimenti Pirelli a Milano, Bollate e Settimo Torinese e il laboratorio per la produzione di arredi in giunco dell'azienda Bonacina1889 a Lurago d'Erba, nei pressi di Como[3].

Il titolo dell'esposizione "the last days in Galliate" si riferisce a Franca Helg, citata attraverso il nome della località a circa un'ora da Milano, affacciata sul lago di Varese e le Prealpi, in cui Helg progettò e costruì nel 1961-1962 la casa di famiglia per i genitori — uno dei pochi esempi di progetti edilizi firmati da lei al di fuori dello studio Albini-Helg — e in cui aveva poi essa stessa vissuto i suoi ultimi anni. La vicenda di Franca Helg, figura chiave della tradizione modernista milanese ed entrata nello studio Albini come socia nel 1951, permette a Leonor Antunes di proseguire la riflessione, centrale nella sua pratica, sul ruolo di artiste, architetti e designer donne che negli anni in cui esercitavano la loro professione rimasero molto spesso isolate o in posizioni secondarie in quello che era un ambiente lavorativo dominato in prevalenza da uomini. Nonostante il pieno riconoscimento del suo ruolo da parte di Franco Albini — che dichiarava apertamente: "il fatto che lo studio sia intestato ad entrambi i nomi è la conferma di questa partecipazione a pari livello e in un rapporto di scambievole fiducia"[4] — e nonostante la sua notorietà in Italia, la figura di Helg è indubbiamente meno conosciuta sulla scena dell'archiettura internazionale.

"The last days in Galliate" allude anche nel titolo a un'altra personalità pionieristica, la designer cubana Clara Porset (1895-1981), il cui approccio innovativo al design d'interni era stato al centro di una mostra di Antunes al Museo Tamayo di Città del Messico (2018) e in una precedente personale organizzata presso la Kunsthalle di Basilea nel 2013. Similmente intitolata "the last days in chimalistac", dal nome del quartiere a Città del Messico in cui Porset aveva trascorso i suoi ultimi anni di vita, la mostra di Basilea rappresentava il primo progetto espositivo in cui Leonor Antunes indagava e rifletteva sulla figura e l'opera di Anni Albers (1899-1994), designer di origine tedesca costretta a fuggire negli Stati Uniti dopo la chiusura per mano dei nazisti della scuola del Bauhaus, e oggi considerata tra le figure più rilevanti del Novecento per la sua ricerca d'avanguardia nell'arte grafica e tessile.

La mostra milanese riunisce per la prima volta queste tre figure — Franca Helg, Clara Porset, Anni Albers — appartenenti a contesti geografici, culturali e temporali distanti tra loro, ma che condividono sia una spiccata e innovativa sensibilità verso l'integrazione tra arti tradizionali da un lato e il design e l'architettura modernista dall'altro, sia la fondamentale consapevolezza di lavorare in un'ottica di emancipazione e rinnovamento culturale.

Una delle prime opere che si incontrano nel percorso espositivo, e il cui titolo è omonimo dell'intera mostra, *the last days in Galliate* [gli ultimi giorni a Galliate, 2018] riproduce fedelmente un particolare della casa di Franca Helg a Galliate Lombardo restituito a partire dalle sue coordinate spaziali e temporali[5]. Composta da un lungo tubo di alluminio rivestito di cuoio nero, l'opera rispecchia la forma e le misure (quasi sei metri di lunghezza) del corrimano disegnato da Helg per la scala di Galliate, ma la linea nera del suo volume, privato della funzione di sostegno, attraversa lo spazio collassando dal soffitto fino ad adagiarsi sul pavimento. Antunes sceglie un elemento architettonico caratteristico di molti interventi di Albini e Helg — si ricordi l'iconico corrimano disegnato nel 1961 per le stazioni della metropolitana di Milano — e ne interpreta la forma sottoponendola a invisibili forze interne ed esterne quali il peso e la gravità, che esulano dalle misurazioni precise e dalle osservazioni iniziali fatte dall'artista, introducendo piuttosto un elemento di casualità che certamente è memore degli esperimenti di Marcel Duchamp sull'idea di un'unità di misura non puramente razionale o standardizzata[6].

Il medesimo approccio libero rispetto a un presunto "originale" si trova nelle sculture *Clara 2* e *Clara 4* (2018). Parte di una serie più ampia, queste opere in legno e corda sono poste direttamente a pavimento e omaggiano Clara Porset. Allieva di Josef Albers (1888-1976) al Black Mountain College in North Carolina, e divenuta grande amica sua e della moglie Anni, Porset era scappata da Cuba negli anni trenta in opposizone al regime militare reazionario di Fulgencio Batista e rifugiatasi in Messico aveva intrapreso un'appassionata ricerca sul folklore locale. È proprio lo studio di Porset sulla tradizionale forma di sedia ribassata messicana nota col nome di *butaques* alla base della serie di sculture di Leonor Antunes, anch'esse realizzate a mano in legno e corda pur tuttavia prive di funzionalità pratica.

Elemento unificante tra opere così diverse e storie apparentemente distanti è il grandioso intervento a pavimento *modified double impression* [doppia impressione modificata, 2018]. L'opera site-specific copre interamente i 1.400 metri quadrati dello spazio espositivo dello Shed ed è l'esito dell'unione di elementi e fonti differenti: si tratta infatti di un gigantesco intarsio di tasselli in linoleum giallo, nero e grigio composto a partire dal disegno di una stampa di Anni Albers del 1978 intitolata *Double Impression I*, qui duplicato e riproporzionato rispetto allo spazio. Già in occasione di mostre precedenti, tra cui l'installazione per la 57ma Biennale di Venezia nel 2017, Leonor Antunes aveva creato grandi opere a pavimento, ma è a Milano che per la prima volta non viene impiegato il sughero come materiale di rivestimento principale — spesso associato a intarsi o incisioni in altri materiali tra cui l'ottone — bensì appunto il linoleum. L'opera parte dall'iconico pavimento commissionato a Gio Ponti per il grattacielo Pirelli nel 1960, per il quale venne impiegato un materiale industriale e standardizzato dell'epoca, il linoleum, ma rinnovandolo nell'uso ardito del colore bianco e nero e accostato al cosiddetto "giallo fantastico", mescolato secondo il principio del dripping a ottenere un effetto marmorizzato. Antunes adotta per il pavimento dello Shed una cromia simile (giallo, nero e grigio) e, grazie all'intersezione tra i colori non convenzionali di Gio Ponti e il dinamismo e movimento che risultano dalla scala ampliata del disegno di Albers, crea un nuovo volume e ambiente. L'uso del colore giallo introduce anche una nuova nota nella palette solitamente utilizzata dall'artista, che solo in rari casi utilizza colori primari, privilegiando piuttosto le tinte naturali dei materiali utilizzati — come nel caso della corda, il legno, la pelle, l'ottone, la gomma o il sughero[7].

Non è solo il contesto culturale e storico in cui l'artista agisce a dare linfa alle sue ricerche, ma anche quello prettamente architettonico. Leonor Antunes si relaziona in modo sistematico e dettagliatamente meditato allo spazio espositivo, creando opere site-specific in cui ogni elemento dell'architettura esistente viene preso in considerazione e concorre alla disposizione e composizione finale degli elementi scultorei. Ogni mostra risulta dunque essere sia un tributo a un determinato contesto, sia un unico ambiente immersivo e un'opera d'arte totale essa stessa. Parte essenziale e integrante del processo creativo è il posizionamento delle opere nello spazio, in un'operazione che vede l'artista impiegata in tempi lunghissimi a sistemare e ordinare i singoli pezzi, ad annodare personalmente corde ed elementi al soffitto fino a raggiungere un'armonia e un allestimento estremamente preciso e calcolato, che trasforma completamente lo spazio pur senza la costruzione di pareti divisorie o muri posticci. In questo contesto tutte le opere coesisitono e risulta pressoché impossibile vedere un'opera separata dalle altre, in un gioco di livelli sovrapposti e di trasparenze.

L'ambiente creato negli spazi di Pirelli HangarBicocca dall'intervento a terra appena descritto *modified double impression* e l'utilizzo dello spazio secondo uno schema non convenzionale diventano un processo ancor più immersivo grazie alla creazione, accanto a uno spazio che si sviluppa interamente in senso orizzontale, di un sistema complesso formato da opere che procedono anche su un asse verticale, tra il pavimento e il soffitto. Con *enlarged rods* [aste ingrandite, 2018] — opera composta da ventiquattro elementi longilinei in legno con basi e cime in ottone, raggruppati in nuclei di tre o quattro e uniti attraverso un intreccio di corda in fibra di cotone — l'artista crea un sistema modulare di paraventi disseminati nello Shed. Ispirati ai montanti in mogano progettati nel 1956 dallo studio Albini-Helg come strutture flessibili e modulari per l'allestimento del negozio Olivetti a Parigi, ma privi delle mensole triangolari che li caratterizzavano e sulle quali, a diverse altezze, venivano esposte le macchine da scrivere e da calcolo Olivetti, simboli del nuovo boom economico dell'Italia del dopoguerra, gli elementi verticali disegnati da Antunes sono espansi fino a coincidere con l'altezza dello spazio espositivo e diventano strumenti attraverso cui guardare, lenti o diaframmi che nella loro ripetizione rompono la simmetria dell'ambiente, richiamando temi centrali nella scultura minimalista, quali l'idea di modularità e il concetto di serialità.

La relazione triangolare che si instaura tra l'oggetto, lo spazio e lo spettatore è centrale anche per *shed* (2018), opera il cui titolo restituisce alla lettera il contesto in cui nasce, ovvero la galleria espositiva di Pirelli HangarBicocca denominata appunto Shed. Come *enlarged rods*, *shed* parte da un elemento progettato dallo studio Albini-Helg. La libreria LB7, celebre per le infinite possibilità di assemblaggio, utilizzava un sistema predeterminato di elementi verticali e mensole orizzontali senza la necessità di ancoraggio a muro, potendo quindi essere posizionata liberamente nello spazio semplicemente fissata a pressione tra il pavimento e il soffitto. I trentadue elementi in alluminio bianco e ottone di *shed*, ingranditi rispetto alle proporzioni originali a occupare perfettamente la distanza tra il pavimento e le travi in metallo del soffitto, vengono divisi in due gruppi simmetrici e speculari e distribuiti uno accanto all'altro in concomitanza del carroponte che attraversa longitudinalmente lo spazio. Nell'intersecarsi con l'architettura esistente creano delle divisioni e degli ambienti più intimi e momenti di pausa.

Assieme alle opere, e naturalmente allo spettatore che vi dialoga, è la luce a concorrere alla creazione di volumi, utilizzata come elemento scultoreo e di scansione temporale, lontana da qualsiasi sistema di illuminotecnica tradizionale museale. La mostra viene illuminata dall'artista attraverso *lamps* [lampade, 2018], una serie di ventitré lampade. Realizzate con un tubolare in ottone che si dispiega in un'unica linea ininterrotta dalla base alla sommità su cui si fissa il bulbo, la cui altezza corrisponde a quella di una ipotetica figura umana, queste sculture creano con la loro illuminazione ambientale e composta degli spazi intimi e dall'aria più domestica in contrapposizione con la vastità dell'ambiente circostante. Parallelamente, e oltre all'intervento sul pavimento esistente, lo spazio è totalmente trasformato dall'apertura di otto lucernari che portano eccezionalmente, e per la prima volta, luce naturale zenitale all'interno dello Shed. I raggi luminosi — o l'oscurità nei momenti serali — penetrano dalle aperture a soffitto, modificando costantemente la percezione e l'atmosfera all'interno dell'ambiente a seconda della loro intensità e del momento del giorno, o del mese, in cui avviene la visita.

Interessata alle caratteristiche di unicità e di conoscenza di una specifica competenza tecnica e a lavorazioni manuali che necessariamente esulano da processi industriali di produzione massiva e rapida, per la mostra "the last days in Galliate" Leonor Antunes sperimenta per la prima volta due nuovi materiali: il giunco, le cui canne possono essere curvate a mano mediante l'utilizzo del calore, e il midollino, più fine e duttile e utilizzato in fili che tessono e si intrecciano attorno al giunco. Approfondendo la collaborazione che ebbe luogo negli anni cinquanta e sessanta tra lo studio Albini-Helg e l'azienda Vittorio Bonacina — una delle ultime manifatture rimaste attive in Europa per la produzione di mobili in fibra naturale — l'artista ha creato la serie di sei sculture sospese *Franca* (2018). Per Antunes è stato importante sia lavorare con la stessa azienda con cui avevano collaborato Albini e Helg sia l'idea che fossero le medesime persone a occuparsene. La manifattura, che oggi si chiama Bonacina1889, è infatti ancora condotta dalla terza generazione della famiglia, e l'attuale proprietario Mario Bonacina aveva lavorato con, e conosciuto personalmente, Franca Helg. Per la realizzazione delle sue sculture, che ingrandiscono — fino a raggiungere quasi quattro metri di lunghezza — il dettaglio della gamba di un tavolino e i ganci di un appendiabito progettati da Helg nel 1955 e 1959, Leonor Antunes ha proceduto volutamente nello stesso modo con cui aveva operato Franca Helg, ovvero riportando su carta in scala reale il disegno bidimensionale dell'oggetto (la scultura nel caso di Antunes) e utilizzandolo poi come guida per la piegatura delle canne. In questo processo di stretta collaborazione con gli artigiani di Bonacina1889, e come anche era stato per Franca Helg, si è reso necessario adattare il disegno del progetto originario alle caratteristiche e ai limiti imposti dai materiali, così come affidarsi alle competenze e abilità di chi realizza le opere. In mostra le sculture *Franca* si accompagnano a un'ulteriore serie di opere che ne duplica le forme ma che si discosta nell'uso del materiale di realizzazione, l'ottone, e conseguentemente nel metodo di lavorazione. Discrepanza sottolineata anche nel titolo, *discrepancies with F.H.* [discrepanze con F.H., 2018].

Nella mostra di Pirelli HangarBicocca il catalogo può essere a tutti gli effetti inteso non solo come una testimonianza documentale, bensì come parte integrante del progetto espositivo, a sottolinearne la natura concettuale. Innanzitutto, il formato del catalogo così come la scelta della carta e della rilegatura riprendono quelli della "Rivista Pirelli", iconico periodo pubblicato da Pirelli tra il 1948 e il 1972 in cui l'informazione tecnica e scientifica si integrava al più attuale dibattito sociale e culturale. Sulla rivista, distribuita in edicola e dunque concepita per una diffusione capillare e non elitaria, contribuivano intellettuali come Italo Calvino, Umberto Eco o Eugenio Montale e sovente si ritrovavano immagini di campagne pubblicitarie o di progetti commissionati da Pirelli ad artisti e designer tra cui Bruno Munari. Leonor Antunes è stata immediatamente affascinata dalla storia raccolta in queste pagine e l'idea di citare la rivista attraverso il catalogo della mostra è stata una scelta quasi naturale. A testimonianza di alcuni momenti e luoghi incontrati durante la genesi della mostra, e in aggiunta alle vedute dell'esposizione fotografata da Nick Ash, il catalogo contiene immagini scattate da Heinz Peter Knes a Galliate Lombardo, Milano, Settimo Torinese e Lurago d'Erba. Come le opere di Antunes non sono mai una citazione didascalica, così il riferimento e l'inclusione di immagini relative ai processi di lavoro non è diretta, piuttosto ne restituisce l'atmosfera attraverso dettagli e frammenti. Una sequenza di particolari che trovano eco nelle opere in mostra: il libro si apre con fotografie della casa e del giardino progettati da Franca Helg a Galliate Lombardo e oggi custoditi dall'architetto Antonio Piva, suo allievo al Politecnico e successivamente divenuto partner nello studio Albini-Helg; per proseguire con scatti all'interno degli stabilimenti Pirelli a Bollate, Milano e Settimo Torinese in cui lo sguardo si ferma sui materiali utilizzati come la gomma naturale e il filo di rame che, pur nel processo industriale di produzione di pneumatici, ricordano passaggi manuali e di definizione personalizzata; per poi continuare con istantanee della lavorazione di canne di giunco presso il laboratorio di Bonacina1889 a Lurago d'Erba.

Lo spirito della rivista e del catalogo che documenta "the last days in Galliate" diventa quindi un tutt'uno con le figure protagoniste e le opere, concorrendo alla riflessione della mostra sul tempo. In un articolo pubblicato nel 1952 sulla "Rivista Pirelli" e intitolato *Tutto al mondo deve essere coloratissimo*, Gio Ponti esprime il suo amore per l'uso del colore e l'idea che quanto viene considerato "tradizionale" sia frutto di ardite sperimentazioni: "Tutta la gente più 'vestita in grigio', più in 'scuro', più distinta (quella gente ch'io detesto) parla sempre della 'tradizione', ha sempre in bocca la 'tradizione' ed ignora, poveretta, che la tradizione è stata sempre l'eccezione (cioè il capolavoro che fa regola), è stata sempre salute, forza, vita, cioè colore e non ha mai vestito pantaloni grigi, giacche grigie, paltò grigi, cose tutte che poi fan le facce grigie, gli spiriti grigi, le vite grigie. La tradizione vera, quella che adoro, quella della quale son depositari i novatori, è stata sempre colorata e sanguigna."[8] Allo stesso modo, le opere di Leonor Antunes attribuiscono il medesimo valore al concetto di tradizione, ritrovando in certe tecniche artigianali e vernacolari un'idea radicale di innovazione e conoscenza.

ROBERTA TENCONI

1 Cfr. Adam Szymczyk, *Thinking Objects*, in *Leonor Antunes: the last days in chimalistac*, a cura di Adam Szymczyk, catalogo della mostra, Kunsthalle Basel, Basel - BOM DIA BOA TARDE BOA NOITE, Berlin 2016.

2 Leonor Antunes, in Jennifer Higgie, *Sculptors discuss Sculpture*, in "Frieze", 147, maggio 2012, pp. 204–206.

3 Altri luoghi visitati da Leonor Antunes sono stati la Fondazione Piero Portaluppi, lo Studio Achille Castiglioni, Casa Boschi di Stefano, Villa Necchi Campiglio, l'appartamento privato un tempo abitato dall'architetto Piero Portaluppi presso la Casa degli Atellani, in cui è ancora conservata la sua collezione di marmi, la Fondazione Studio Museo Vico Magistretti, nonché le mostre di Amalia Del Ponte presso il Museo del Novecento, "Lucio Fontana. Ambienti/Environments" in Pirelli HangarBicocca ed "Ettore Sottsass. There is a Planet" in Triennale. Penso sia utile tenere traccia di questi luoghi e storie come indice del processo di assimilazione e di successiva sintesi attuato dall'artista in fase di definizione del progetto espositivo.

4 Franco Albini, *Introduzione* alla tesi di Franca Helg per l'abilitazione all'insegnamento di Composizione Architettonica presso il Politecnico di Milano. Documento datato 13 luglio 1966, conservato presso la Fondazione Franco Albini, Milano e pubblicato in Vittorio Prina, *Franca Helg a Galliate Lombardo*, Alinea, Firenze 2006, pp. 21–22.

5 A proposito della relazione e delle modalità con cui Leonor Antunes si approccia a elementi esistenti per trasporli in opere del tutto nuove, è interessante rileggere le sue parole: "Nella mia produzione alludo spesso a particolari case o edifici pubblici, però non documento mai questi luoghi, limitandomi a misurarli. Questo processo mi aiuta a programmare il lavoro successivo in termini di dimensioni, peso, massa e gravità" (cfr. Jennifer Higgie, *Sculptors discuss Sculpture*, cit., pp. 204–206).

6 In particolare si veda l'opera di Marcel Duchamp *3 Standard Stoppages* del 1913-1914 con cui l'artista propone una personale versione dell'unità di misura del metro. L'opera nasce infatti facendo cadere tre fili lunghi un metro su una tela posta orizzontalmente, che viene quindi tagliata in tre strisce seguendo le curve casuali assunte dal filo durante la caduta, suggerendo così una nuova idea di lunghezza.

7 È opportuno tuttavia notare che, nella stessa mostra, la serie di quattro sculture appese e modulari *altereted climbing form* [*forma rampicante alterata*] *I*, *II*, *III* (2017) e *IV* (2018), realizzate in ottone dipinto, oltre al colore ocra, bianco, oro e nero presentano l'uso del verde. Ispirata a un rilievo astratto di Mary Martin, artista esponente del costruttivismo britannico, l'opera si presenta come uno schermo fluttuante composto da svariati tasselli rettangolari sospesi e uniti da sottilissimi cavi in metallo, in un omaggio alla tradizione minimalista e ai suoi pattern di forme e superfici geometriche. Mi piace inoltre pensare che la scelta di un colore così brillante e vivido come il giallo sia stato in modo più o meno inconscio influenzata anche dalla mostra sugli "Ambienti/Environments" di Lucio Fontana, visitata da Leonor Antunes durante il primo sopralluogo in Pirelli HangarBicocca.

8 Pubblicato in "Rivista Pirelli", 5, 1952. Disponibile online: http://search.fondazionepirelli.org/bookreader/riviste/RivistaPirelli/1952_5.html#page/26/mode/2up.

PIRELLI PLANTS
SETTIMO TORINESE
AND BOLLATE, 2018

PHOTOS BY
HEINZ PETER KNES

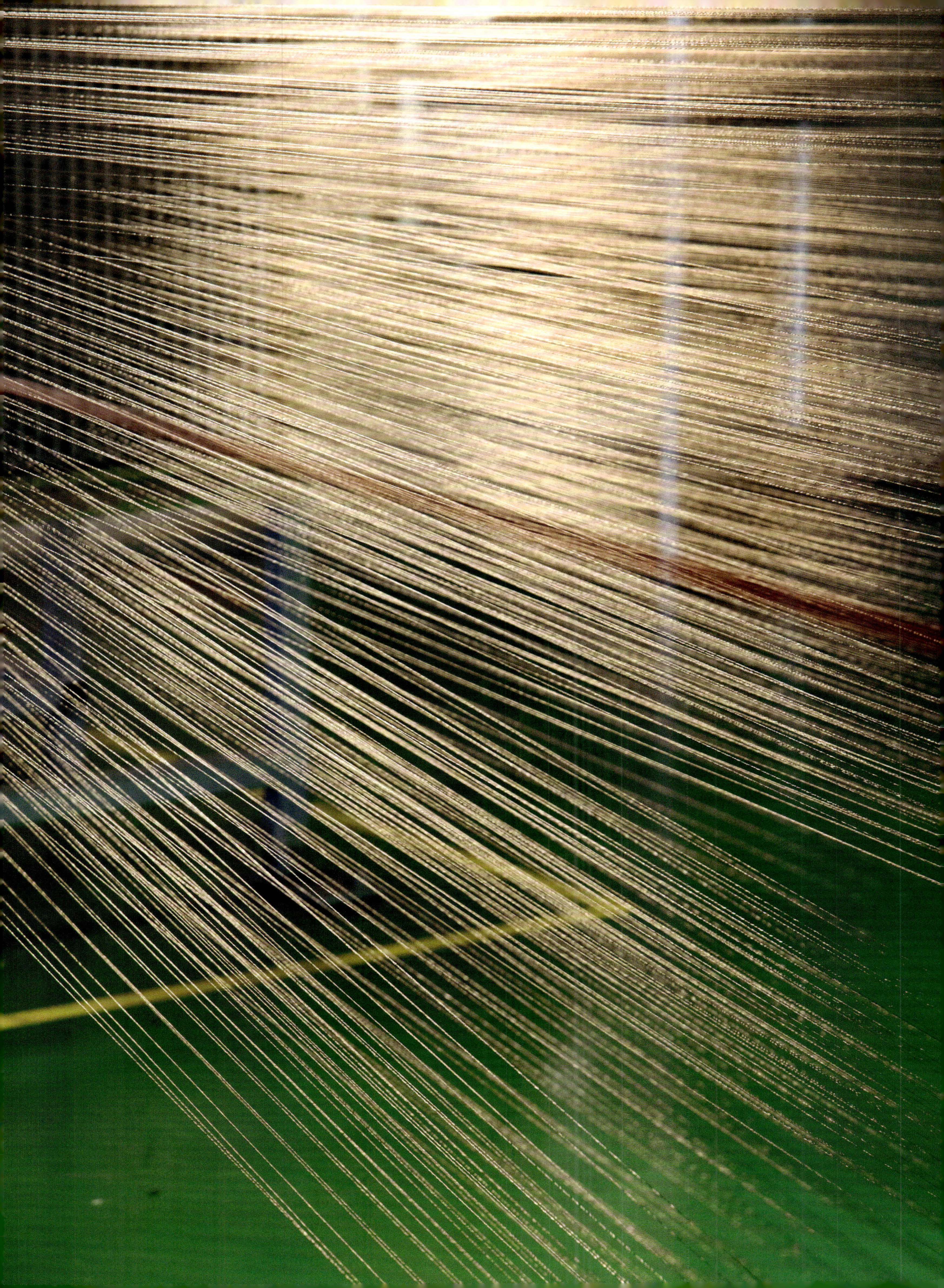

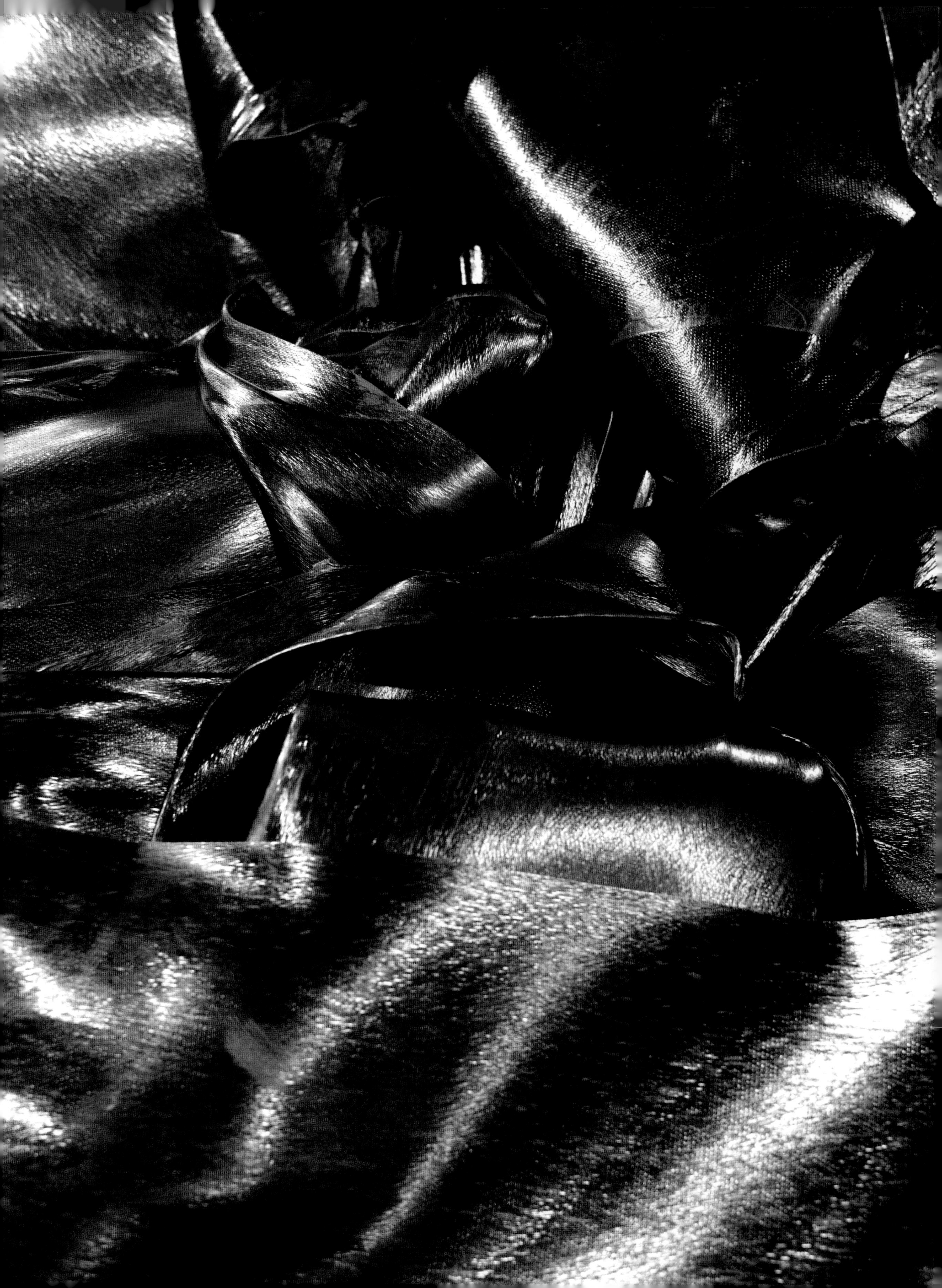

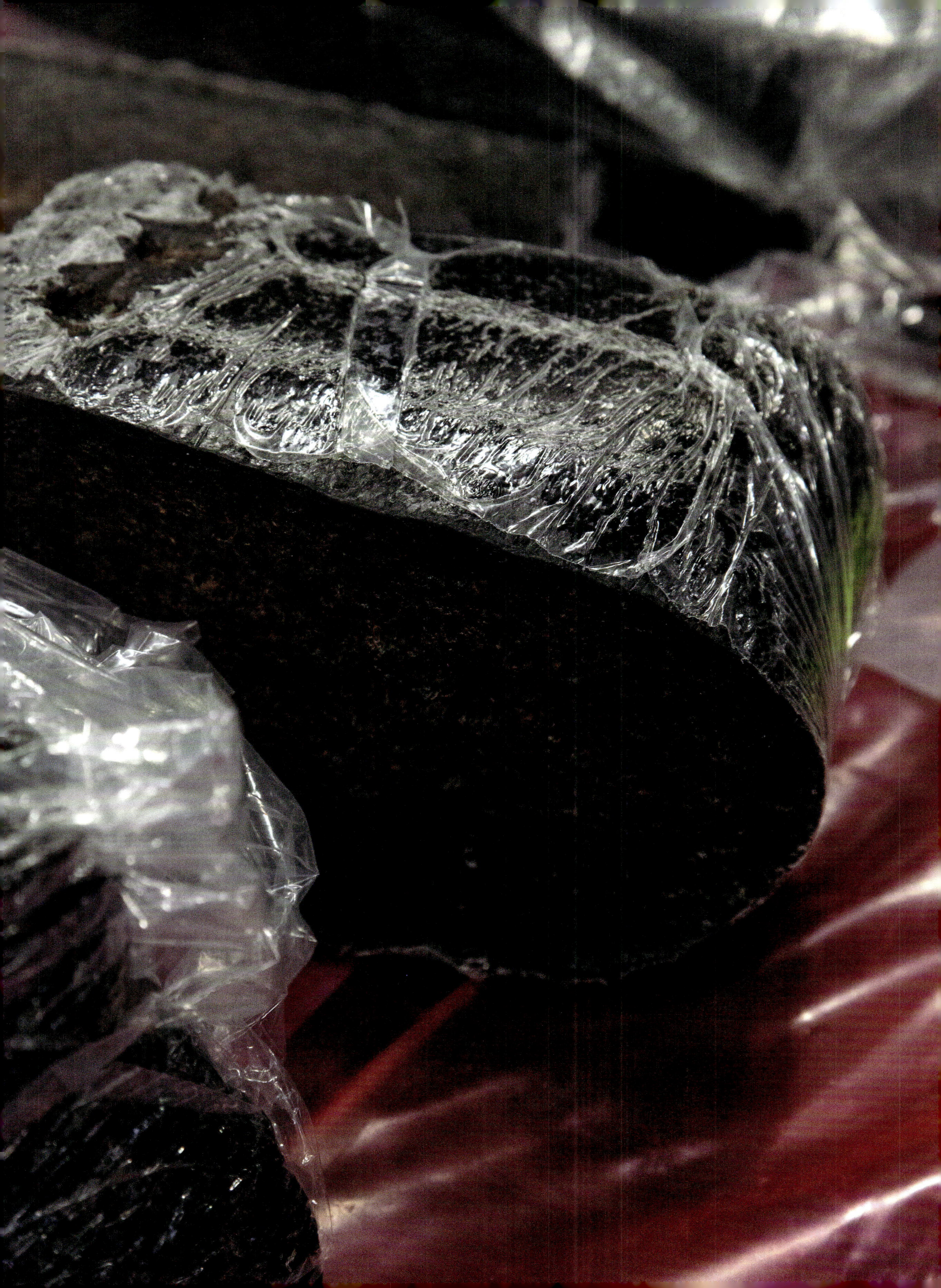

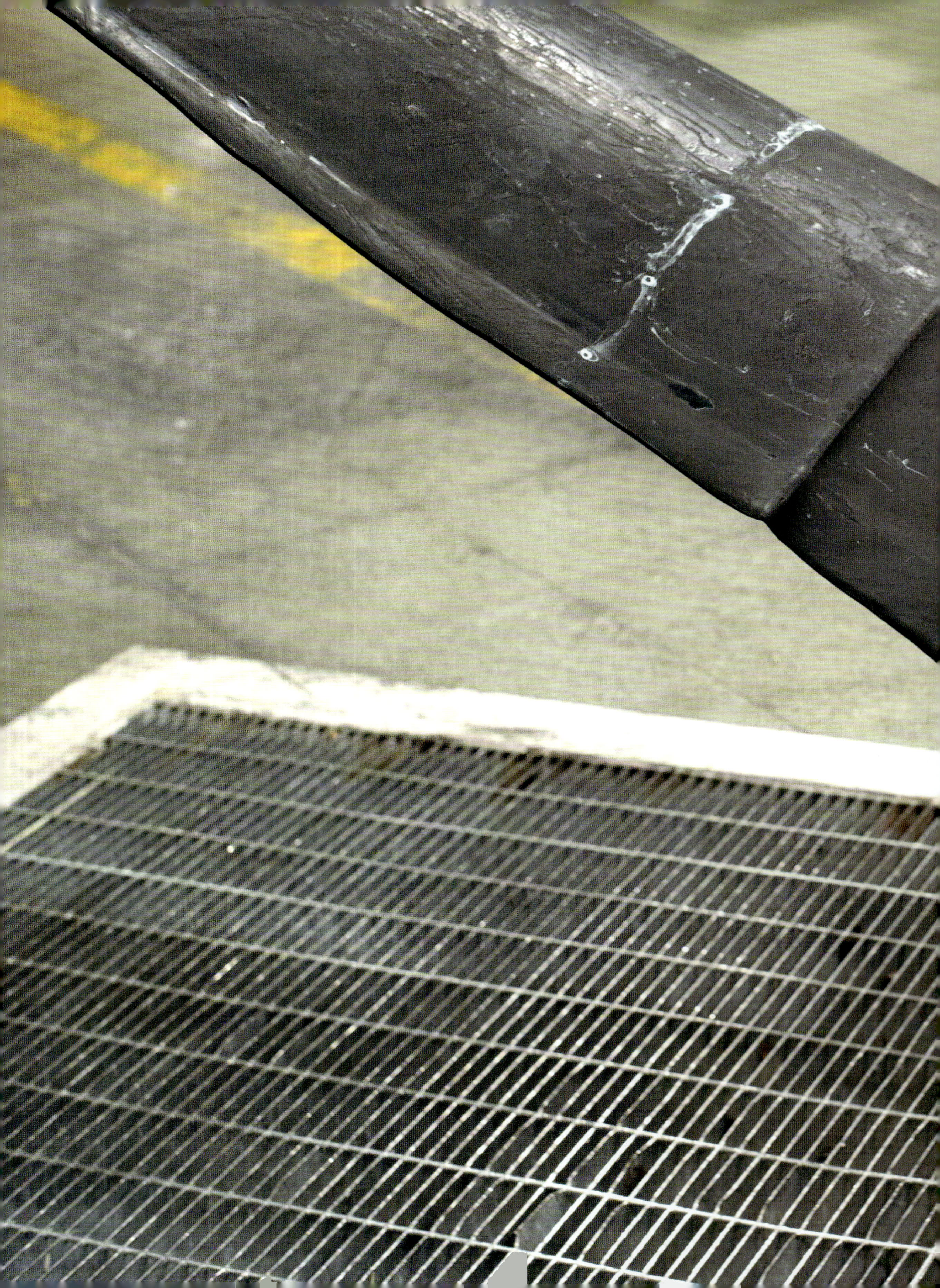

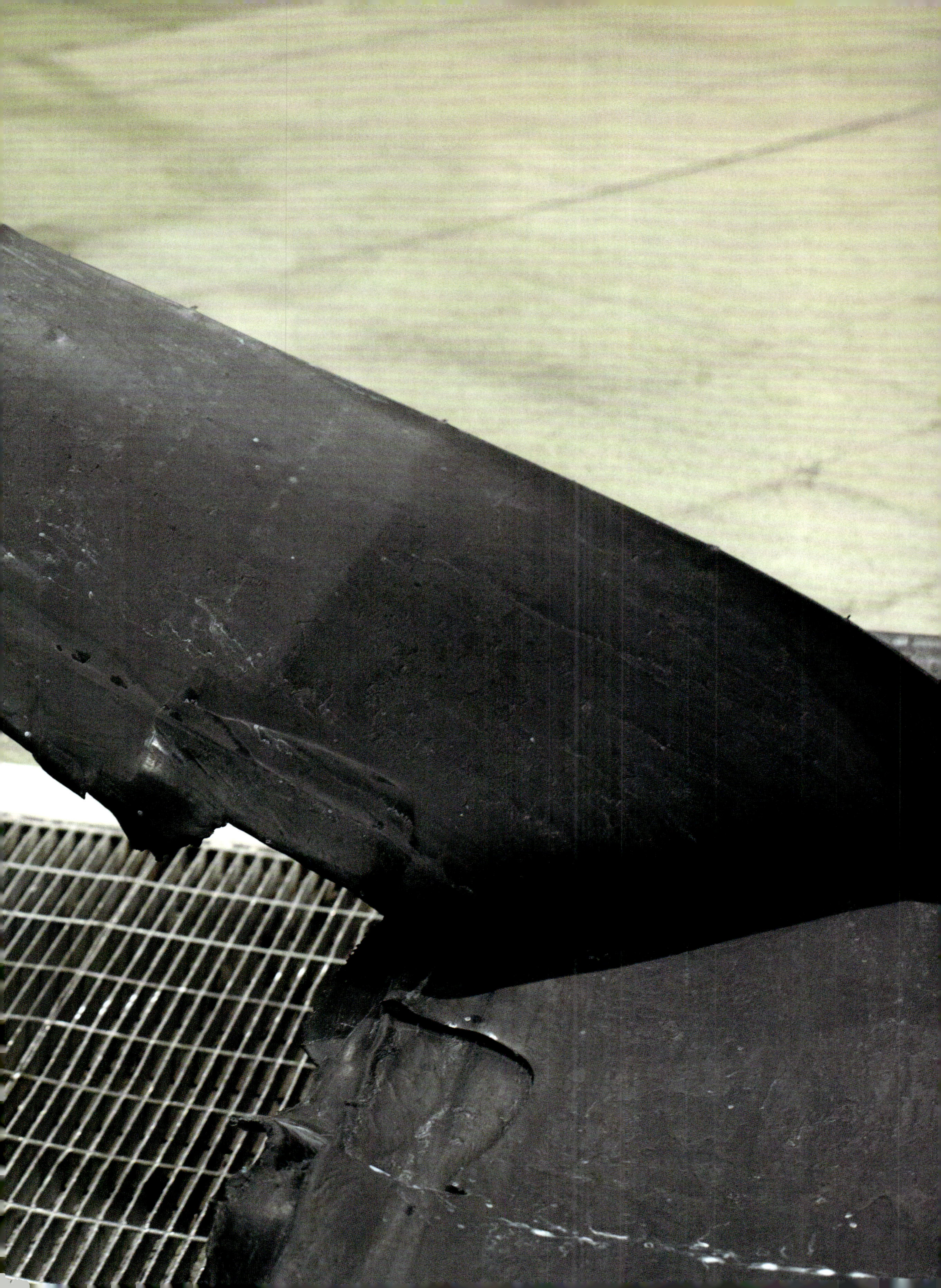

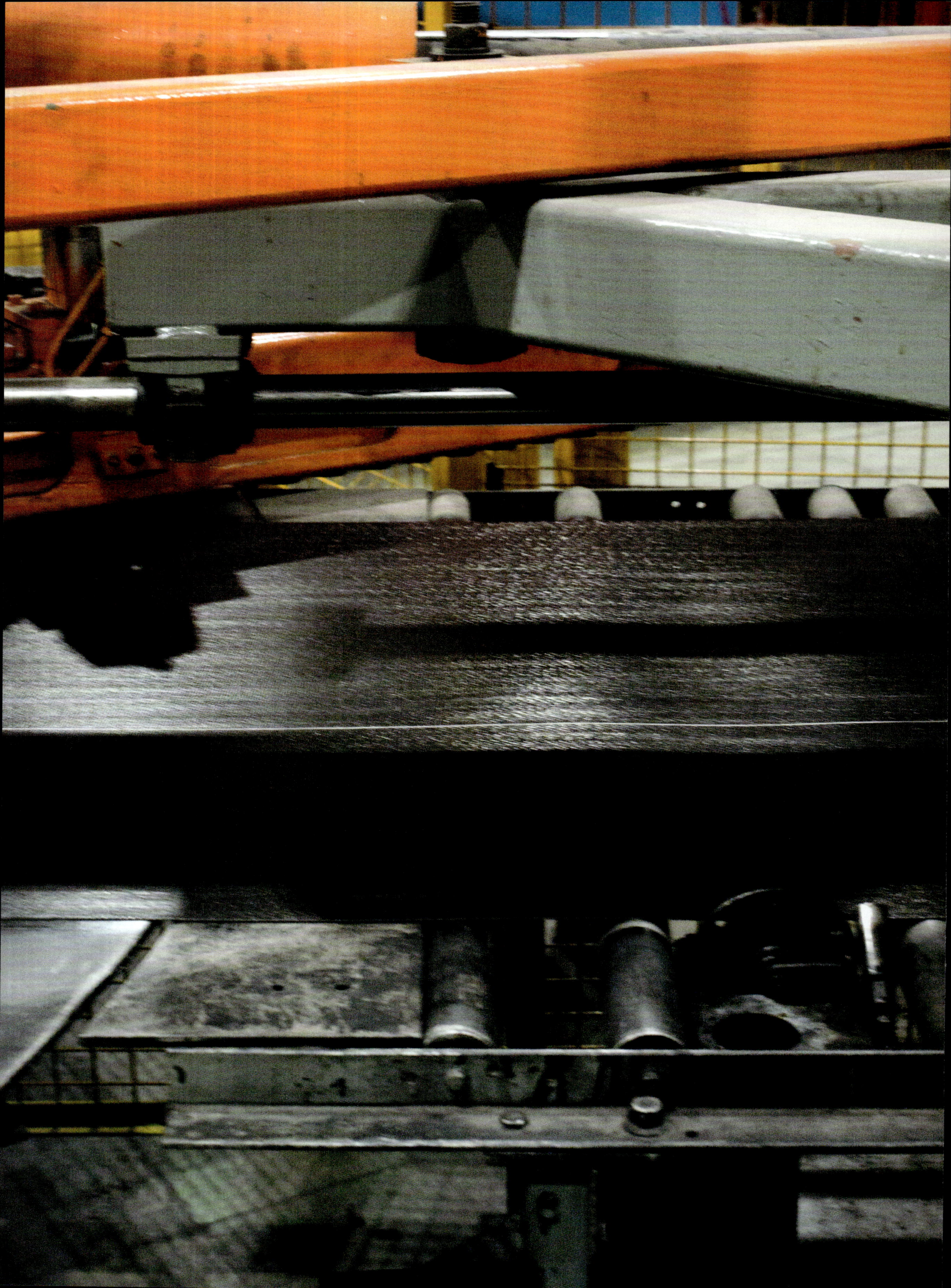

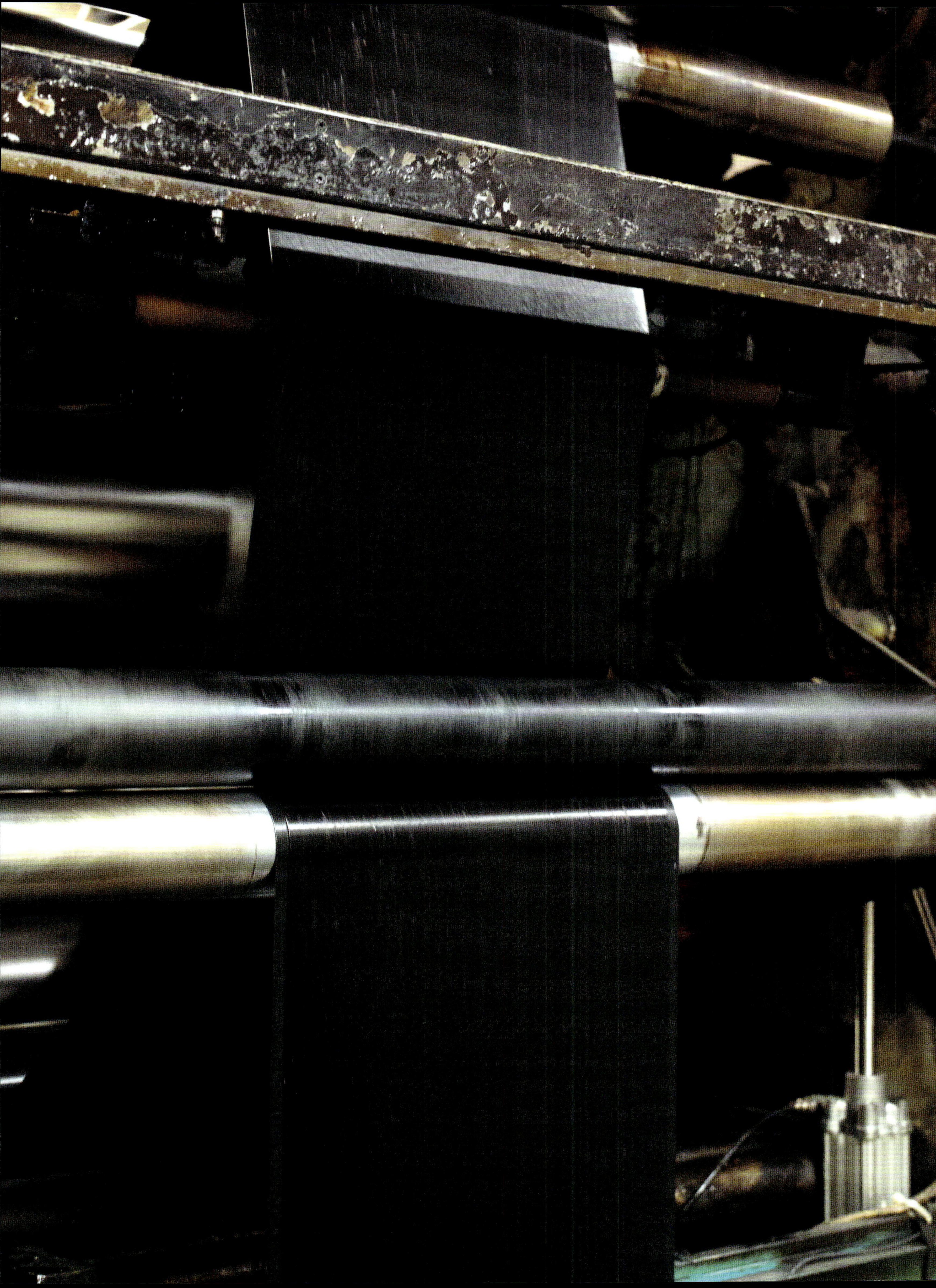

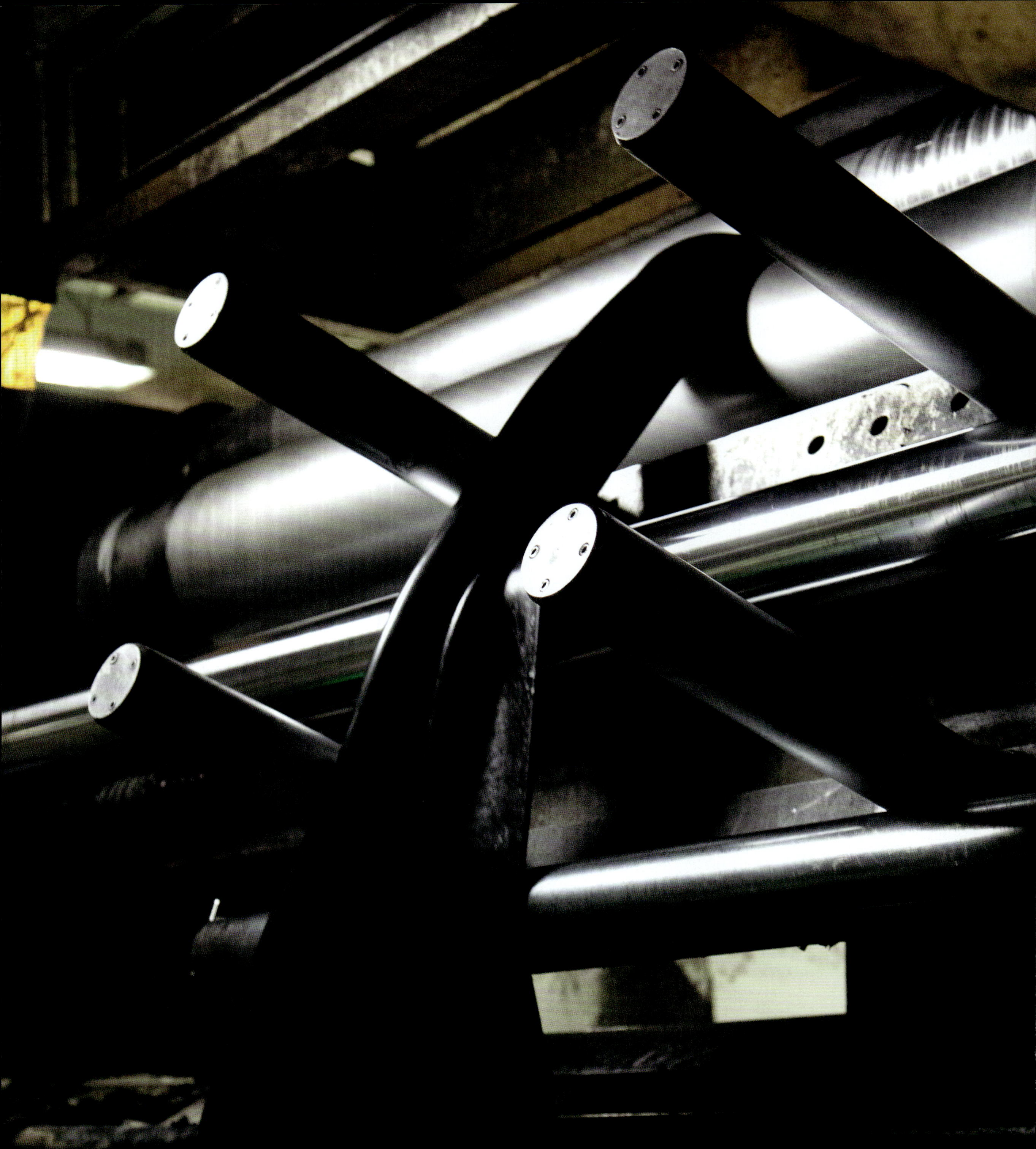

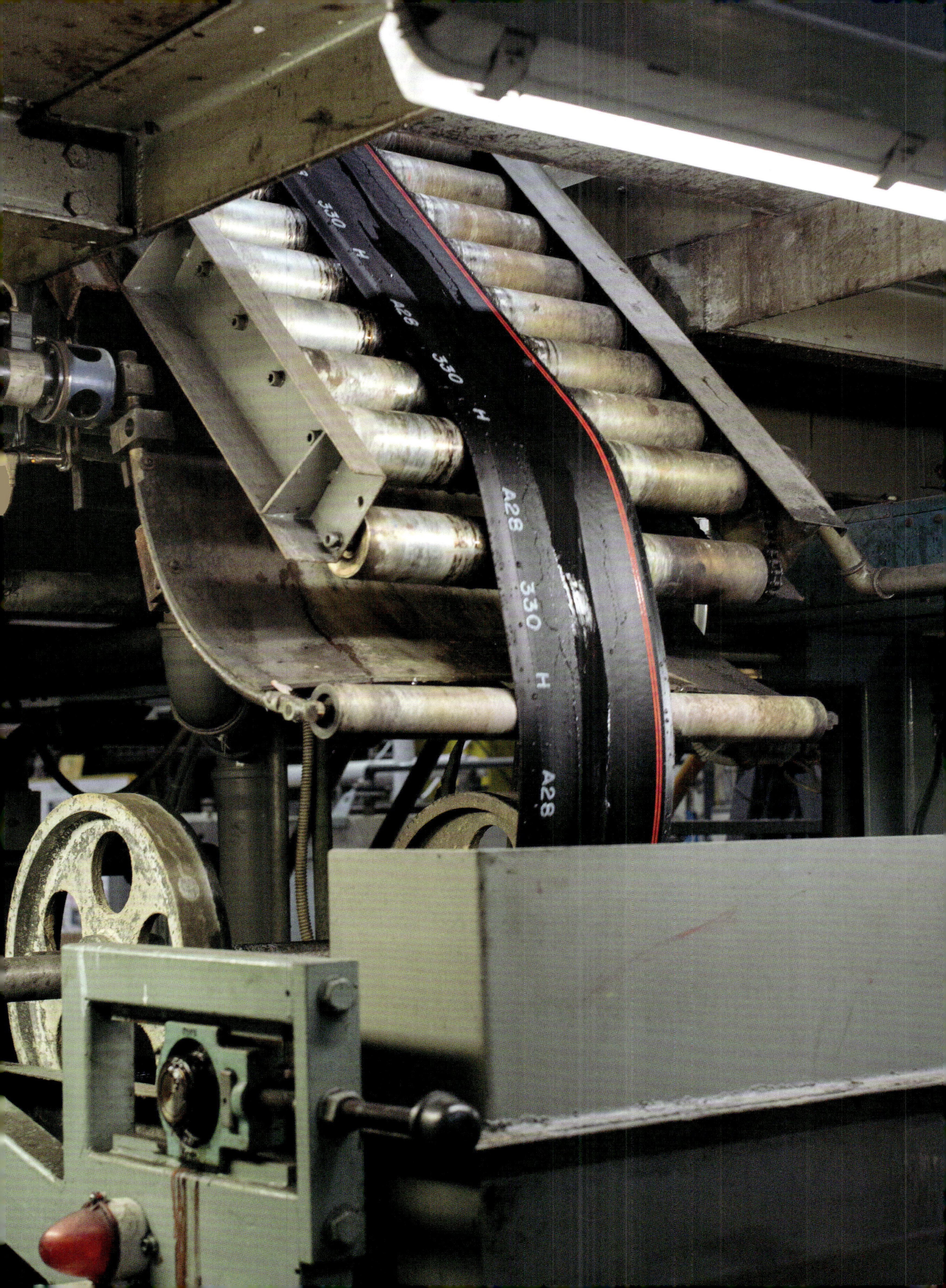

330 H
A28 330 H
A28 330 H
A28

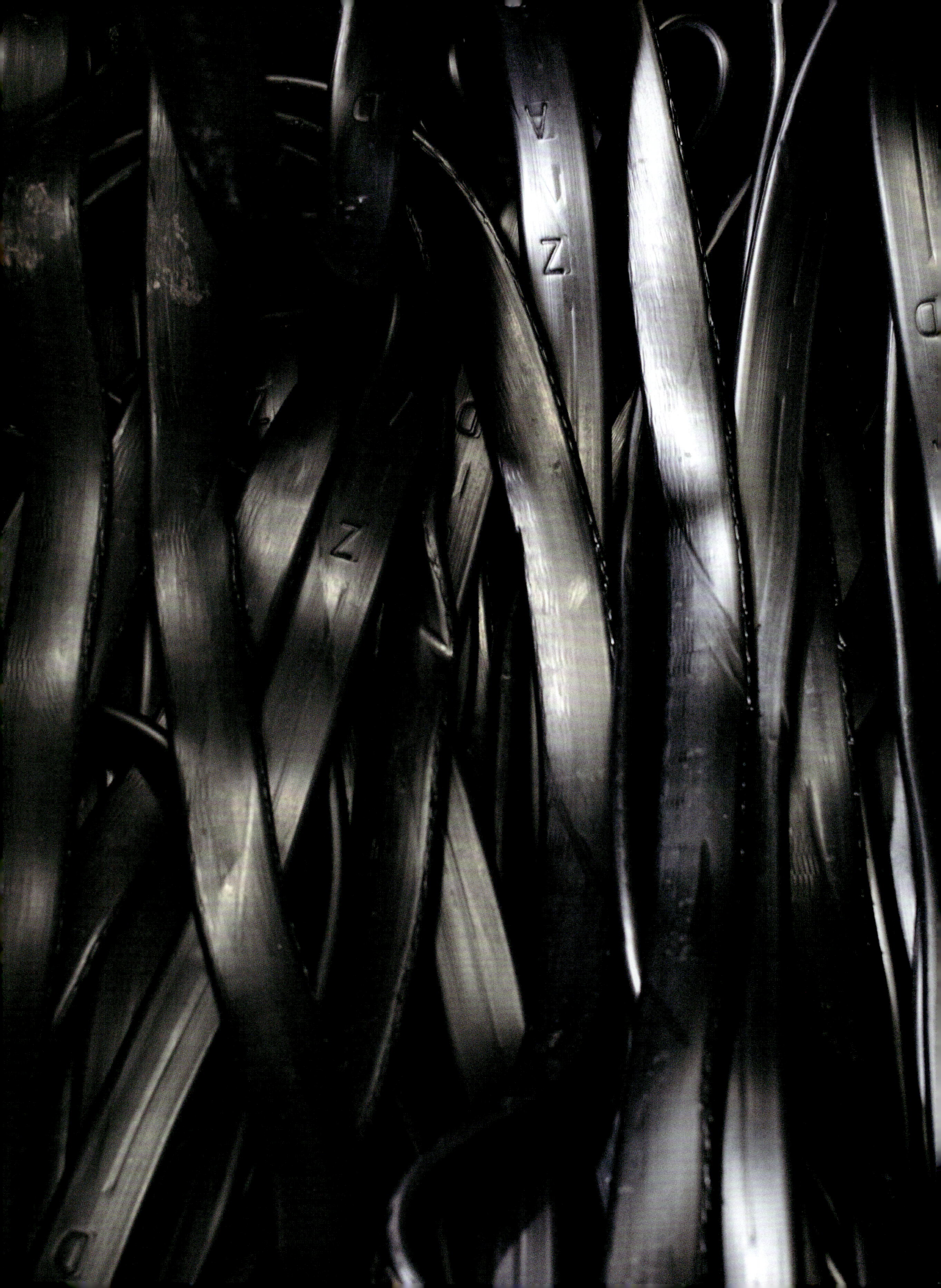

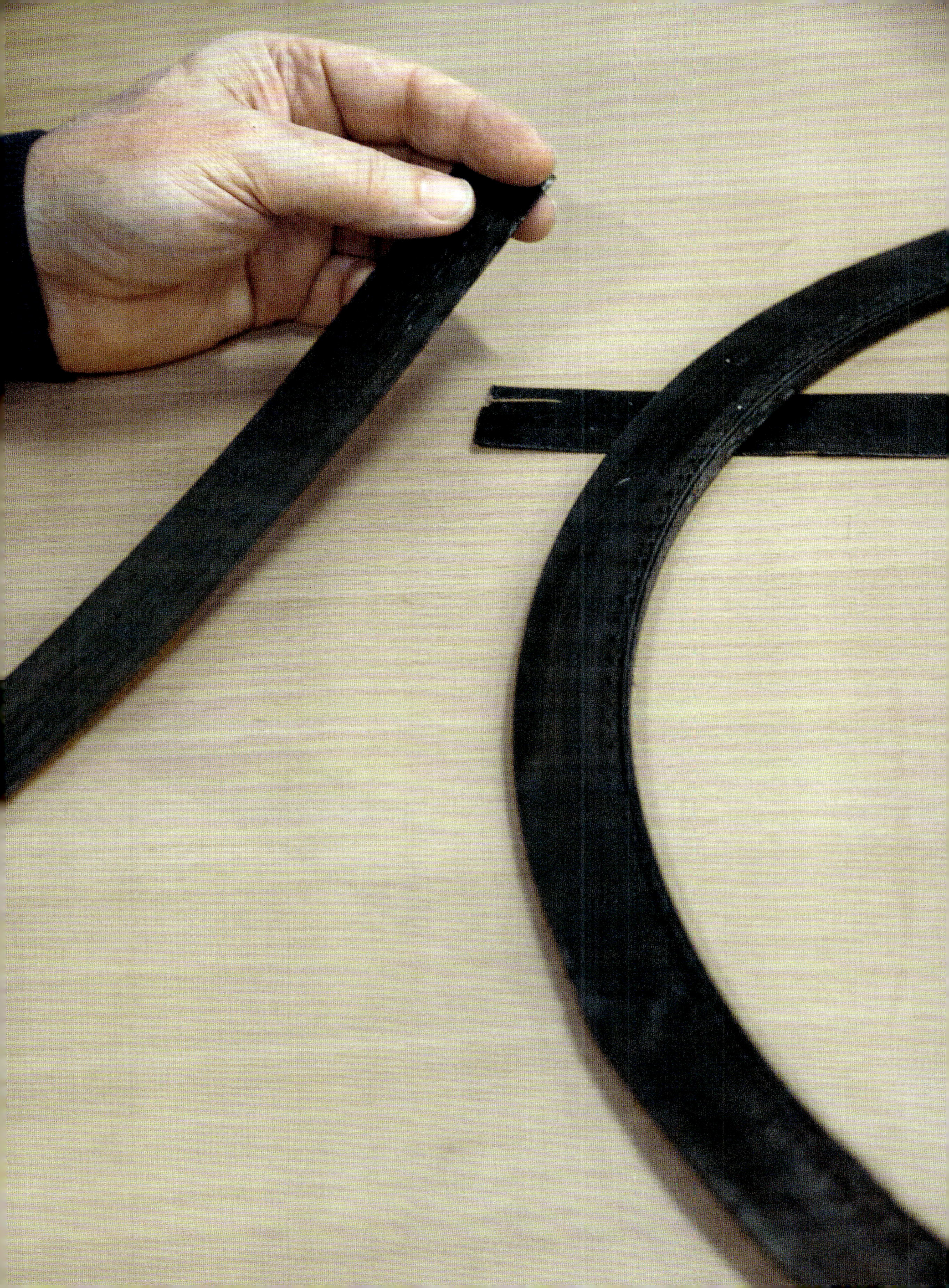

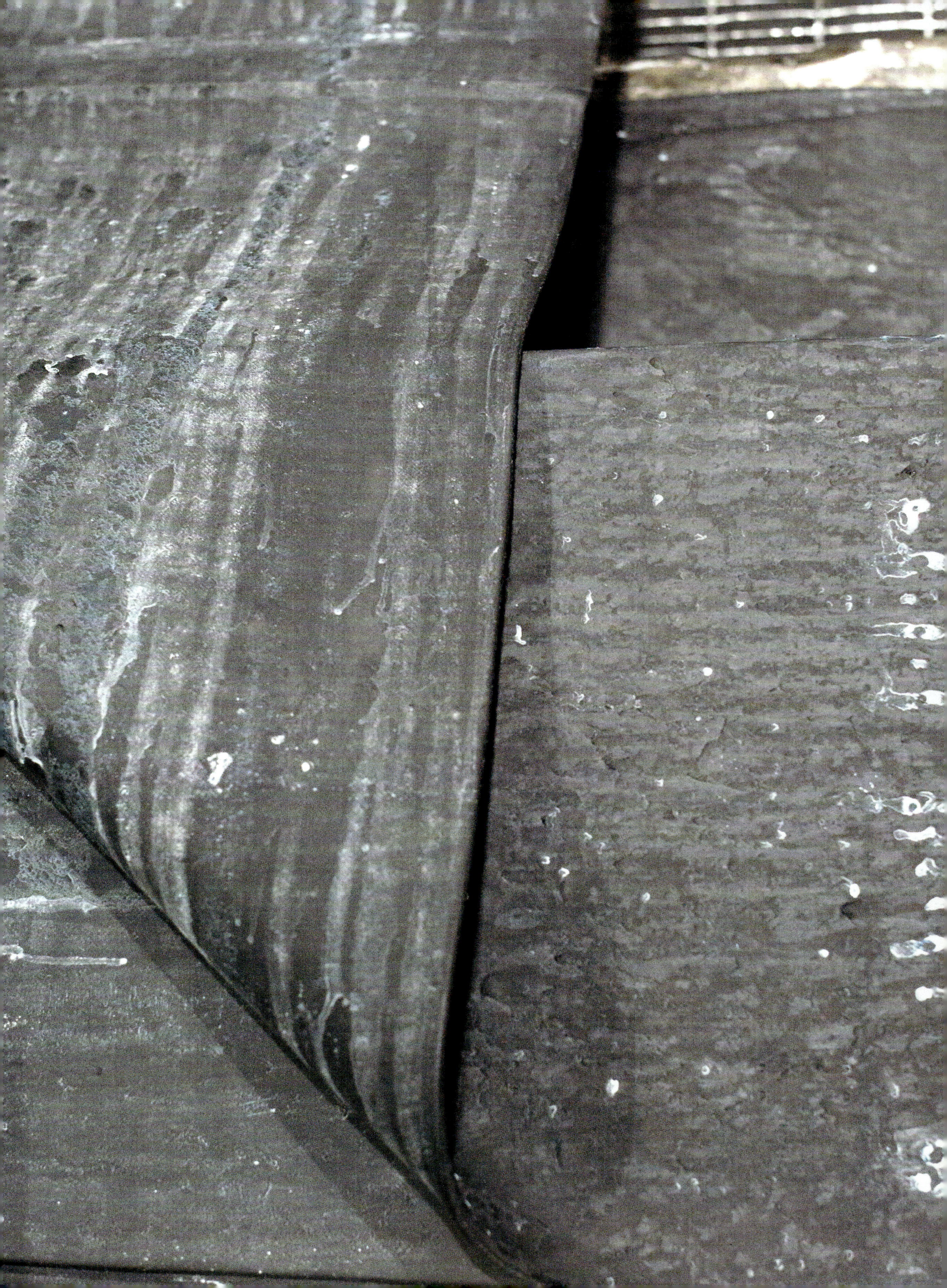

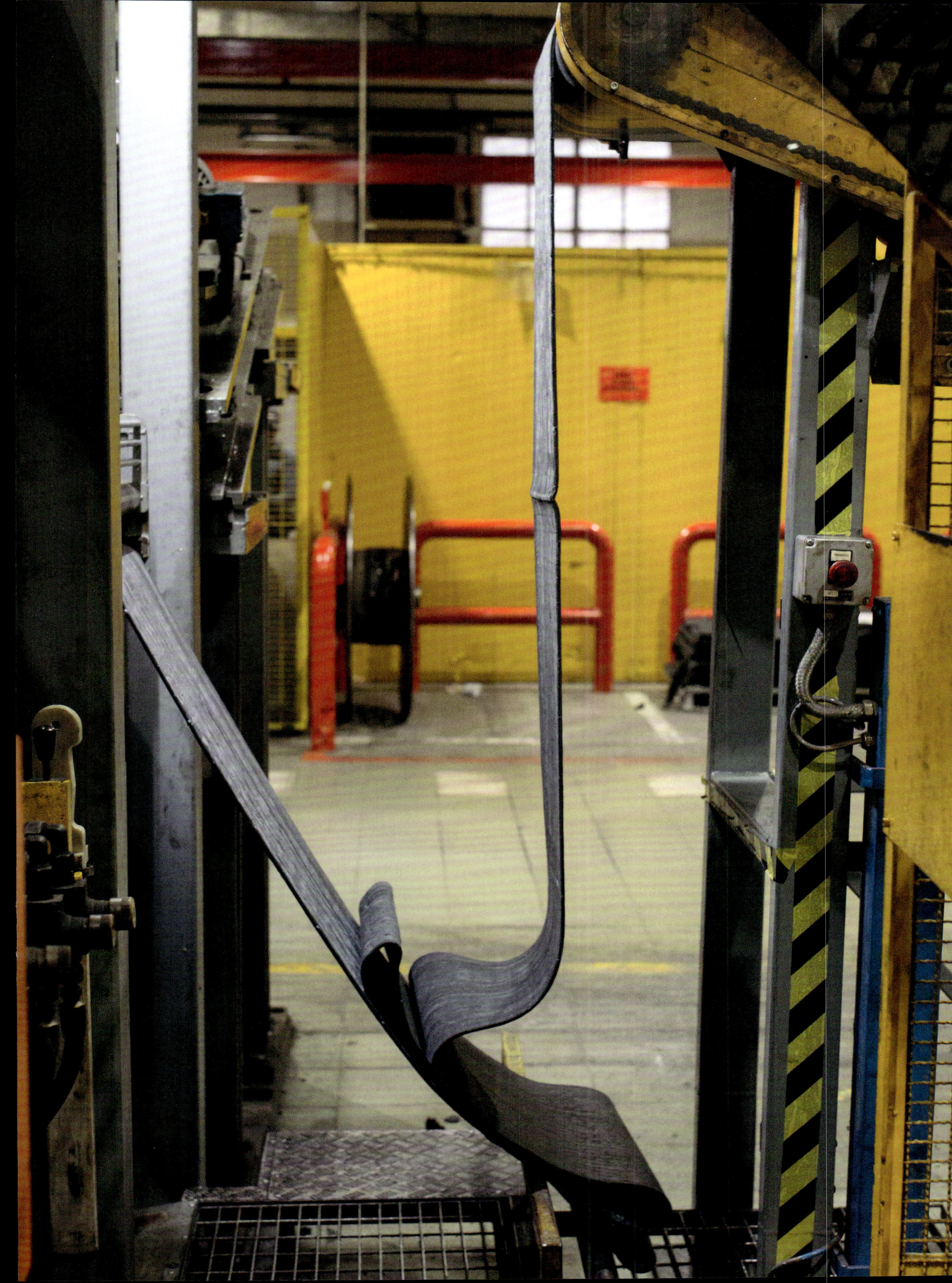

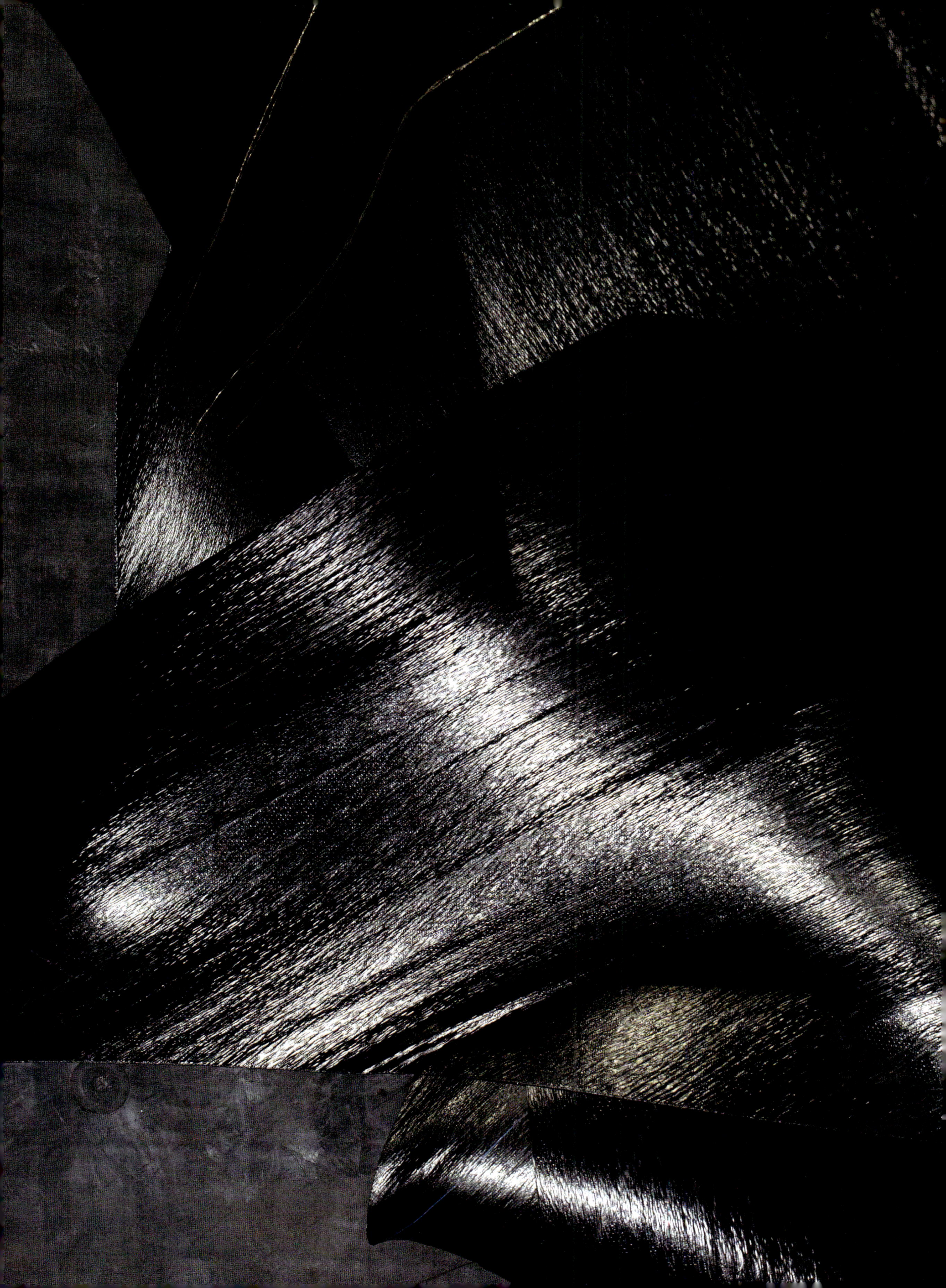

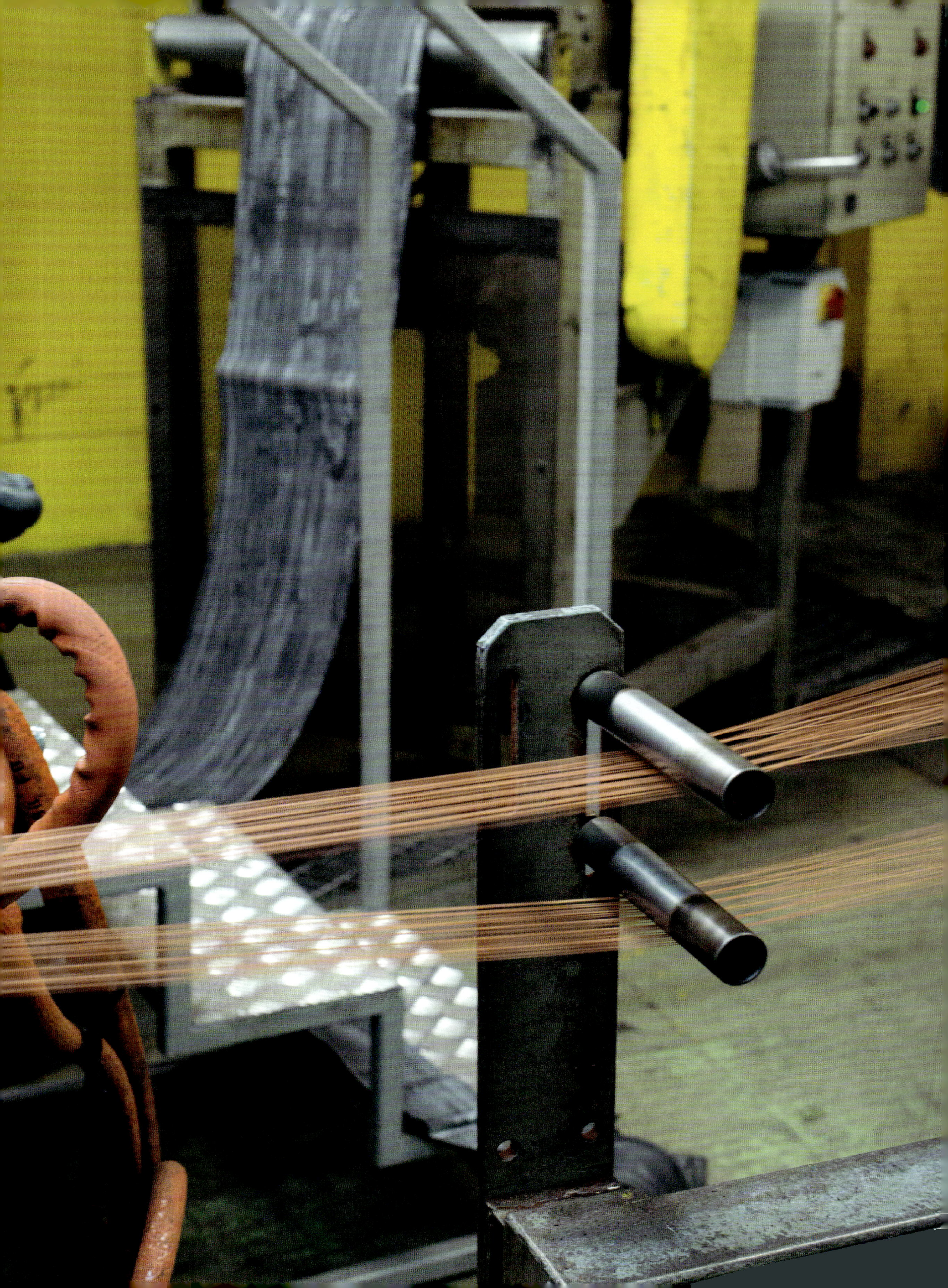

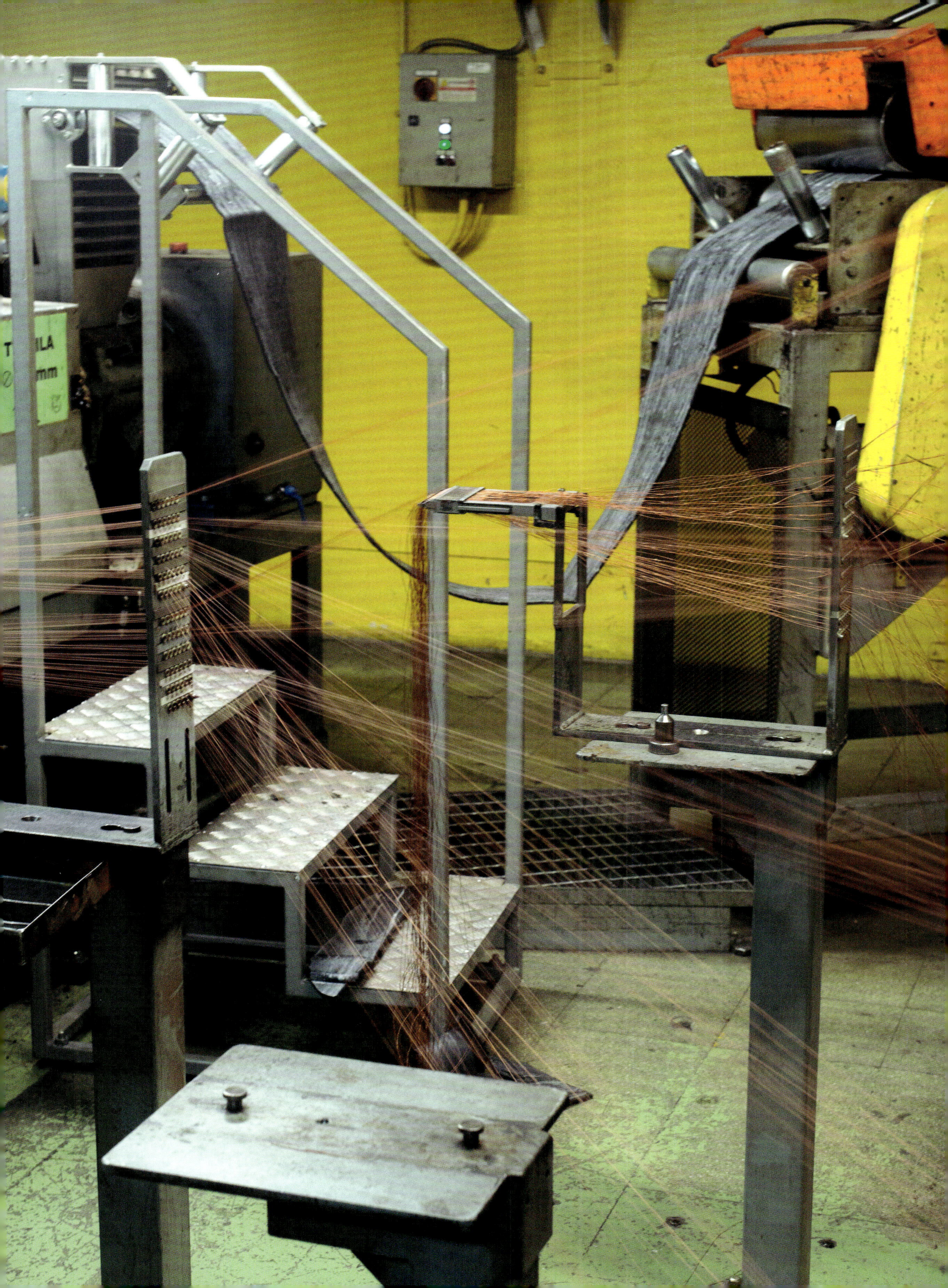

A number of striking features repeat in Leonor Antunes's work, often recurring in multiple variations. A spare formal economy is modified by a constant and insistent sense of differentiation. This is especially clear in the proliferation of knots and joints of one kind or another; in the upright or hanging structures, often emphatically elongated and vertical, that activate the space between floor and ceiling as well as in the many modular arrangements and structures, sometimes forming larger partitions. The deliberate mixing of geometric with biomorphic elements, occasionally morphing into one other, introduces further unpredictable—even rogue—effects. These features vary in their distribution and depending on different installations but continue to return in a body of work that is characteristically very formal and hybrid at the same time.

Despite the tight vocabulary of modernist forms and formats, its effects are strongly corporeal. And yet Leonor Antunes's objects are not in the least abject in any explicit sense but often custom-made or artisanally produced to a high standard. The precision finish is often understated but still reminiscent of, and a deliberate counter to, more familiar materials and effects of modern fetishism. These kinds of transposition are important. Rather than shiny tubular steel, for example, the installation at Pirelli HangarBicocca is punctuated by brass tubes contorted into any number of different suspended abstract forms. These, in turn, relate to the lampstands for the lights that are scattered amongst the other works, as if a sculpture and a piece of furniture were different versions of the same basic morphology rather than defined by separate and mutually exclusive realms. The knots and entangled ropes add to the sense of modernism's vascular circuits, exposed as bits of its remaindered phantasmatic body.

The organic aspect of Leonor Antunes's work has to do with its material constituents and parts but also with the fundamental material processes that are set in train: whereby forms and materials, as well as objects and architectures, often enter into a relation of near-mimicry with each other. I mean mimicry here in Roger Caillois's sense, not the traditional sense of the mimetic function of representation in figurative painting and sculpture. Caillois's concern was with the question of distinction, that is, what demarcated an organism from its surroundings or environment. So instances of mimicry in nature, like an insect camouflaged on a leaf or a twig, were instances of forms adapting to their environment in what he insisted was a "mutual arrangement" or "reciprocal mapping."[1] Distinctions between things get confused in the process.

In Leonor Antunes's hands, mimicry has a clear architectural dimension that is both imaginary and actual. It follows that her work both adapts and reacts to the setting for which it was initially produced or, equally, in which it finds itself. At Pirelli HangarBicocca there are some works that have been especially made in response to the specific conditions of the building. *Shed* (2018) is almost camouflaged, placed at right angles to a riveted steel column, creating a temporary partition wall. The painted aluminum panels, hinged like a folding screen, connect to the floor and to the ceiling with brass fixtures. So the structure is both fastened to its surroundings and apparently rhythmic and moveable at the same time. The concertina's surface of *shed* is differentiated from that of its "host" column as smooth is to rough. But the two entities are also conjoined, literally, as if one were an extension to the other, with both likenesses and differences succumbing, as Caillois would have it, to the lure of space.[2] And so it goes on, sometimes explicitly, but mostly in subtle doublings that also characterize the relationships between smaller groups of works.

Leonor Antunes's formal vocabulary is not pre-set or pre-given but evolving and cumulative. She continually absorbs aspects of the visual syntaxes she engages with. What I would call the work that goes into the work is often a process of investigation into modernist design and its historicities, especially as they attach to a specific place—in this instance, Milanese design in the 1950s and 1960s. Leonor Antunes works with and through facets of the historical material that draws her—often, but by no means exclusively, women designers and artists that have tended to be edged out of mainstream or canonic histories. These can be fairly hybrid and indirect rather, subliminal, even, rather than literal. An example is the figuring of the ground in the linoleum floor that is *modified double impression* (2018), the basic schema of which represents a vast scaling up of a print by Anni Albers. In a building belonging to Pirelli, the manufacturers once known for the production of linoleum, the material is at once at home and uncannily transformed. The floor is inlaid, but so are the layers of association that accrue to it. She has taken one schema and grafted it onto another, in this instance through color, notably introducing the "giallo fantastico" or fantastic yellow that Gio Ponti used for the extravagant marbled patterning on the linoleum floor he designed for his famous Pirelli Tower.[3]

Adding layers in this way is equally matched or even surpassed by all the taking away and editing out. If it weren't, Leonor Antunes's work would have none of the understatement that it characteristically has. Naturally, mimicry of this type does not draw attention to itself. Sometimes it's noticeable and sometimes it's not. Rather, the blending becomes strategic and incremental. The relationships of call and response that seem to be set up between the works also mimic those interactions that we might have with them. The effects are strongly spatial but also temporal, as other works that have been shown in other contexts are seen again and so re-presented. Caillois's epigram "Beware; Whoever pretends to be a ghost will eventually turn into one"[4] seems all the more relevant when it comes to such re-presentations or the frequent moments of déjà vu. The *Claras* (2018), for example, that lie prone against the linoleum floor now articulate the ground quite differently from the way they did at the Museo Tamayo in Mexico City earlier on in 2018. Likewise, the three *alterated climbing form* (2017–2018) enter into a new set of relations with the industrial architecture of the Shed as semi-open partitions or permeable walls that you can also walk through.

When Leonor Antunes titles her works she often does so with reference to historical figures, for example, *Clara 1, 2, 3, 4, 5, 6, 7*, with reference to the Cuban-born designer Clara Porset who lived most of her life in Mexico. Others are more coded, like the reference to the title of a work by the British Constructive artist Mary Martin, *Climbing Form* (1954); or more cryptic still, in *discrepancies with F.H.* (2018), the initials are those of Milanese architect and designer Franca Helg who haunts so much of the installation at Pirelli HangarBicocca. Dead artists and designers are far from dead in Leonor Antunes's work, but they live on there in complex ways and not simply as reference points or as causal explanations of it. Certainly, the artist investigates these often marginalized figures in order to make the material out of which she makes a work—but even that process seems a more intricate process of inlaying and even more crucially, even, *excising* (there's much more taking out arguably than adding in). The looping between the lost and the found, between what's forgotten and what's remembered, scrambles conventional linear narratives. The naming of names dramatizes a larger pattern of temporal disruption that is being played out. There is no doubting the interest of these figures—nor their cultural significance as a source of design innovation—but *in the work*, which is what matters most here, the names, or clues to names, do more to plot a parallel *mise-en-scène* of imaginary protagonists to which the work both attaches and from which it also breaks away.

It is unusual for an artist to people her work in this way, as if to render her imaginary world transparent. Leonor Antunes reveals many of her sources but not in order to explain the work: rather, to add to is opacity, perhaps. She shares with us the extraordinary archive that she has explored of Franca Helg, for example, the designer who worked with Franco Albini and the lesser-known half of the design partnership Albini-Helg. But the "source" is only a clue, as likely to be turned or twisted as the form the work takes as sculpture. *The last days in Galliate* (2018) takes as its initial template the shape of a handrail for the spiral staircase of the lakeside house Helg designed for her parents. Following its measurements exactly, an aluminum tube has been tightly covered with leather stitched together using artisanal techniques traditionally associated with saddle-making in Leonor Antunes's native Portugal. What remains of that measure, on the other hand, when the spiral has been allowed to fall and drop towards the floor in a tangle of loops, is far more awkward and intensely sculptural. If a spiral staircase is a connecting structure between floors, then a hanging sculpture both is and is not one.

A sculptural language is very strongly articulated. Of course, this isn't a language of mass and volume but relates to that other trajectory within twentieth-century art. Think of the first "thinning out" of sculptural form in the spindly casts of Giacometti's figures or Brancusi's forest of vertical, soaring bronzes. Or more important still for Leonor Antunes, think of the reorientation of sculpture's gravitational pull towards falling or collapsing, especially vividly seen in the work of North American artists such as Eva Hesse, Richard Serra, and Bruce Nauman towards the end of the 1960s, a moment that marked nothing less than a complete remapping of sculpture in accordance with a bodily topography.[5] Hesse's own drawing in space, using fine threads of latex and fiberglass as literal, materializations of a graphic line strung across a space verges on the visceral despite the fact that it barely reached the threshold of what a sculpture could be.

If Leonor Antunes seems to continue with such a sculptural project, then her material and corporeal preoccupations are also very different. There is a precision in her relationship to materials that are often sensual and tactile. Whether it is tightly sewn leather or painted brass there is no doubt that we are encountering an array of different textures. The tactile is often thought about in terms of enclosure of one sort or another, as if to be surrounded by cloth or textiles were the index of touch understood as sensual perception. When the early twentieth-century architect and writer Adolf Loos famously pictured an "enclosing room" he imagined a chair in which "to feel the material, the wood, to see it, touch it."[6] In contrast, rather than a cocoon-like enclosure, tactility is directly exposed here as a seam or a surface, a hinge or a knot.

On closer inspection, all of her materials are actively haptic and are often two-edged. Graphic forms and linear silhouettes in *alterated knot (4, 5, 6, 7)* (2018) transform as you approach them into palpable materials with some parts bound in black nylon yarn, other parts in leather. The materials are familiar—linoleum, brass, leather, painted aluminum, rope, mahogany, and so on—but made strange in experience. This relationship between ropes tying things together and the graphic line of drawing has a powerful counterpoint in Anni Albers's drawings of knots from the late 1940s. The knot, as a basic unit of a textile, becomes the tangled counter to the building block. And the methods Leonor Antunes uses are more likely to be artisanal than sculptural in a conventional sense. Or rather, in the series *Franca (#1, #2, #3, #4, #5, #6)* (2018), an artisanal set of skills have been used to make highly sculptural forms that hang from the ceiling as elongated and continuous, yet rigid, curvatures. They draw on Franca Helg's designs for rattan furniture but make radically abstract sculptures. Helg had collaborated with the manufacturers Vittorio Bonacina in the 1950s and 1960s and Leonor Antunes has worked with the same firm to achieve the same high-level of finish. The contour-shapes of rattan-core are reminiscent of a Moebius strip. Interlaced with rattan, they are suggestively both taut and soft, flat and curved.

This to and fro between sculpture, design and architecture has various consequences, including a very different relationship to drawing and to the role of drawing in design in particular. Leonor Antunes has described the way skilled craftsmen at Bonacina1889 (as the firm is known today) used full-size outlines drawn out on paper to "sculpt" the rattan-core to her design, following the same method that Helg's furniture had been produced. Helg had used rattan-core to make a chair or a table, curving the material into complex topological surfaces. The graphic element becomes even more emphatic when you think of the cursive lines of Helg's original drawings, or for that matter, when you think more generally about any drawing in which a line is used to explore the inside of a three-dimensional structure. In turn, their bodily nature is also made clear. Chairs are not just supports for but act as molds of the body, where the material actually yields a little in response to your weight as you sit; coat racks are like inanimate surrogates of ourselves, answering to our height and upright stance. Furniture is full of reminiscences of bodies that have been there, just as coat hooks are more faintly, perhaps, reminiscent of the anthropomorphic traps of Duchamp's readymades.[7]

There is an elastic sense of scaling-up and -down to adapt to new spatial dimensions. The cursive loops in the series *Franca* are based on blown-up details from several designs by Franca Helg, including a hook from her design for a freestanding coat rack (taken from the many permutations on rattan coatracks she produced). The detail is not just a descriptive term here but becomes a vital part of Leonor Antunes's own morphology. Details are taken and removed from their original context, their meaning transformed in the process. She treats them, crucially, as if they were architectural details, which is very different from the way a "detail" is regarded in common usage as simply a small part of a larger whole. In architecture, the detail is specific and distinct from the elements. Whilst the word "detail" has tended to be lost from the discourses of modern sculpture it has been productively mobilized in architecture and in particular in relation to the Italian architect Carlo Scarpa, notably by Marco Frascari, who began his career working in Scarpa's office.

If my first suggestion was about the role of something like mimicry, my second suggestion is this: Leonor Antunes revives the architectural detail and returns it to sculpture as a motivating device. As Frascari has argued, architects like Carlo Scarpa showed how details could be generators, a role previously ascribed to the plan. The emphasis on detail marks a shift away from the classical architectural elements—understood, that is, as doors, staircases, walls and so on. The architectural element is the staircase, but the detail is the handrail. And the handrail, of course, is not an abstraction but the bit you touch. It is a motif that Leonor Antunes has used before as she transposed on the rope bannisters the Hungarian modernist architect Ernö Goldfinger had designed for his house at 2 Willow Road (1939) in Hampstead, London.[8] As Walter Benjamin wrote: "Tactile appropriation is accomplished not so much by attention as by habit."[9] From this point of view, familiar details such as a handrail or a coat-hook are also important as tokens of touch. Then as you look closely they have been made using traditional craft skills like saddle-stitch. The leather skin acts not so much as a substitute for, or referent to, human skin so much as it uncannily invokes the tightness of a leather glove on a finger. The anthropomorphism is not literal but powerful and unavoidable.

Maybe it's this sense of the detail that is so distinctive in Leonor Antunes's approach to sculpture. Again and again, it is the detail that has been removed from its usual context and transformed. It's not the spiral staircase from the house at Galliate but the handrail that has been taken as a template, with its distinctive detailing at the base, suspended on rope from the ceiling and falling to the floor to make a new form in the process. And then, in an even more compelling case of the detail being transposed, *enlarged rods* (2018) concentrates attention on the joints of the tall slender structures. She has drawn on a specific project here but also made something much stranger, as a sculpture, out of it—sculptural groupings that are larger, higher, with different fixtures top and bottom, but still recursively bound to the original scheme by Albini-Helg studio for the Olivetti shop in Paris. Designed in 1956, the vertical rods were part of a modular shelving system supporting triangular shelves to display the typewriter range. Antunes interprets the vertical poles, typically taking the support and prizing it away from its supporting role.

One register of display—the shelving system to show off products—has been translated into another—that of the artwork. It's not the display parts that command our attention but instead the interest, aside from the polished mahogany of the tall curved modular structures, is displaced onto the details of the triangular joints and the brass metal legs top and bottom. These are the supports to the supports, as it were, as the "prop" parts are broken down still further. It's these minimal units that, as Frascari stresses, that offer "the minimal unit in the process of signification."[10] As he says, the role of details is as generators taking over the role traditionally ascribed to the plan. Stripped of their use value and displaced from their original function, Leonor Antunes makes sculpture out of detail of the kind Frascari described in relation to Scarpa: "Each detail tells the story of its making, its placing, and of its dimensioning."[11]

It turns out that the corporeal dimension of Leonor Antunes's work, then, is less about infrastructure, that is to say, less about the circuitry of veins and arteries, as if modernism were a metaphorical body; rather, the logic of the work is driven by the parts and joints, detached or residual. Or perhaps as spectators, it's we who circuit through and around these pivotal points. And as we enter the space and move through it, things tend to disperse. Partitions block some ways through, and open others. Shiny facets of metal reflect and refract the structures and surfaces outside it. Work made in other contexts is brought together with new work, sparking off one another to create new morphological relations. Fixed referents to place and time get lost in the process. Historical episodes within modernist design—as well as the names that become their protagonists like Helg or Martin or Albers or Porset—are re-arranged and reconfigured, inviting us to think again about how things live in the world.

BRIONY FER

1 Roger Caillois, "Mimicry and Legendary Psychasthenia," in *The Edge of Surrealism A Caillois Reader* (Durham: Duke University Press, 2003), p. 96.
2 Ibid., p. 96.
3 Gio Ponti designed the 32-floor Pirelli Tower in Milan in 1950.
4 Roger Caillois, "Mimicry and Legendary Psychasthenia," Op. cit., p. 91.
5 I'm thinking of works like Hesse's *Right After* (fiberglass, 1969). This sculptural "fall" has been extensively discussed, see for example Briony Fer, *The Infinite Line* (New Haven: Yale University Press, 2004) pp. 117–144.
6 Adolf Loos, "On Thrift," in Adolf Opel and Daniel Opel (eds.), *Adolf Loos: On Architecture*, trans. Michael Mitchell (Riverside, CA: Ariadne Press, 1995), p. 178.
7 For example, Marcel Duchamp *Trap (Trebuchet)* (1917), a readymade coat rack that was placed directly on the floor, or *Hat-rack (Tout-fait)* (1916), which was suspended from the ceiling. Both were lost and remade in editions in the 1960s.
8 Lydia Yee and Habda Rashid (eds.), *Leonor Antunes: The Frisson of the Togetherness* (London: Whitechapel Gallery, 2017).
9 Walter Benjamin, "The Work of Art in the Age of Mechanical Reproduction," in *Illuminations* (New York: Schocken Books, 1969), p. 240.
10 Marco Frascari, "The Tell-tale Detail," in *Via 7: The Building of Architecture* (Cambridge: The MIT Press, 1984), p. 23.
11 Ibid., p. 29.

Nella produzione di Leonor Antunes ricorrono alcuni elementi singolari, spesso ripetuti in molteplici variazioni. Una sobria economia formale è modificata da un costante e insistente senso di differenziazione, come emerge chiaramente soprattutto dalla proliferazione di nodi e giunti di vario tipo e dalle strutture diritte o sospese, spesso enfaticamente allungate e verticali, che movimentano lo spazio tra pavimento e soffitto, oltre che dalle numerose composizioni e strutture modulari, che talvolta formano divisori più grandi. L'accostamento intenzionale di elementi geometrici e biomorfi, che di tanto in tanto si trasformano l'uno nell'altro, introduce ulteriori effetti imprevedibili, se non addirittura devianti. Questi elementi variano nella distribuzione e secondo l'installazione, ma continuano a riproporsi in un corpus di opere che, peculiarmente, è al tempo stesso molto formale e ibrido.

Nonostante il vocabolario conciso delle forme e dei formati modernisti, gli effetti sono fortemente corporei. Gli oggetti di Leonor Antunes, tuttavia, non sono affatto dozzinali, ma spesso personalizzati o frutto di una produzione artigianale di alto livello. Non di rado la rifinitura di precisione è sottovalutata, ma echeggia ancora i materiali e gli effetti più familiari del feticismo moderno, facendo loro da deliberato contrappunto. Questi tipi di trasposizione sono importanti. Invece del lucido acciaio tubolare, per esempio, l'installazione in Pirelli HangarBicocca è punteggiata di tubi d'ottone che si contorcono in una serie di forme astratte sospese, tutte diverse tra loro. Queste, a loro volta, alludono agli steli delle lampade sparpagliate tra le opere, come se una scultura e un complemento d'arredo fossero versioni differenti della stessa morfologia di base, anziché definiti da ambiti separati che si escludono a vicenda. I nodi e le corde aggrovigliate accentuano la sensazione di guardare circuiti vascolari del modernismo, esposti come frammenti residui del suo corpo fantasmatico.

L'aspetto organico della produzione di Leonor Antunes ha a che fare con le sue parti e le sue componenti fisiche, ma anche con i fondamentali processi corporei messi in moto, in virtù dei quali le forme e i materiali, gli oggetti e le architetture instaurano spesso una relazione quasi mimetica tra loro. Qui uso il termine mimetismo con il significato che gli attribuisce Roger Caillois, non con quello tradizionale della funzione mimetica della rappresentazione nella pittura e nella scultura figurative. Caillois è interessato all'aspetto della distinzione, cioè di cosa delimiti un organismo dall'ambiente circostante. Così i casi di mimetismo naturale, come un insetto mimetizzato su una foglia o su un ramoscello, sono esempi di forme capaci di adattarsi all'ambiente in quello che, a suo parere, è un "accordo comune" o una "mappatura reciproca"[1]. In questo processo le distinzioni tra le cose si confondono.

Nella pratica di Leonor Antunes il mimetismo acquisisce una chiara dimensione architettonica, insieme immaginaria e reale. Ne consegue che la sua produzione si adatta e reagisce al contesto per cui è stata creata inizialmente o, parimenti, in cui è inserita. In Pirelli HangarBicocca sono esposte alcune opere realizzate appositamente in risposta alle condizioni specifiche dell'edificio. *Shed* (2018) è quasi mimetizzato, collocato esattamente all'angolo rispetto a una colonna di placche di acciaio, creando un divisorio temporaneo. I pannelli di alluminio dipinti, muniti di cerniere come un paravento, sono collegati al pavimento e al soffitto da dispositivi di fissaggio in ottone. Dunque la struttura è sia assicurata allo spazio sia apparentemente ritmica e mobile. La superficie a fisarmonica di *shed* si differenzia da quella della colonna "ospite" quanto il liscio dal ruvido. Le due entità, tuttavia, sono anche letteralmente unite, come se fossero l'una un'estensione dell'altra, con analogie e differenze che cedono entrambe, come direbbe Caillois, al richiamo dello spazio[2]. E così via, talvolta esplicitamente, ma perlopiù in impercettibili sdoppiamenti che caratterizzano anche i rapporti tra gruppi più piccoli di opere.

Il vocabolario formale di Leonor Antunes non è prestabilito né preesistente, bensì evolutivo e cumulativo. L'artista assorbe senza sosta aspetti delle sintassi visive con cui si confronta. Quella che chiamerei l'opera che confluisce nell'opera è, non di rado, un processo di indagine sul design modernista e sulle sue storicità, specialmente quando riferite a un luogo specifico, in questo caso il design milanese degli anni cinquanta e sessanta. Leonor Antunes lavora con le sfaccettature del materiale storico che stimola la sua curiosità: spesso, ma non certo in via esclusiva, con designer e artiste donne che sono state perlopiù emarginate dalle storie tradizionali o canoniche, storie che possono essere abbastanza ibride e indirette, o addirittura subliminali, anziché letterali. Un esempio è il rivestimento a pavimento in linoleum di *modified double impression* [doppia impressione modificata, 2018], il cui schema di base rappresenta l'enorme ingrandimento di una stampa di Anni Albers. In un edificio di proprietà di Pirelli, azienda un tempo nota per la produzione di linoleum, il materiale è inserito nel suo contesto e, contemporaneamente, subisce una misteriosa metamorfosi. Il pavimento è intarsiato, ma ciò vale anche per gli strati di associazioni che lo intridono. L'artista ha preso uno schema e, attraverso il colore, l'ha innestato su un altro, introducendo, in particolare, il "giallo fantastico" usato da Gio Ponti per lo stravagante motivo marmorizzato del pavimento di linoleum che ideò per il famoso grattacielo Pirelli[3].

Questa aggiunta di strati è compensata, se non addirittura superata, dalla sottrazione e dall'eliminazione. Se così non fosse, la produzione di Leonor Antunes non avrebbe nulla dell'understatement che la contraddistingue. Naturalmente, un mimetismo di questo tipo non attira l'attenzione su di sé. Ora è palese, ora no. Piuttosto, la fusione diventa strategica e incrementale. I rapporti di botta e risposta che paiono instaurarsi tra le opere imitano anche le interazioni che noi potremmo avere con esse. Gli effetti sono marcatamente spaziali, ma anche temporali, perché si rivedono e si ripresentano altre opere che sono state esposte in contesti differenti. L'epigramma di Caillois — "Sta' in guardia. Chi finge di essere un fantasma alla fine lo diventa"[4] — sembra ancora più pertinente quando si tratta di simili ripresentazioni o dei frequenti episodi di déjà-vu. Per esempio, le *Clara* (2018) prone sul linoleum scandiscono il pavimento in modo molto diverso da come facevano al Museo Tamayo di Città del Messico nei precedenti mesi del 2018. Analogamente, le tre *alterated climbing forms* [forme rampicanti alterate, 2017-2018] stabiliscono una nuova serie di rapporti con l'architettura industriale dello Shed sotto forma di divisori semiaperti o di pareti permeabili che si possono anche attraversare.

Quando Leonor Antunes intitola le sue opere, spesso richiama delle figure storiche. Per esempio, *Clara 1, 2, 3, 4, 5, 6, 7* alludono alla designer cubana Clara Porset, che trascorse quasi tutta la vita a Città del Messico. Altri riferimenti sono più velati — come quello al titolo di un'opera dell'artista costruttivista britannica Mary Martin, *Climbing Form* (1954) — o ancora più criptici, come *discrepancies with F.H.* [discrepanze con F.H., 2018], dove le iniziali sono quelle dell'architetto e designer milanese Franca Helg, la cui presenza permea gran parte dell'installazione in Pirelli HangarBicocca. Nella produzione di Leonor Antunes artisti e designer scomparsi sono tutt'altro che scomparsi, bensì continuano a vivere in modi complessi, e non semplicemente come punti di riferimento o spiegazioni causali. Senza dubbio l'artista indaga queste figure spesso emarginate per creare il materiale con cui realizza i suoi lavori, ma anche questo metodo sembra più un intricato processo di intarsio e, cosa ancora più cruciale, persino di *asportazione* (probabilmente ci sono più sottrazioni che aggiunte). Il ciclo tra ciò che è perso e ciò che è trovato, tra ciò che si dimentica e ciò che si ricorda, semina scompiglio nei racconti lineari convenzionali. L'imposizione dei nomi drammatizza un più ampio schema di perturbazione temporale che viene messo in scena. Non ci sono dubbi sull'interesse di queste figure né sulla loro rilevanza culturale come fonti di innovazione nell'ambito del design, ma nell'*opera*, che qui è l'aspetto più importante, i nomi, o i relativi indizi, contribuiscono più che altro a tratteggiare una messa in scena parallela di protagonisti fittizi cui i lavori aderiscono e da cui, al contempo, si allontanano.

È insolito che un artista popoli la sua produzione in questo modo, come per rendere trasparente il suo mondo immaginario. Leonor Antunes rivela molte delle sue fonti, ma non per spiegare l'opera, bensì forse per aumentarne l'opacità. Per esempio, esplora e condivide con noi lo straordinario archivio di Franca Helg, la designer che lavorò con Franco Albini, nonché la metà meno nota della partnership Albini-Helg. La "fonte", tuttavia, è soltanto un indizio, soggetto a essere rovesciato o attorcigliato quanto la forma che l'opera assume come scultura. *The last days in Galliate* [gli ultimi giorni a Galliate, 2018] prende a modello la forma del corrimano per la scala a chiocciola della casa sul lago che Helg progettò per i suoi genitori. Seguendo esattamente le sue misurazioni, un tubo di alluminio è stato avvolto in un rivestimento di cuoio compatto, cucito secondo i metodi artigianali tradizionalmente associati alla produzione di selle in Portogallo, il paese natale di Leonor Antunes. Quando la spirale ha la possibilità di precipitare e di cadere verso il pavimento in un groviglio di spire, ciò che rimane di questa misurazione è molto più ingombrante e intensamente scultoreo. Se una scala a chiocciola è una struttura di raccordo tra piani, una scultura sospesa lo è e non lo è.

Il linguaggio scultoreo è fortemente articolato. Naturalmente, questo non è un linguaggio di massa e di volume, ma si lega all'altro indirizzo dell'arte del XX secolo. Si pensi al primo "sfoltimento" della forma scultorea nelle figure affusolate di Giacometti o nella foresta di svettanti bronzi verticali di Brancusi. Oppure, ancora più importante nel caso di Leonor Antunes, al riorientamento della spinta gravitazionale della scultura verso la caduta o il crollo, visibile in modo particolarmente vivido nella produzione di artisti nordamericani come Eva Hesse, Richard Serra e Bruce Nauman verso la fine degli anni sessanta, un momento che addirittura riorganizzò il panorama della scultura in conformità a una topografia del corpo[5]. Il modo in cui Hesse disegna nello spazio, usando sottili fili di lattice e fibra di vetro come materializzazioni letterali di una linea grafica tesa in un ambiente, rasenta il viscerale pur non raggiungendo la soglia di ciò che la scultura potrebbe essere.

Se Leonor Antunes sembra portare avanti un simile progetto scultoreo, le sue ossessioni materiali e corporee sono tuttavia molto diverse. Il suo rapporto con materiali spesso sensuali e tattili si contraddistingue per una certa precisione. A prescindere che si tratti di cuoio dalle cuciture robuste o di ottone dipinto, è innegabile che ci imbattiamo in una serie di texture differenti. Non di rado, il tattile è considerato un involucro, come se essere circondati da una tela o da un tessuto fosse l'indice del tocco inteso come percezione sensuale. Quando Adolf Loos, architetto e scrittore dell'inizio del XX secolo, rappresentò il famoso "spazio racchiudente", immaginò una poltrona in cui "sentire il materiale, il legno, vederlo, toccarlo"[6]. Al contrario, anziché come un guscio simile a un bozzolo, qui la tattilità si rivela direttamente sotto forma di cucitura o superficie, di cerniera o nodo.

A un esame più attento, tutti i materiali sono attivamente aptici e spesso bivalenti. Quando l'osservatore si avvicina, le forme grafiche e i profili lineari di *alterated knot* [nodo alterato] *(4, 5, 6, 7)* (2018) si trasformano in materiali palpabili, con alcune parti legate in filo di nylon nero e altre in cuoio. I materiali sono familiari — linoleum, ottone, cuoio, alluminio dipinto, corda, mogano ecc. — ma resi inusuali durante l'esperienza. Il rapporto tra corde che legano le cose tra loro e la linea grafica del disegno trova un efficace contrappunto nei disegni di nodi realizzati da Anni Albers alla fine degli anni quaranta. Il nodo, come unità fondamentale del tessuto, diventa l'omologo aggrovigliato del mattone. I metodi usati da Leonor Antunes, inoltre, tendono a essere più artigianali che scultorei in senso convenzionale. O meglio, nella serie *Franca (#1, #2, #3, #4, #5, #6)* (2018) l'artista fa ricorso a capacità artigianali per creare forme altamente scultoree, che pendono dal soffitto come curvature allungate e continue ma rigide. Queste ultime attingono dai progetti di Franca Helg per i mobili in giunco, ma sono sculture radicalmente astratte. Helg aveva collaborato con la casa manifatturiera Vittorio Bonacina negli anni cinquanta e sessanta e Leonor Antunes ha lavorato con la stessa azienda per raggiungere un livello altrettanto alto nelle rifiniture. Le forme di midollino ricordano un nastro di Möbius. Intrecciate con il giunco, sono così suggestive da essere insieme dure e morbide, piatte e curve.

Questo andirivieni tra scultura, design e architettura ha varie conseguenze, compreso un rapporto molto diverso con il disegno e con il suo ruolo nel design in particolare. Leonor Antunes descrive il modo in cui gli artigiani esperti della Bonacina1889 (l'attuale nome dell'azienda) hanno utilizzato sagome a grandezza naturale, disegnate su carta, per "scolpire" la canna di giunco del suo modello, adottando lo stesso metodo di produzione usato per i mobili di Helg, che creava sedie o tavoli curvando questo materiale in complesse superfici topologiche. L'elemento grafico diventa ancora più enfatico quando si pensa alle linee fluide dei disegni originali di Helg o, se è per questo, quando si considera, più in generale, qualunque disegno in cui la linea serva a esplorare l'interno di una scultura tridimensionale. Allo stesso tempo, si sottolinea anche la loro natura corporea. Le sedie non sono soltanto supporti per il corpo, ma fungono da stampi in cui il materiale cede leggermente in risposta al peso della persona che si siede; gli appendiabiti sono come sostituti inanimati di noi stessi, rispondendo alla nostra statura e alla nostra posizione eretta. I mobili sono pieni di reminiscenze dei corpi che hanno ospitato, mentre gli appendiabiti ricordano, forse più vagamente, i tranelli antropomorfi dei ready-made di Duchamp[7].

C'è un senso elastico di ingrandimento e rimpicciolimento per adattarsi alle nuove dimensioni spaziali. Le spire fluide della serie *Franca* si basano su dettagli ingranditi di diverse creazioni di Franca Helg, tra cui un gancio del progetto per un appendiabiti autoportante (tratto dalle numerose permutazioni dei suoi modelli in giunco). Qui il dettaglio non è soltanto un termine descrittivo, ma diventa una parte vitale della morfologia di Leonor Antunes. I dettagli vengono presi ed estrapolati dal contesto originale, trasformandone contemporaneamente il significato. L'artista li tratta — è importante sottolinearlo — come se fossero dettagli architettonici, il che è molto diverso dalla concezione comune, secondo cui il "dettaglio" è semplicemente la piccola parte di un insieme più grande. In architettura, esso è un'entità specifica e distinta dagli elementi. Anche se la parola "dettaglio" tende a scomparire dai discorsi della scultura moderna, è stata mobilitata proficuamente in architettura e, in particolare, in relazione all'architetto italiano Carlo Scarpa, soprattutto da Marco Frascari, che iniziò la propria carriera lavorando nel suo studio.

Se la mia prima idea riguarda il ruolo di un fenomeno come il mimetismo, la seconda parte dal presupposto che Leonor Antunes faccia rivivere il dettaglio architettonico e lo restituisca alla scultura sotto forma di espediente motivazionale. Architetti come Carlo Scarpa, dice Frascari, hanno dimostrato che i dettagli possono essere generatori, un compito precedentemente assegnato al progetto. L'accento posto sul dettaglio segna un allontanamento dagli elementi architettonici classici, intesi come porte, scale, pareti e così via. L'elemento architettonico è la scala, ma il dettaglio è il corrimano e, naturalmente, quest'ultimo non è un'astrazione, ma la parte che si tocca. Questo è un motivo che Leonor Antunes aveva già usato per trasporre le balaustre di corda progettate dall'architetto modernista ungherese Ernö Goldfinger per la sua casa al 2 di Willow Road (1939), nel quartiere londinese di Hampstead[8]. Come scrive Walter Benjamin, "la fruizione tattica non avviene tanto sul piano dell'attenzione quanto su quello dell'abitudine"[9]. Da questo punto di vista, dettagli familiari come un corrimano o il gancio di un appendiabiti sono importanti anche come simboli del tatto. Poi, da un esame accurato emerge che sono stati creati ricorrendo a competenze artigianali tradizionali come la cucitura per le selle. Il cuoio non funge da sostituto o da referente della pelle umana, ma invoca misteriosamente l'aderenza di un guanto su un dito. Pur non essendo letterale, l'antropomorfismo è potente e inevitabile.

Forse è questo senso del dettaglio a contraddistinguere l'approccio di Leonor Antunes alla scultura. Volta dopo volta, è il dettaglio a essere rimosso dal suo contesto abituale e trasformato. A fungere da modello non è la scala a chiocciola della casa a Galliate, ma il corrimano, con le sue inconfondibili rifiniture alla base, sospeso a una corda che pende dal soffitto, cadendo fino al pavimento per creare una nuova forma. Poi, in un caso ancora più convincente di trasposizione del dettaglio, *enlarged rods* [aste ingrandite, 2018] punta l'attenzione sui giunti delle strutture alte e snelle. Qui l'artista ha attinto da un progetto specifico, ma ne ha ricavato qualcosa che, in termini scultorei, è molto più bizzarro: gruppi di sculture più grandi, più alte, con diversi dispositivi di fissaggio in cima e alla base, ma ancora legati indissolubilmente allo schema originale dello studio Albini-Helg per il negozio Olivetti a Parigi. Progettati nel 1956, i montanti verticali facevano parte di un sistema di scaffalature che supportava le mensole triangolari su cui era esposta la gamma di macchine da scrivere. Come sempre, Antunes li interpreta prendendo il supporto e strappandolo dal suo ruolo.

Un registro dell'ostentazione — il sistema di scaffalature per esibire i prodotti — si traduce in un altro, quello dell'opera d'arte. A monopolizzare l'attenzione non sono i pezzi esposti; a parte il mogano lucido delle alte strutture modulari curve, infatti, l'interesse si sposta sui dettagli dei giunti triangolari e delle gambe di ottone in cima e in fondo. Questi sono i sostegni dei sostegni, per così dire, perché le parti "sceniche" si scompongono ulteriormente. Come sottolinea Frascari, sono questi elementi di base a rappresentare "l'unità minima del processo di significazione"[10]. Il ruolo dei dettagli, dice, è quello di generatori che assumono la funzione solitamente assegnata al progetto. Spogliandoli del loro valore d'uso e allontanandoli dal loro compito originario, Leonor Antunes crea, partendo dal dettaglio, la scultura che Frascari descrive in relazione a Scarpa: "Ciascun dettaglio racconta la storia della propria genesi e collocazione, del proprio dimensionamento."[11]

Emerge dunque che la dimensione corporea della produzione di Leonor Antunes non riguarda precisamente l'infrastruttura, ossia i circuiti delle vene e delle arterie, come se il modernismo fosse un corpo metaforico; piuttosto, la logica dell'opera è guidata dalle parti e dai giunti, distaccati o residui. O forse siamo noi spettatori a circolare tra questi fulcri. Quando entriamo nello spazio e lo attraversiamo, le cose tendono a disperdersi. I divisori bloccano alcuni passaggi e ne aprono altri. Le luccicanti sfaccettature metalliche riflettono e rifrangono le strutture e le superfici esterne. I risultati prodotti in altri contesti e il nuovo lavoro si uniscono, stimolandosi a vicenda per creare inediti rapporti morfologici. Nel frattempo, i riferimenti fissi al luogo e al tempo si smarriscono. Gli episodi storici del design modernista — oltre ai nomi che diventano i loro protagonisti, come Helg, Martin, Albers o Porset — si ridispongono e si riconfigurano, invitandoci a riflettere nuovamente su come le cose vivono nel mondo.

BRIONY FER

1 Roger Caillois, *Mimicry and Legendary Psychasthenia*, in *The Edge of Surrealism: A Caillois Reader*, Duke University Press, Durham 2003, p. 96.
2 *Ibidem*.
3 Gio Ponti progettò il grattacielo Pirelli a Milano, un edificio di trentadue piani, nel 1950.
4 Roger Caillois, *Mimicry and Legendary Psychasthenia*, cit., p. 91.
5 Penso a opere come *Right After* di Hesse (fibra di vetro, 1969). Questa "caduta" scultorea è stata ampiamente commentata: si veda, per esempio, Briony Fer, *The Infinite Line*, Yale University Press, New Haven 2004, pp. 117-144.
6 Adolf Loos, *On Thrift*, in *On Architecture*, a cura di Adolf Opel e Daniel Opel, traduzione di Michael Mitchell, Ariadne Press, Riverside 1995, p. 178.
7 Per esempio, *Trébuchet* di Marcel Duchamp (1917), un appendiabiti ready-made posizionato direttamente sul pavimento, o *Tout-fait* (1916), che era appeso al soffitto. Entrambi andarono perduti; ne furono realizzate delle repliche negli anni sessanta.
8 *Leonor Antunes: The Frisson of the Togetherness*, a cura di Lydia Yee e Habda Rashid, Whitechapel Gallery, London 2017.
9 Walter Benjamin, *L'opera d'arte nell'epoca della sua riproducibilità tecnica. Arte e società di massa*, Einaudi, Torino 2000, p. 45.
10 Marco Frascari, *The Tell-tale Detail*, in *Via 7: The Building of Architecture*, The MIT Press, Cambridge 1984, p. 23.
11 Ivi, p. 29.

LEONOR ANTUNES
THE LAST DAYS IN GALLIATE

PIRELLI HANGARBICOCCA
MILAN, 2018

PHOTOS BY
NICK ASH

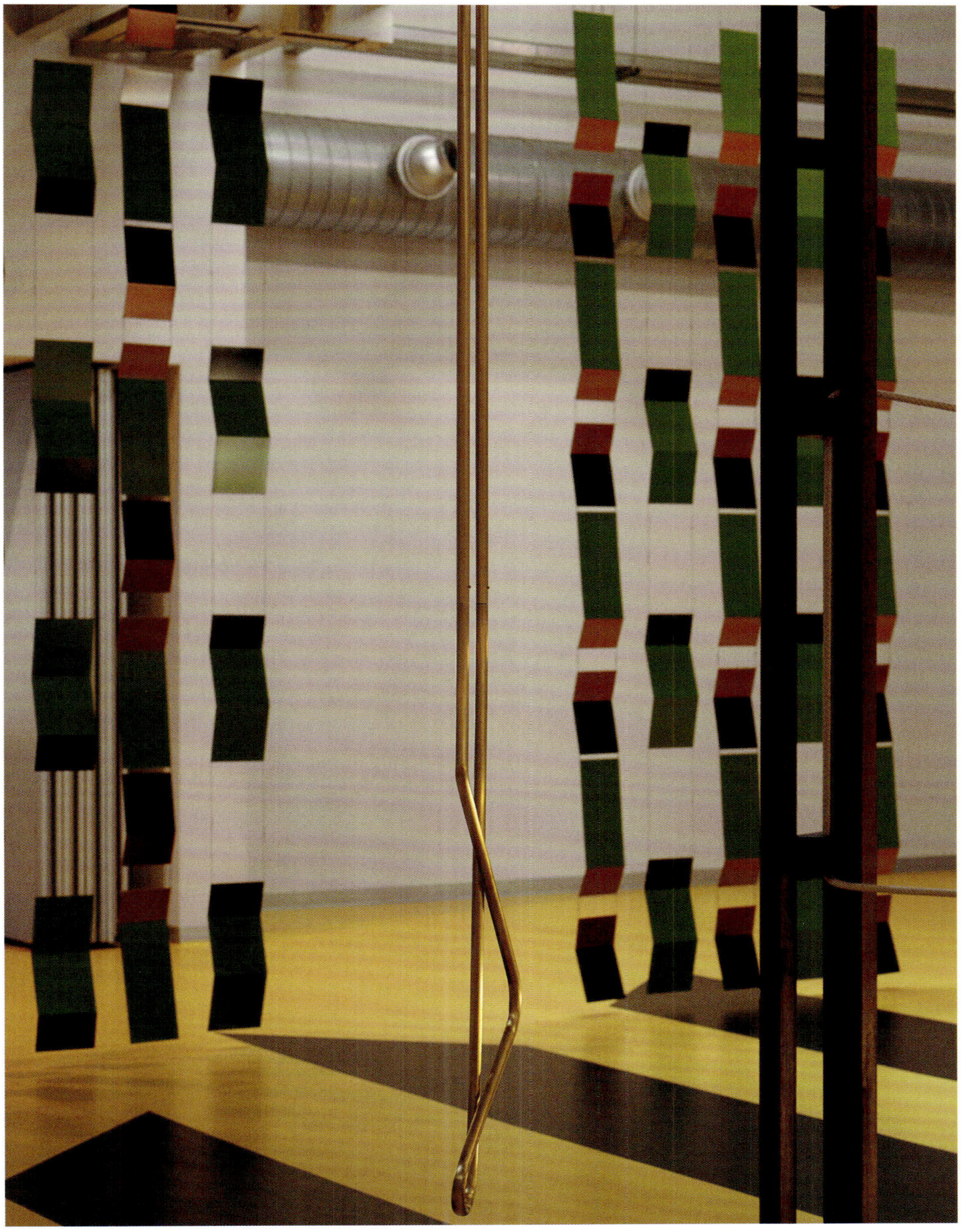

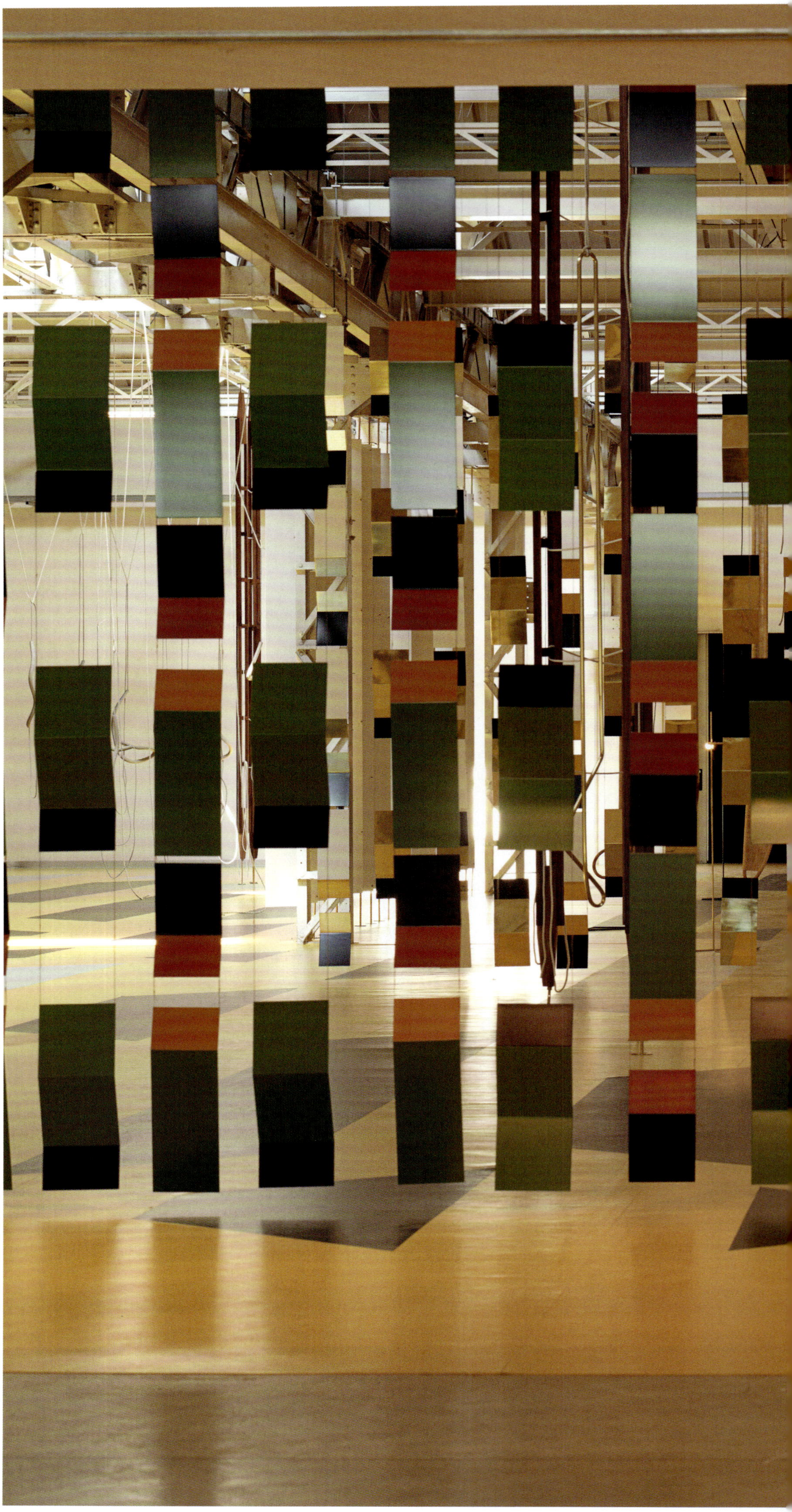

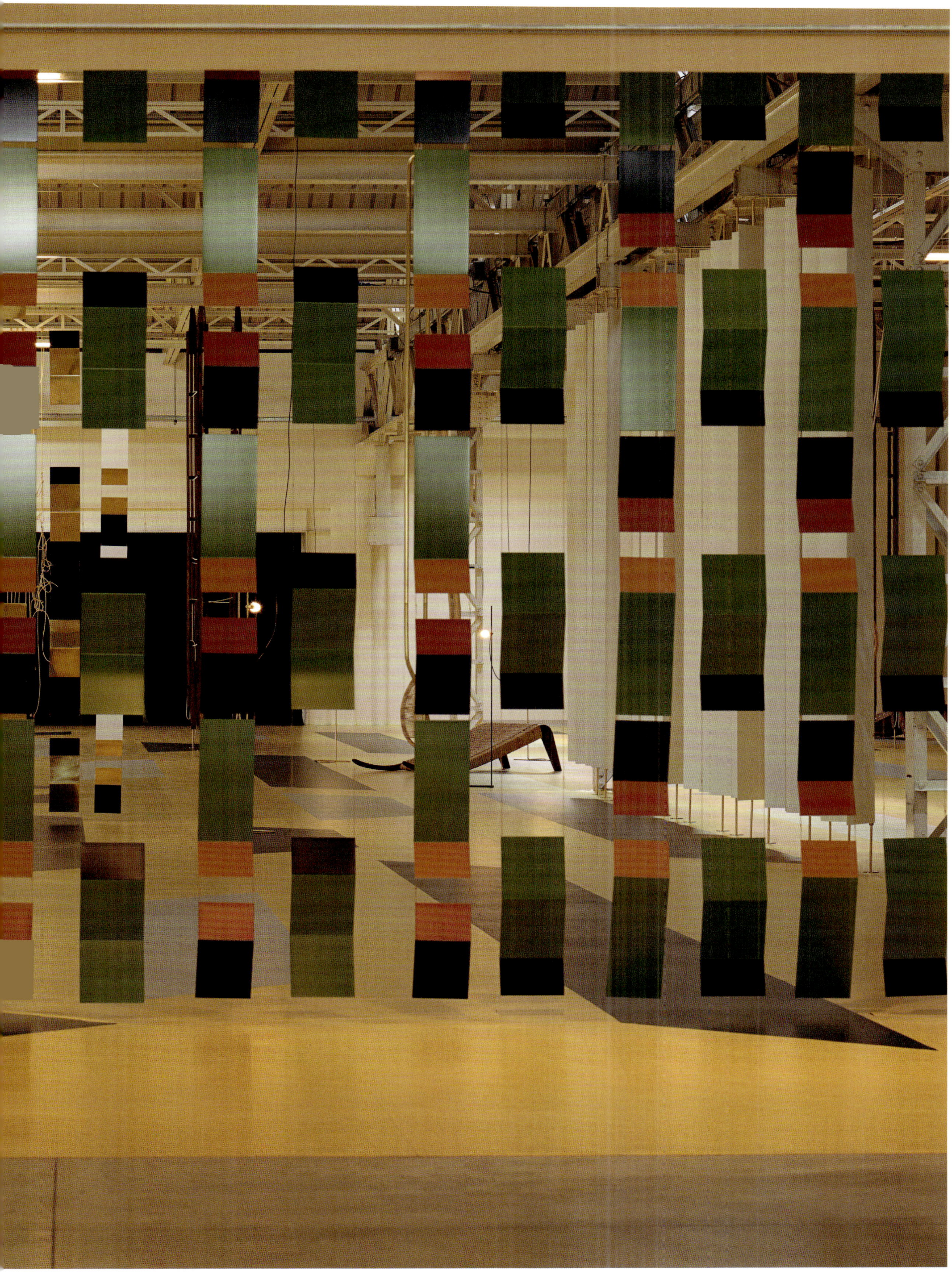

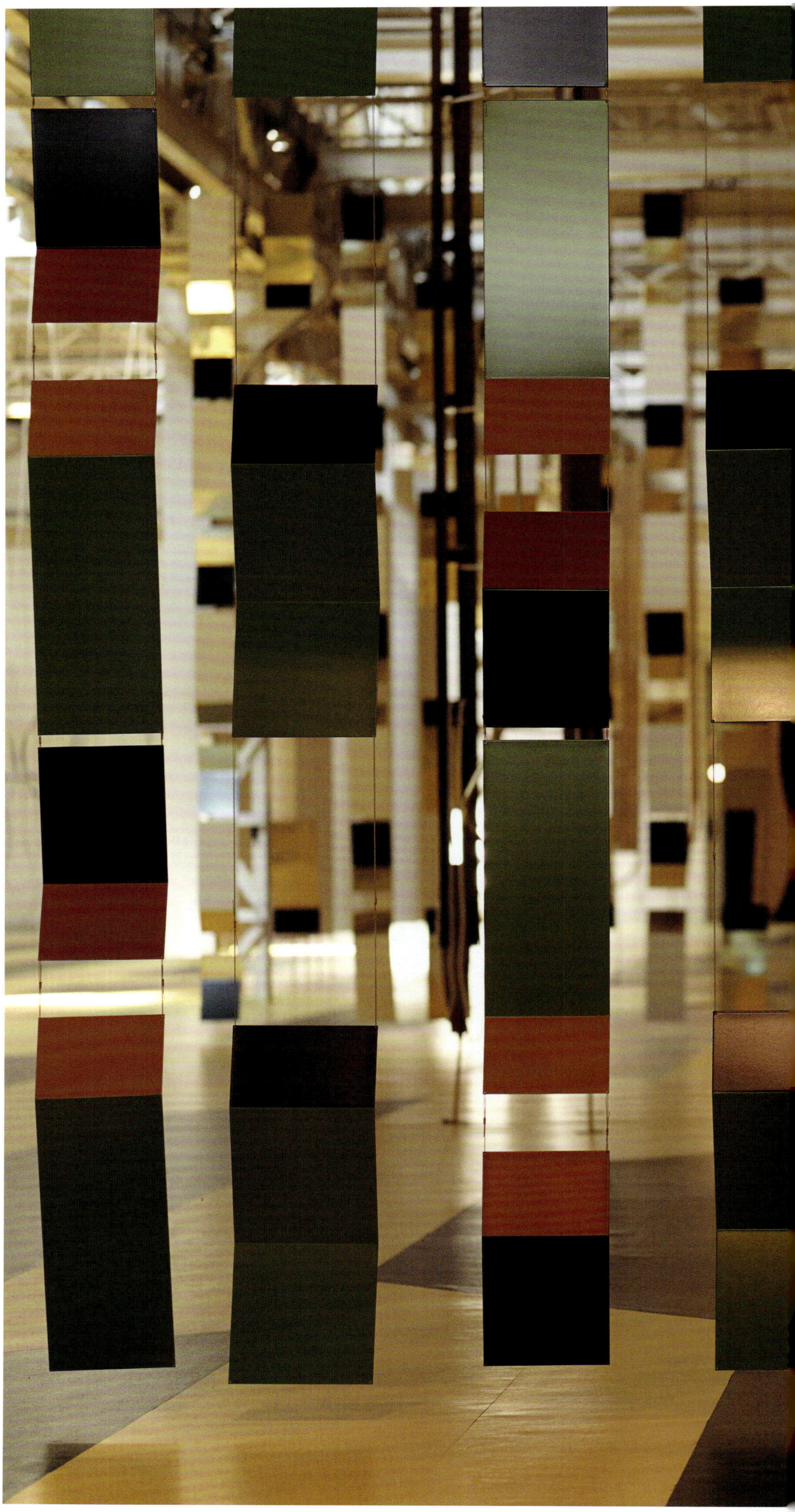

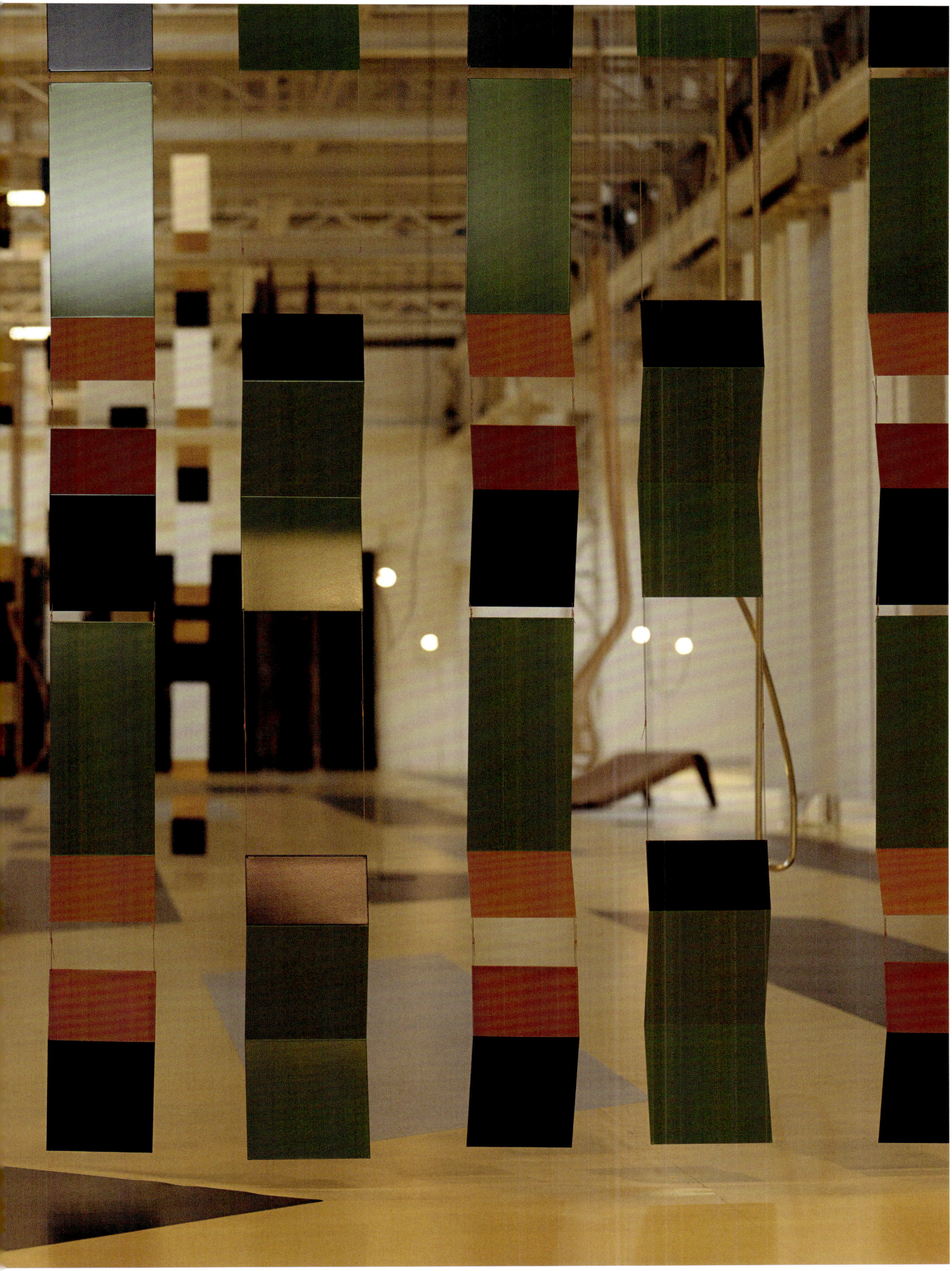

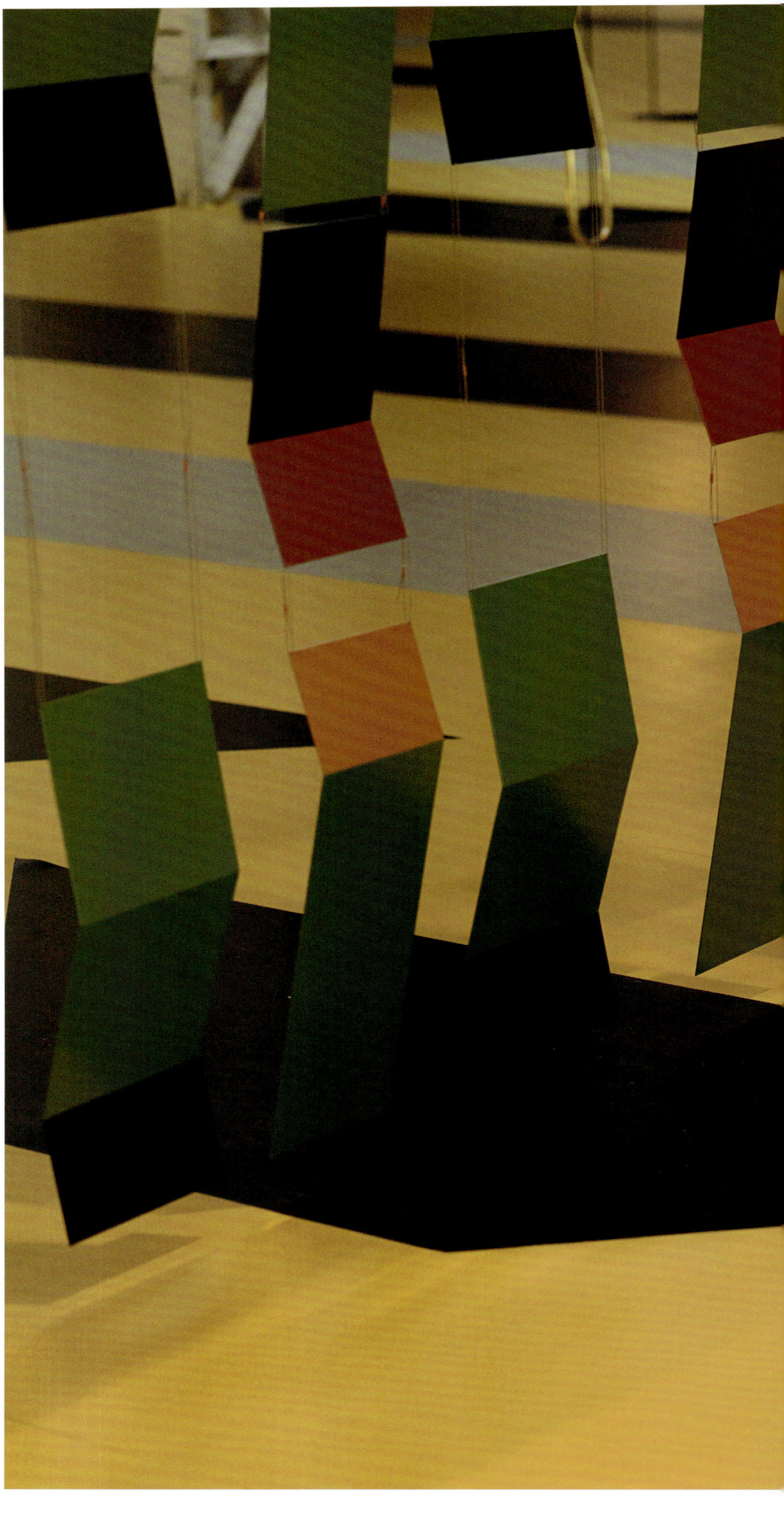

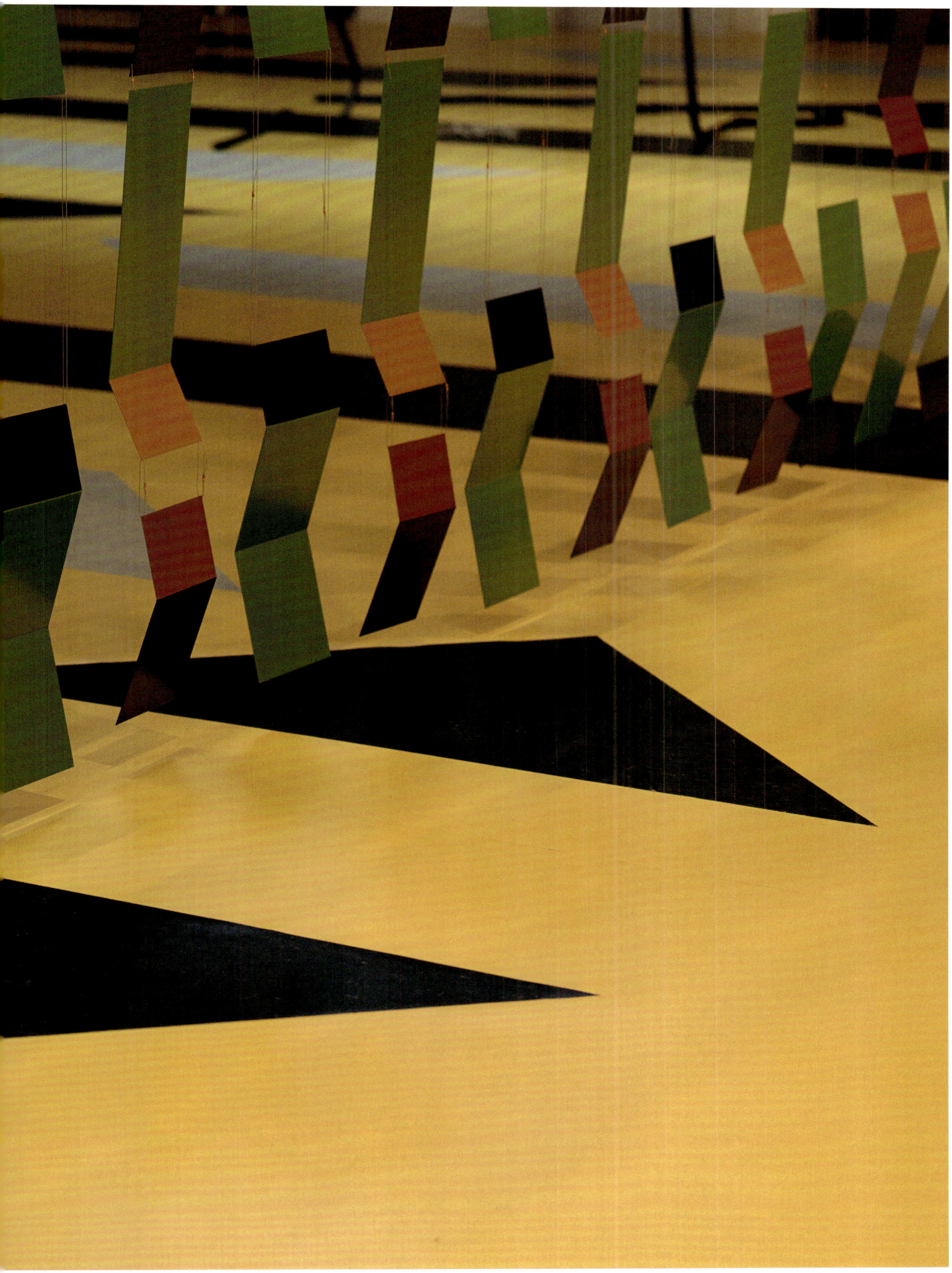

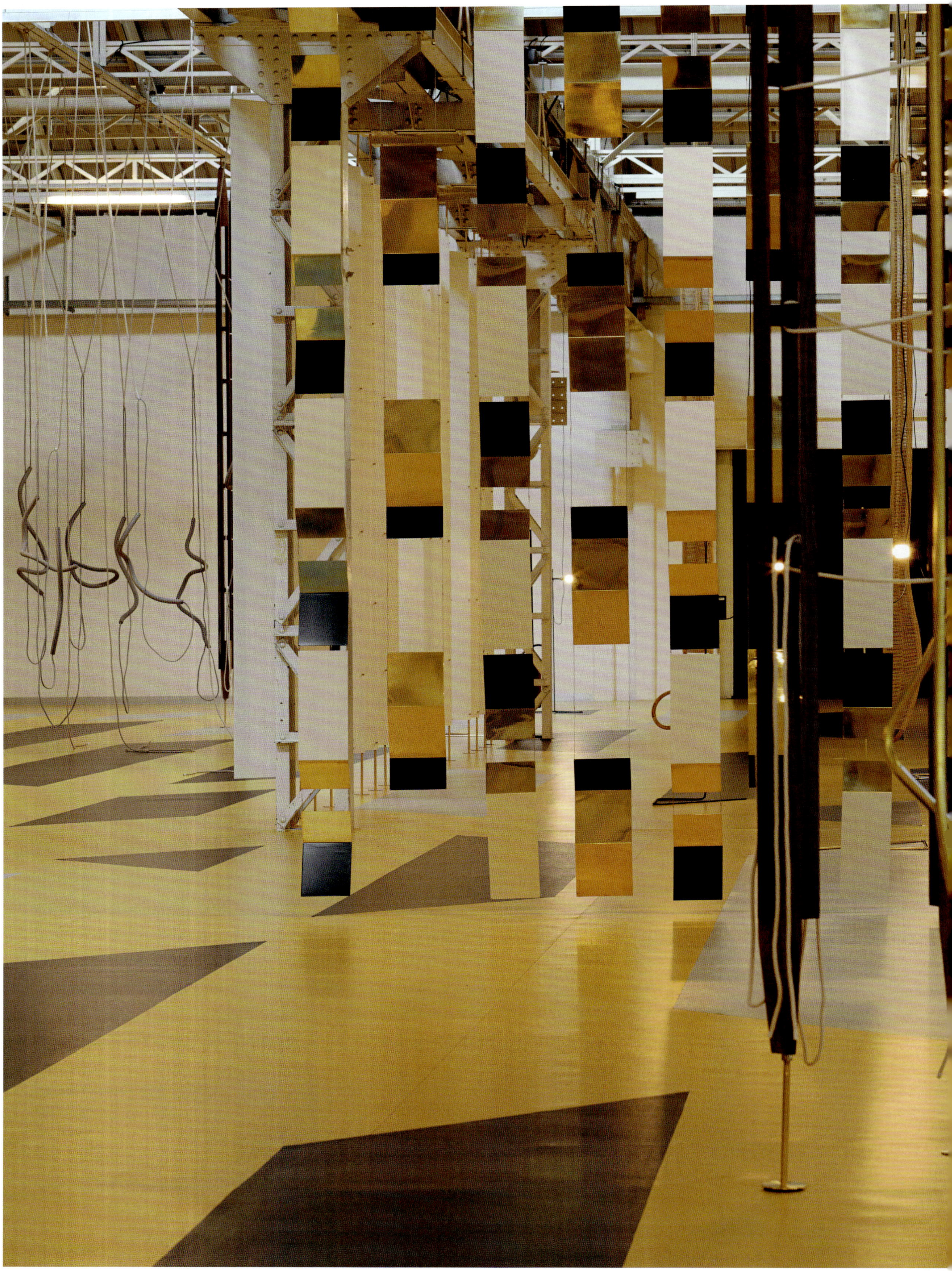

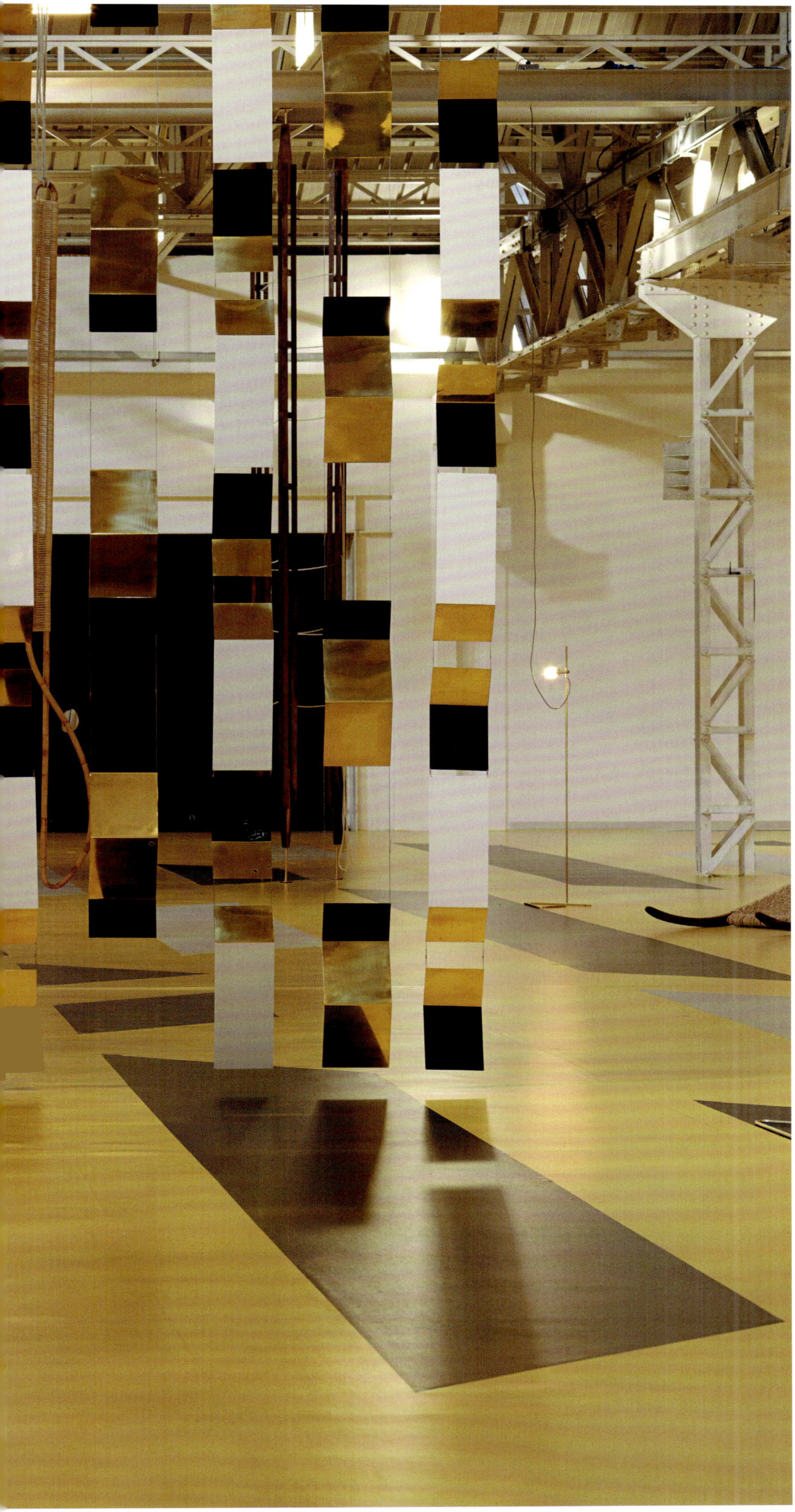

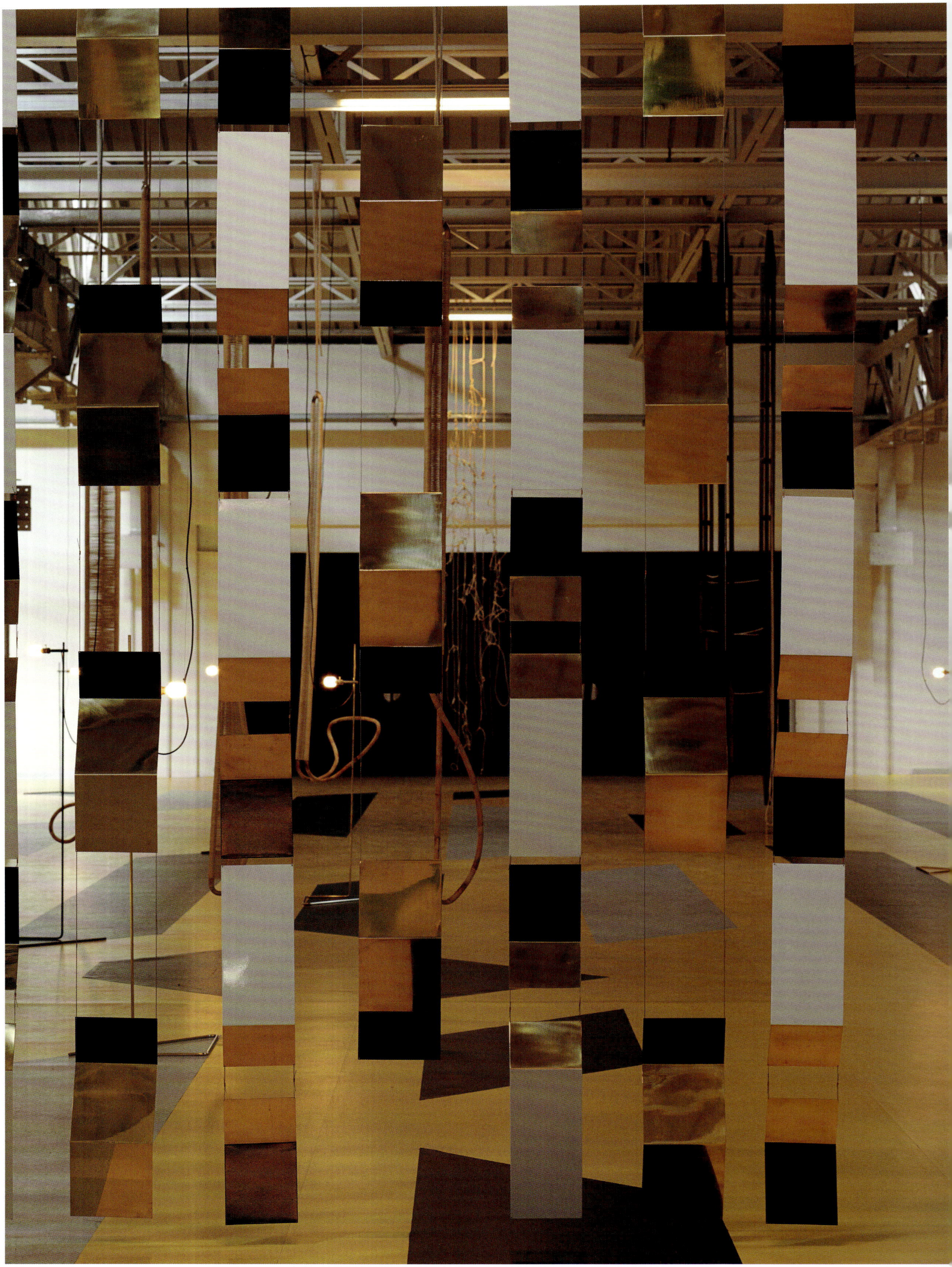

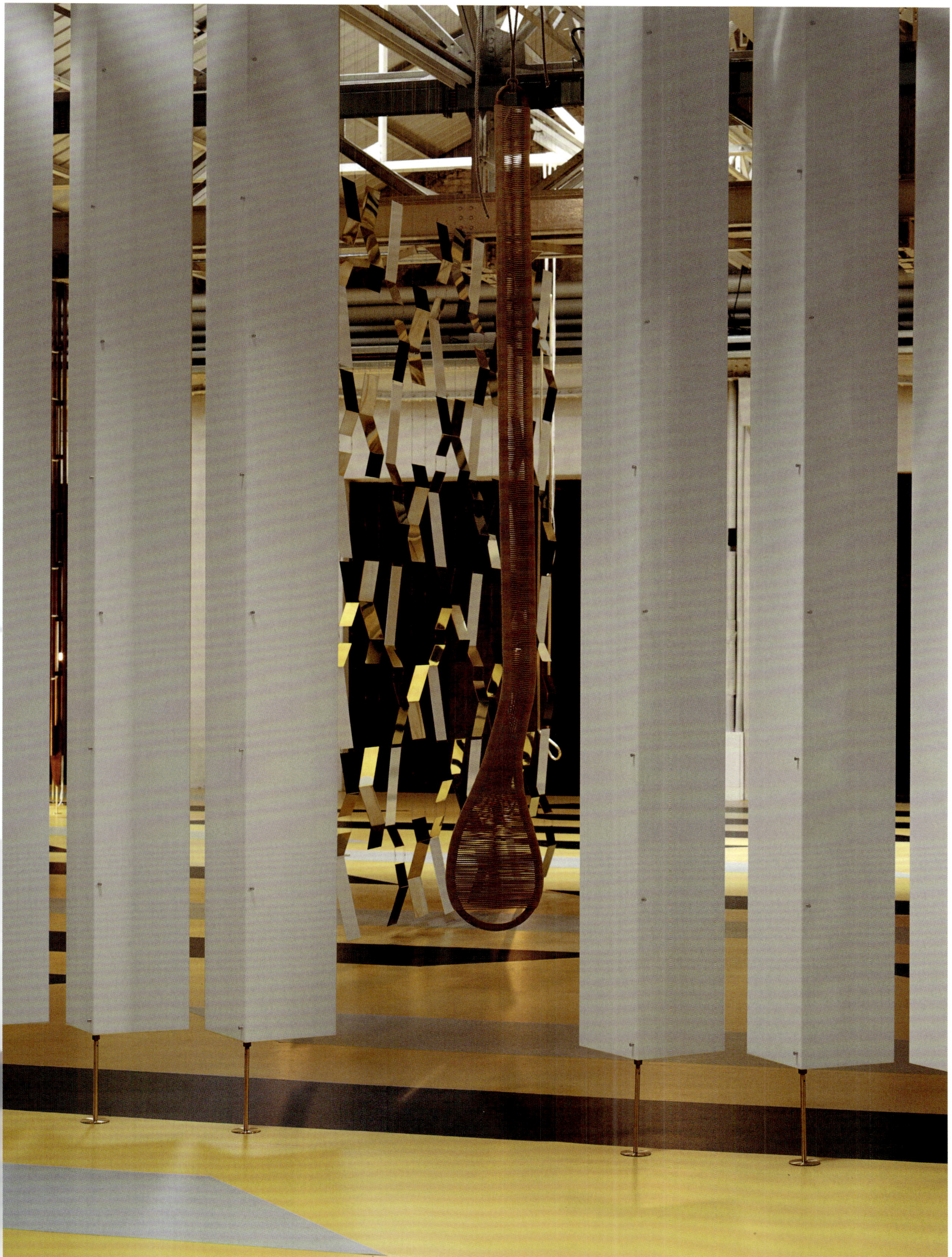

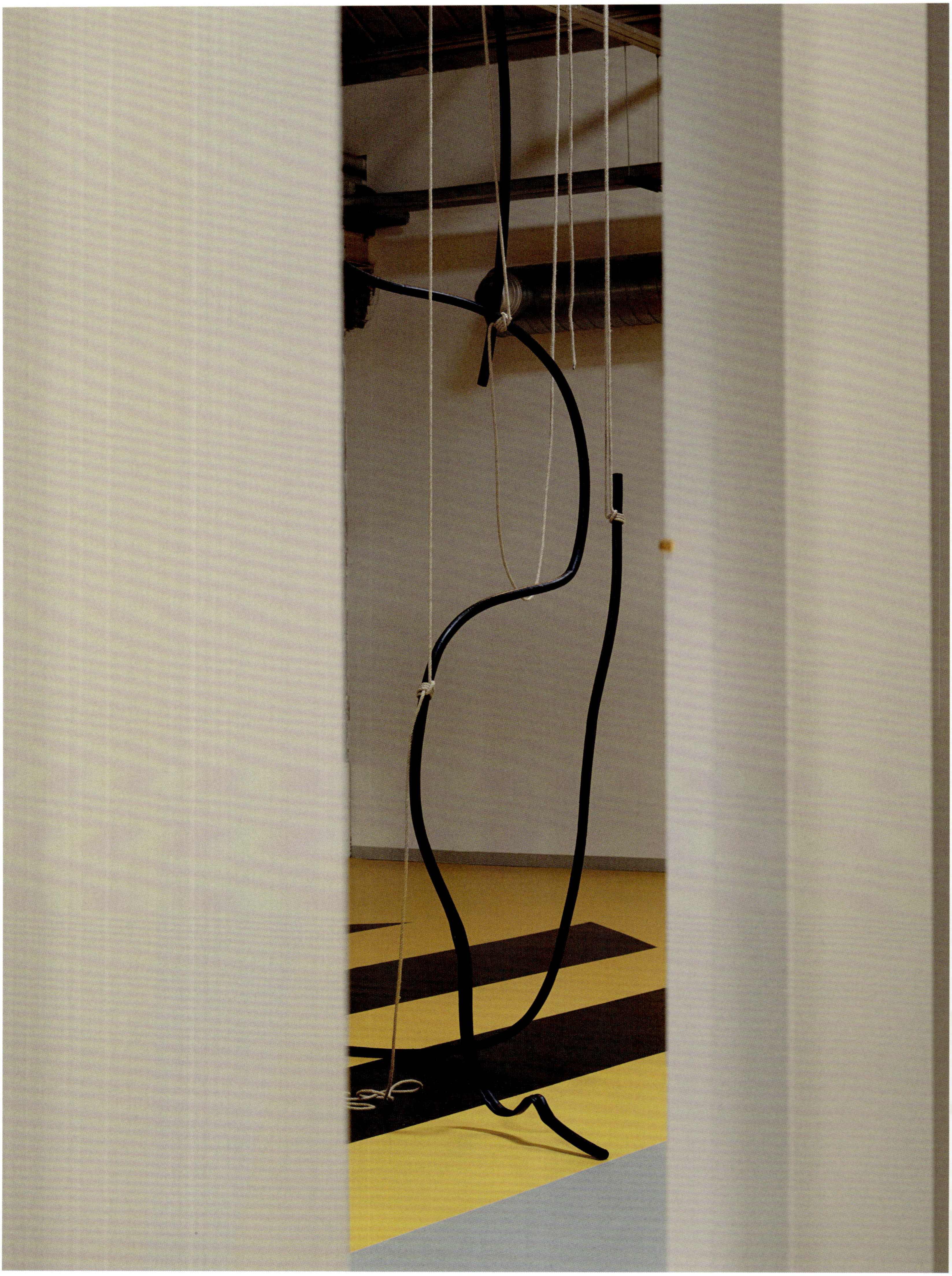

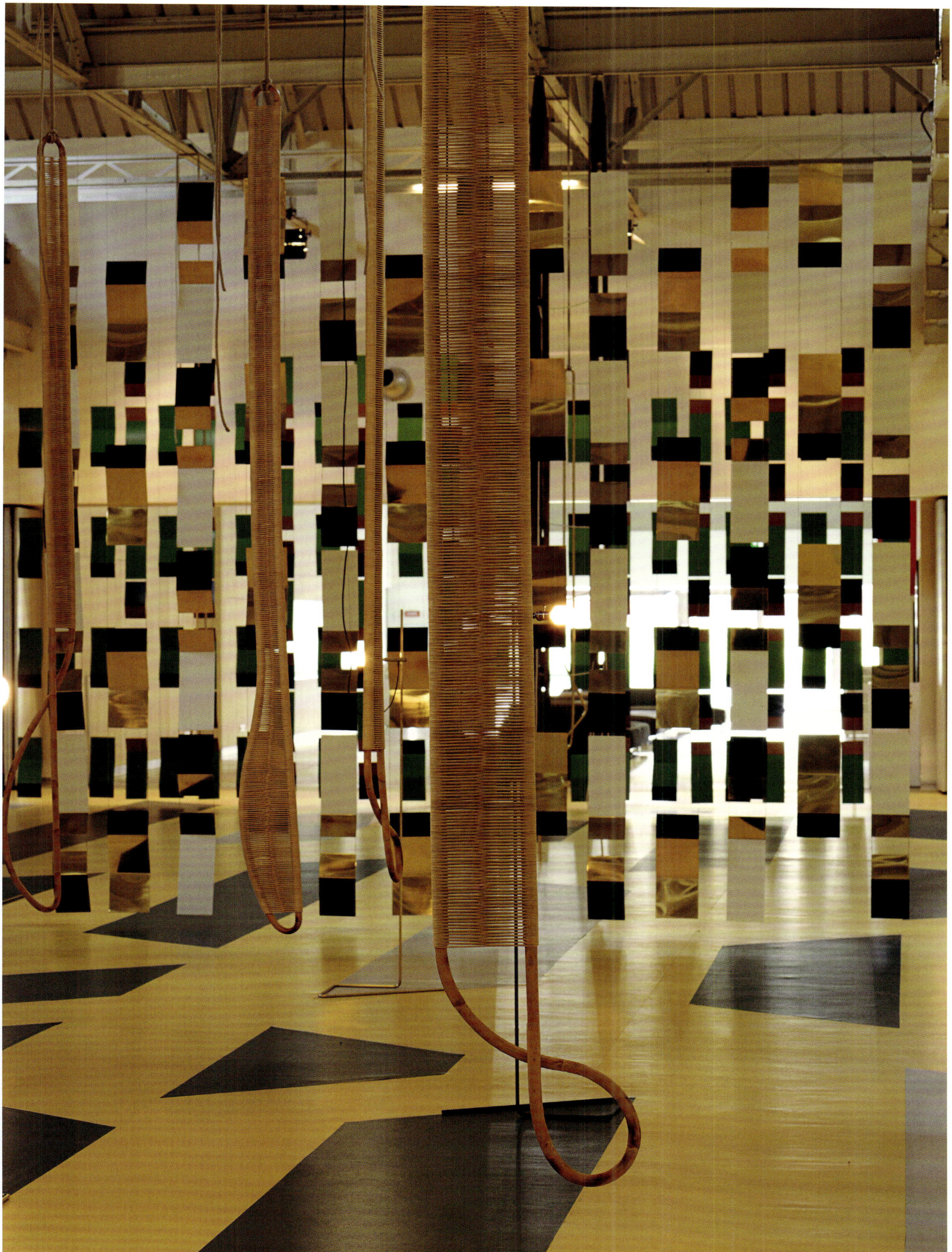

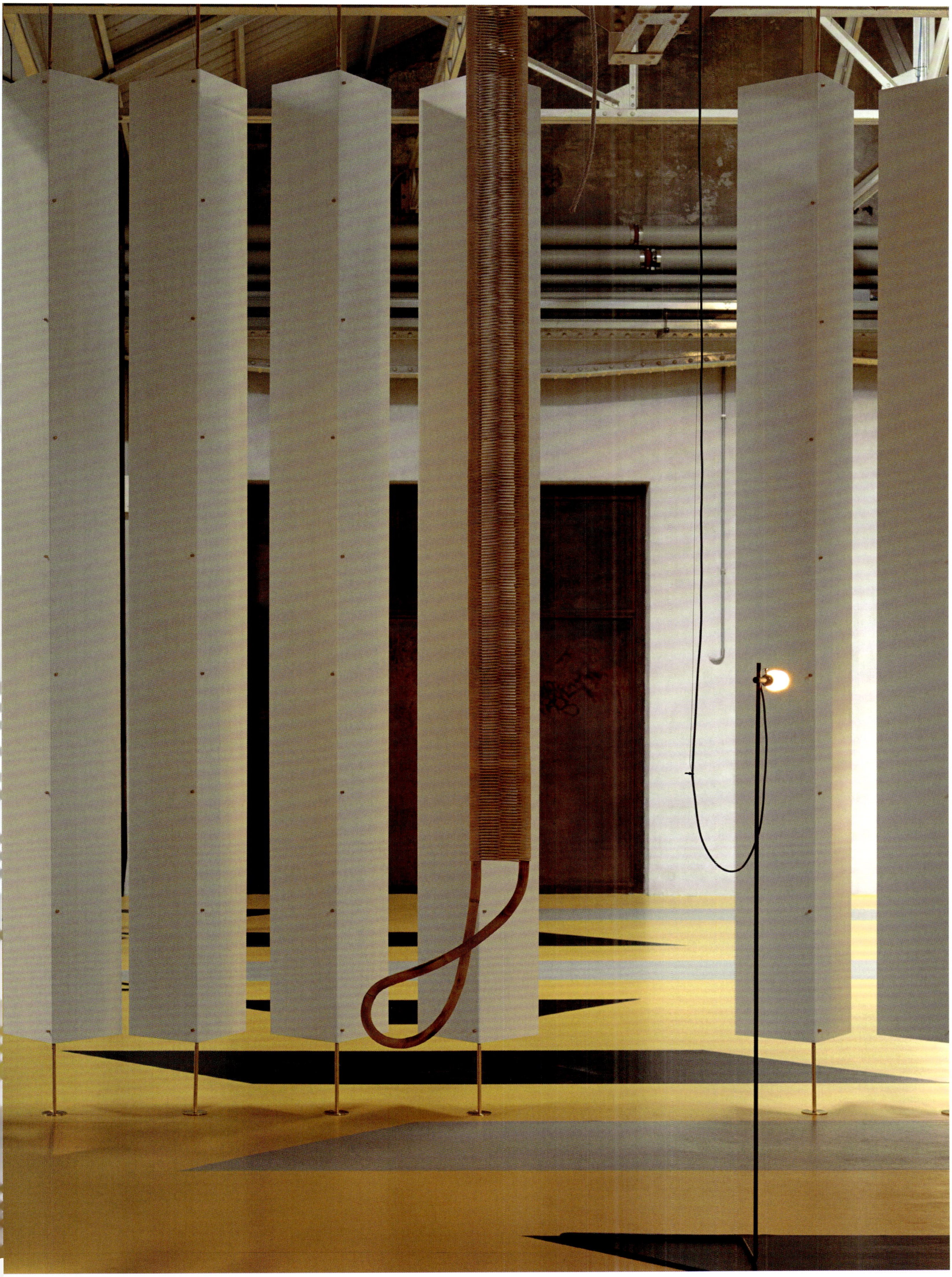

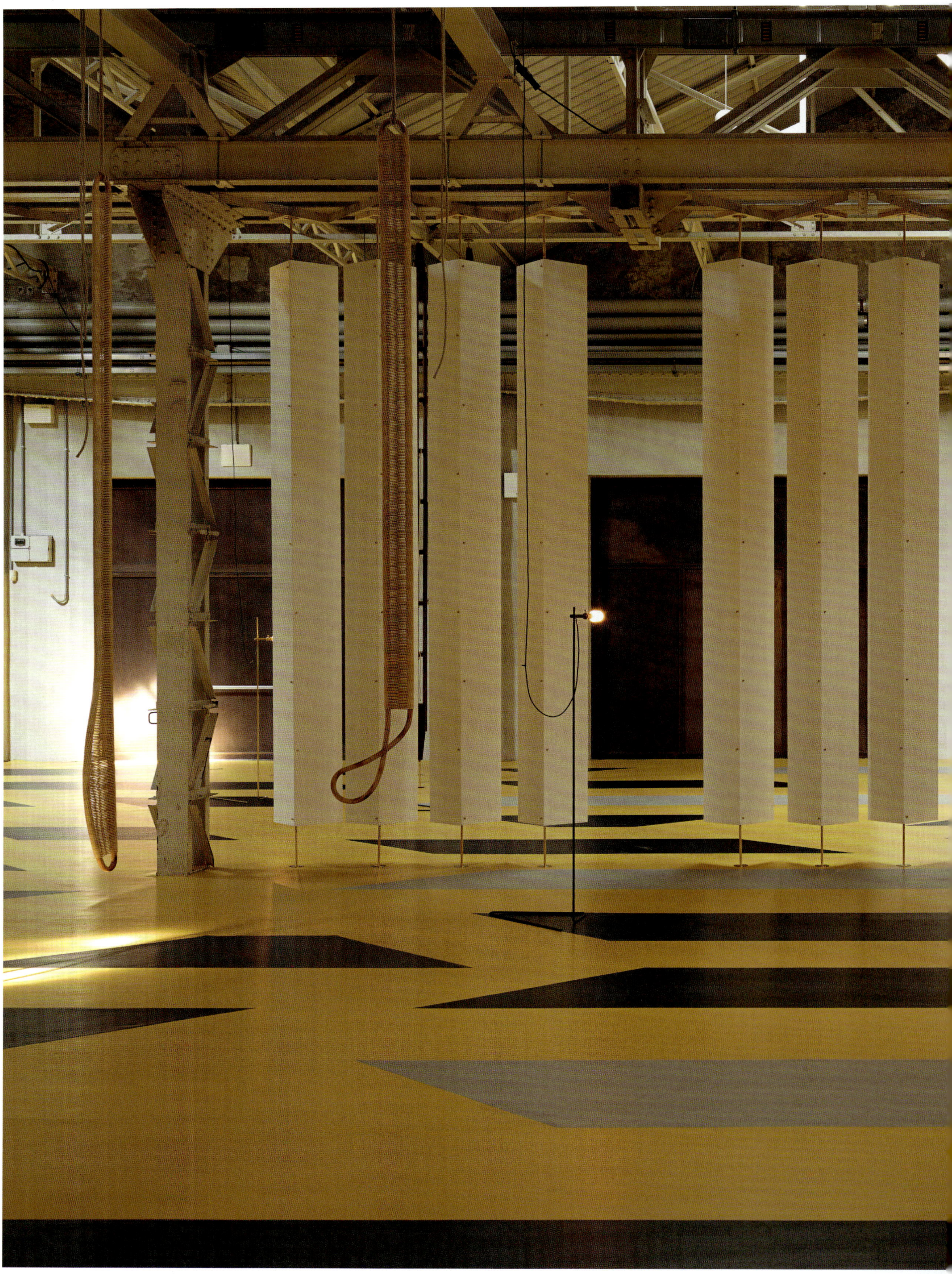

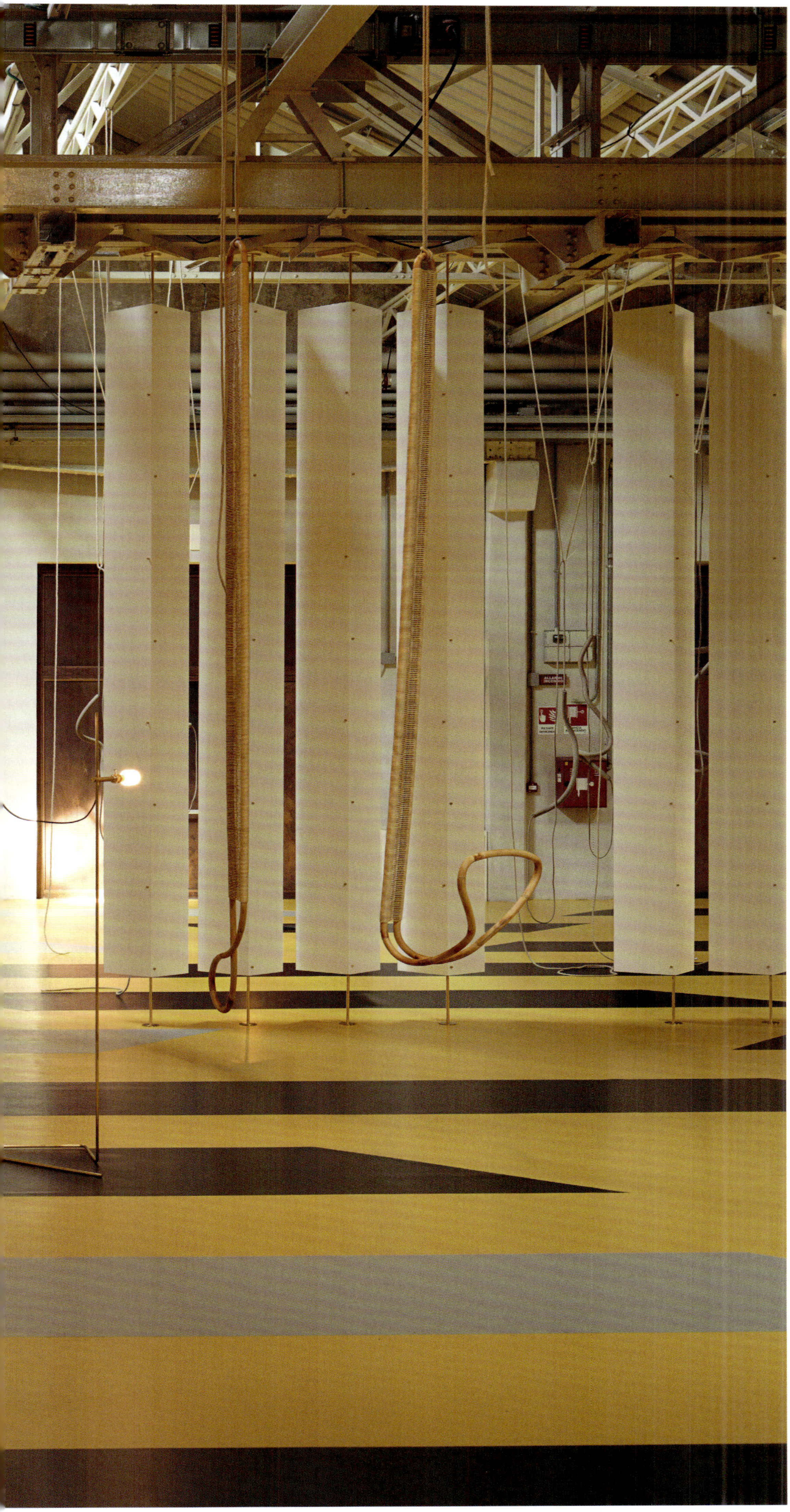

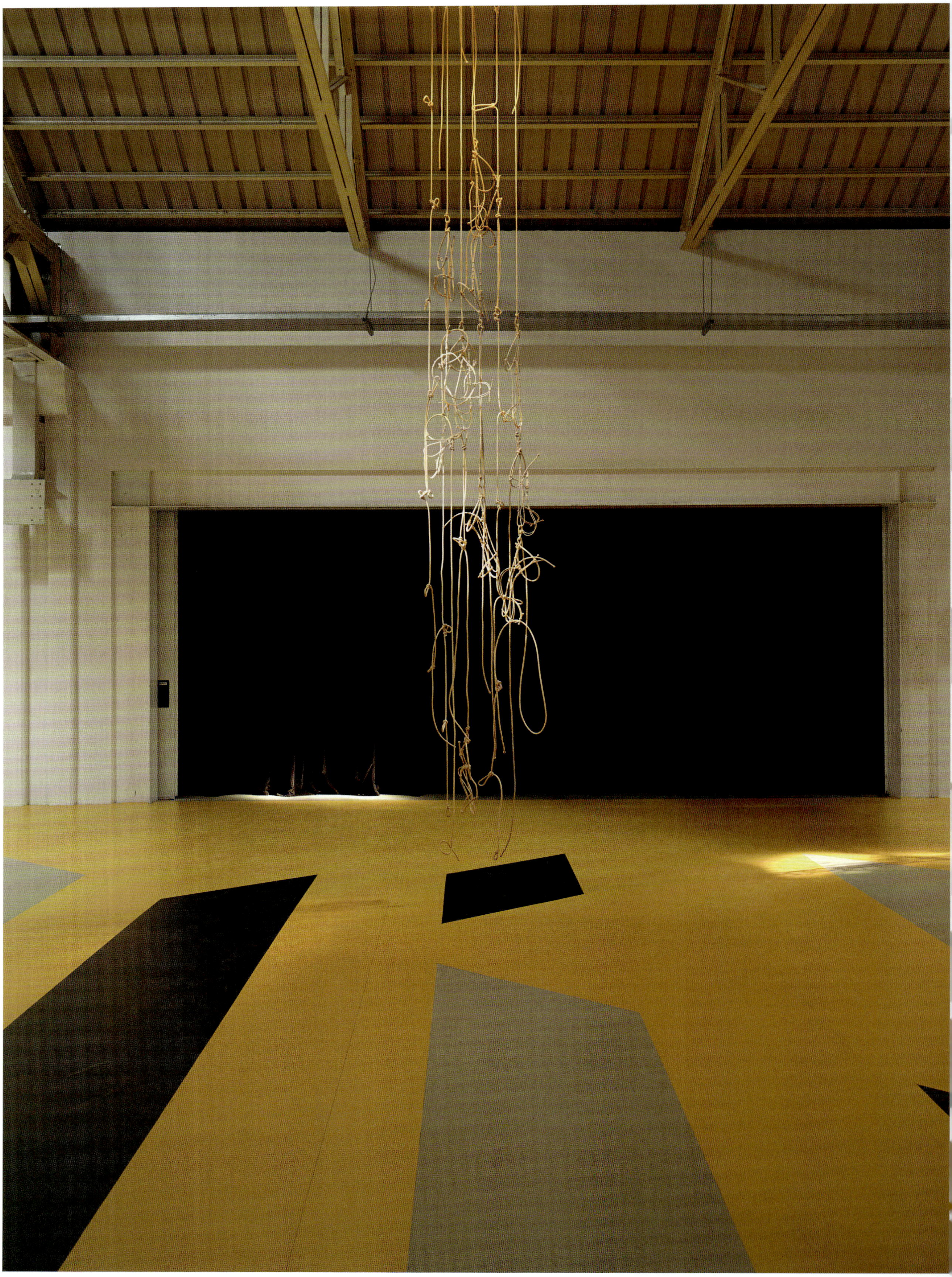

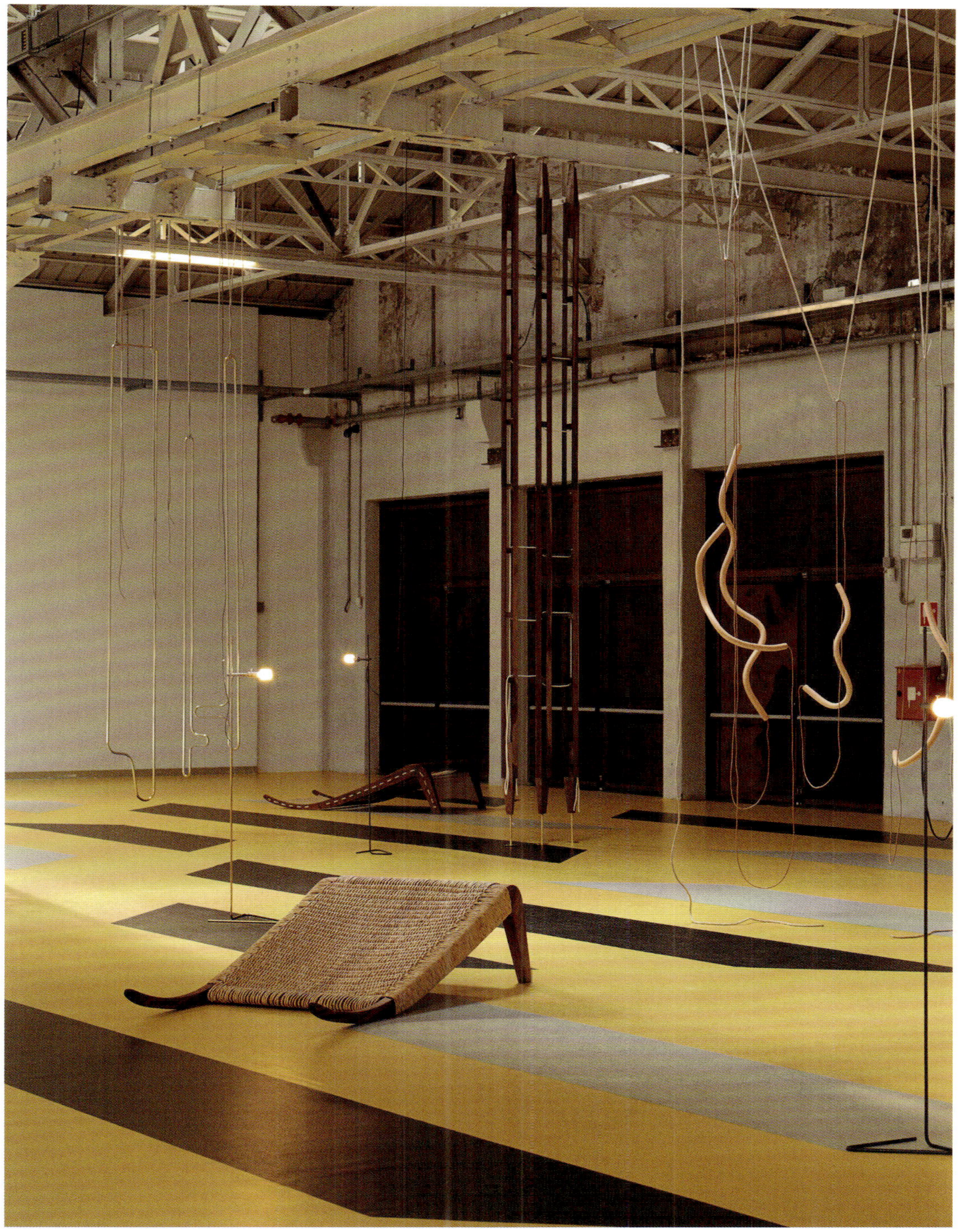

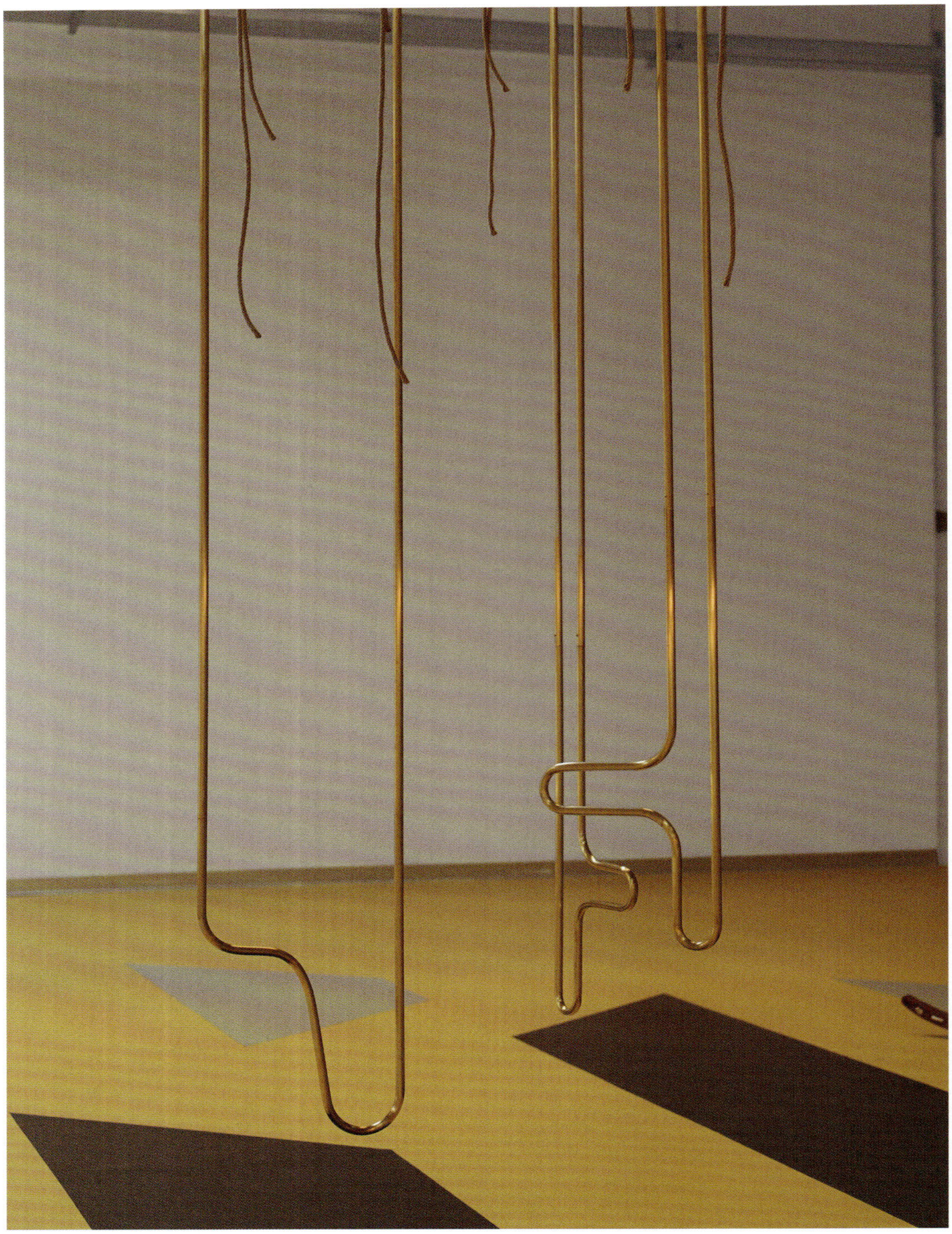

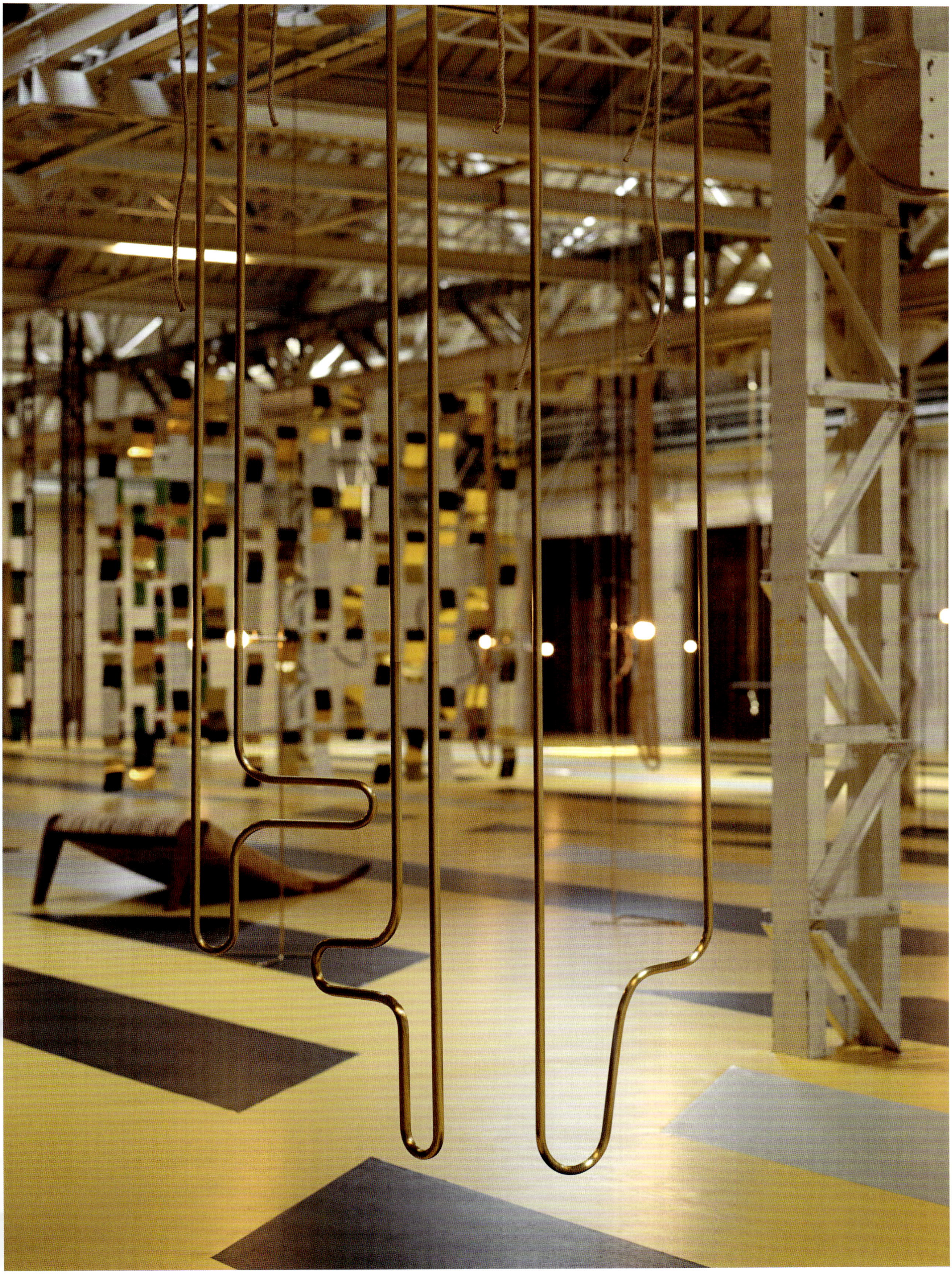

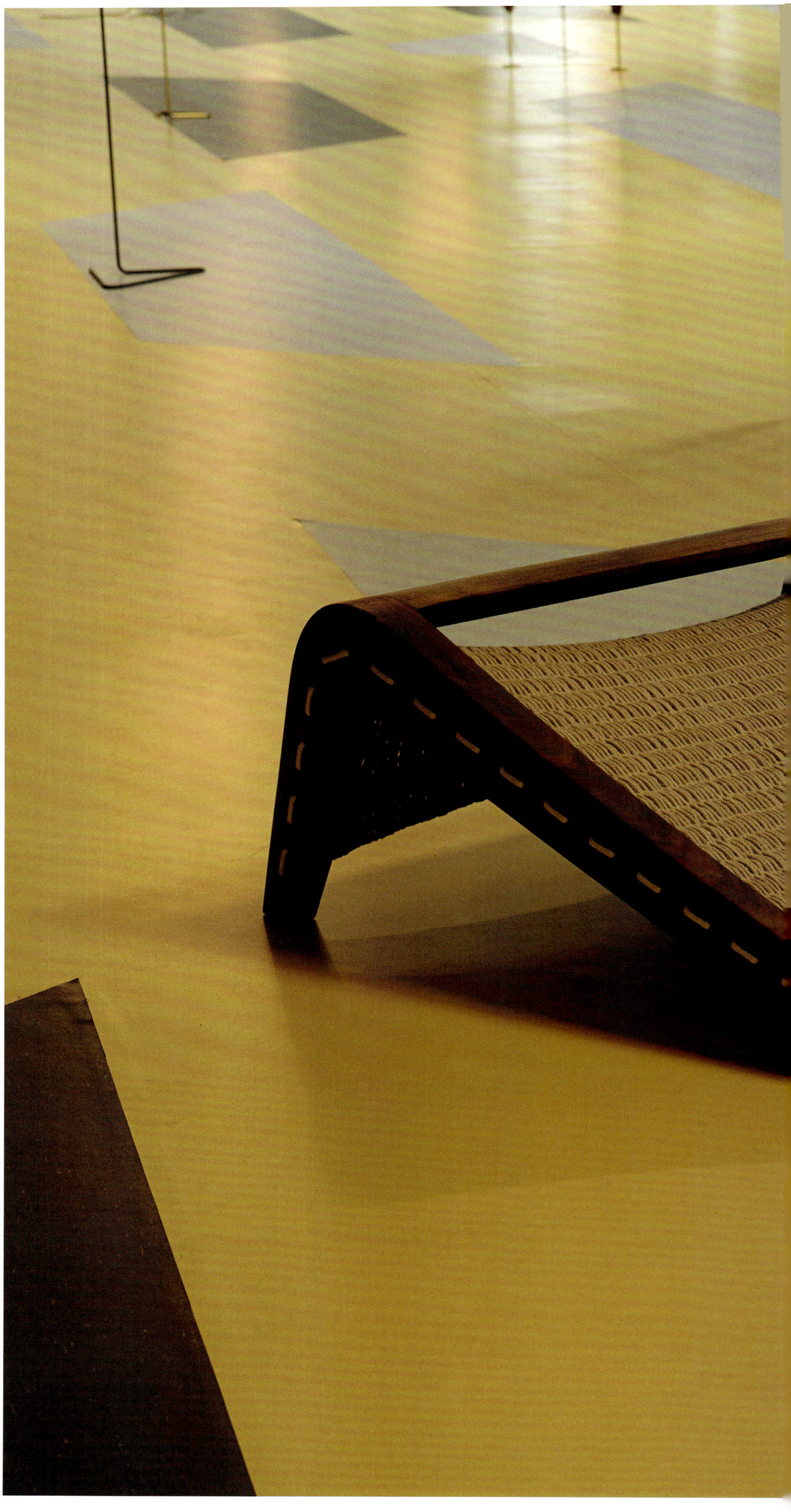

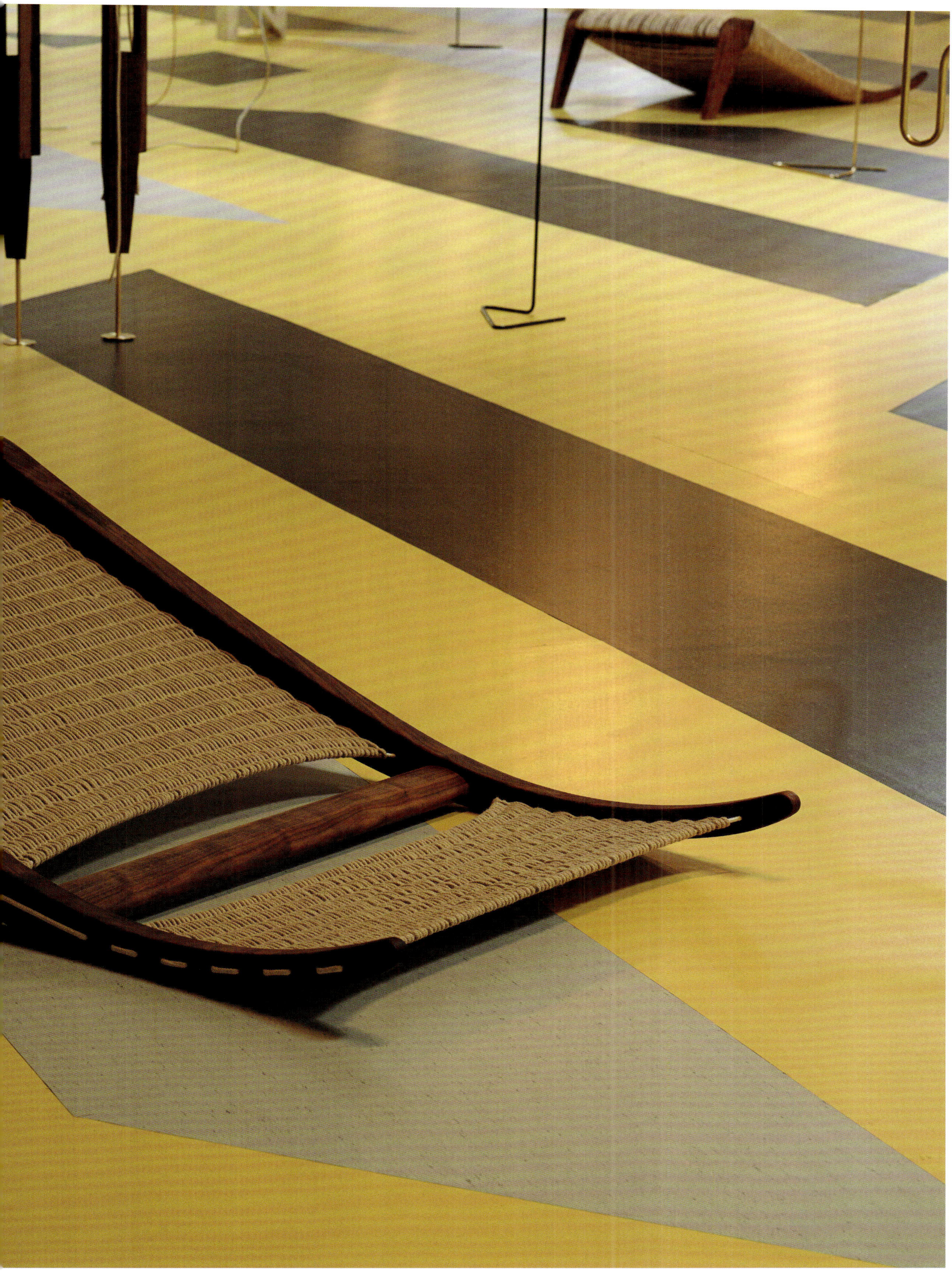

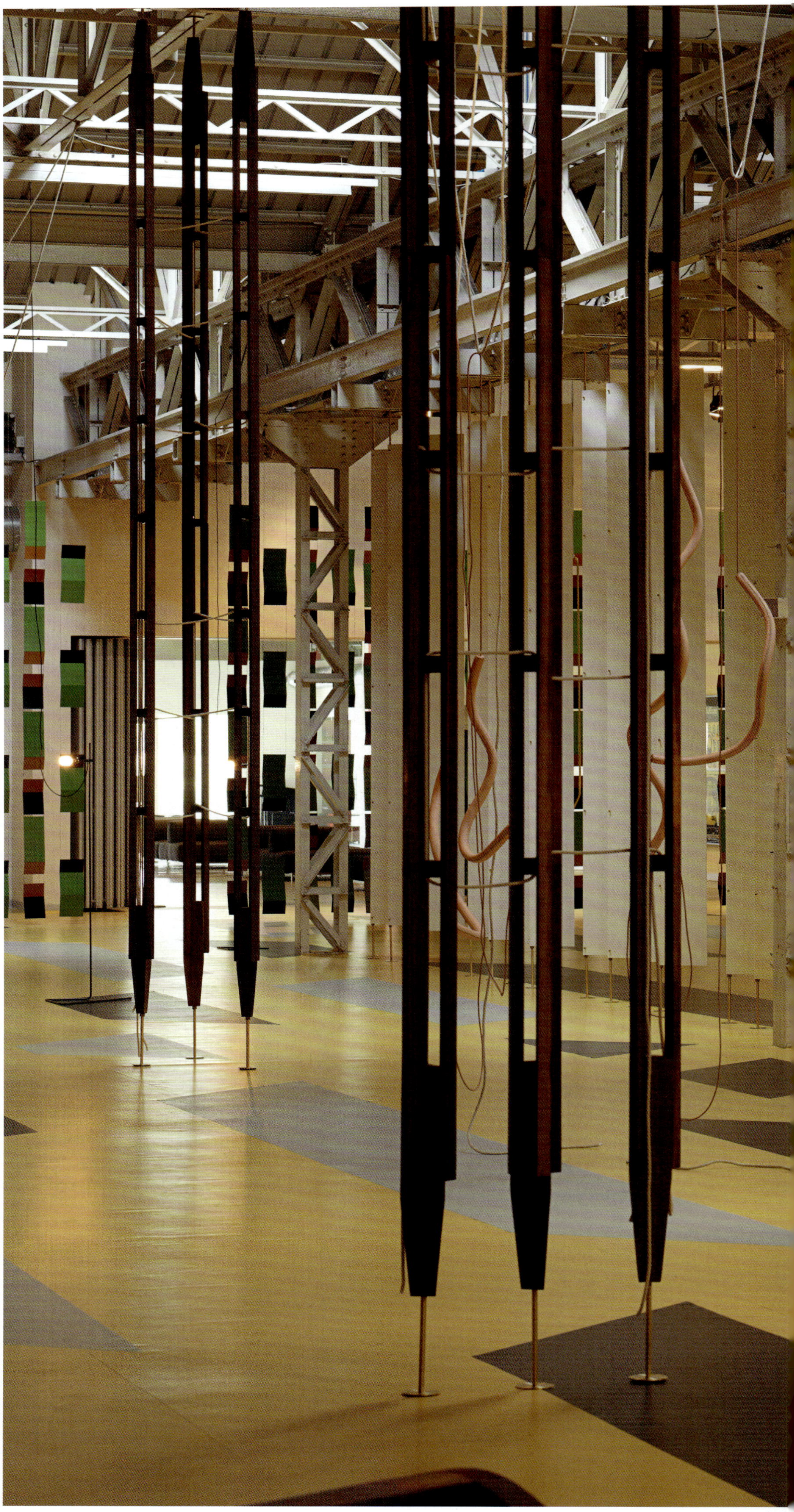

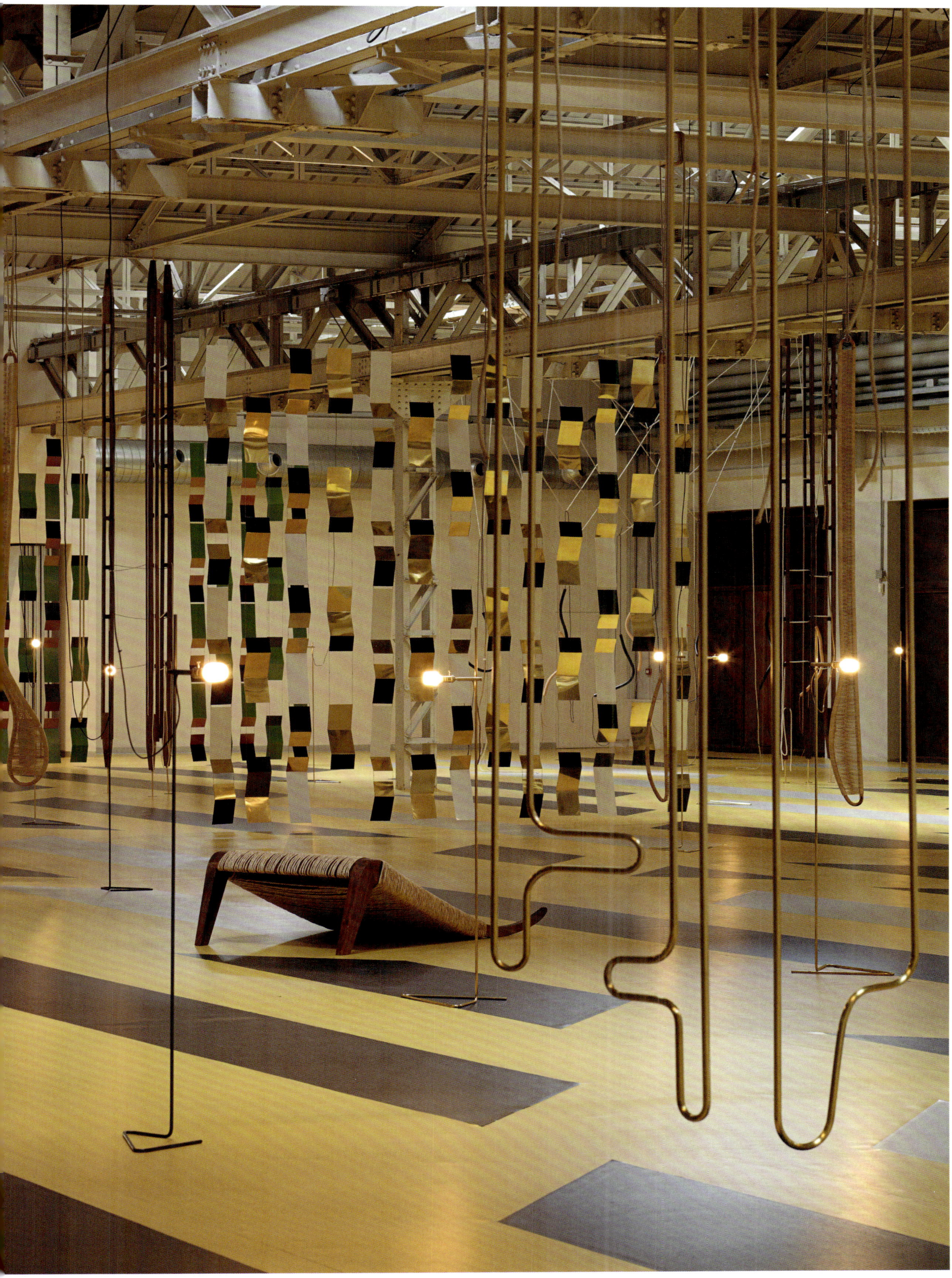

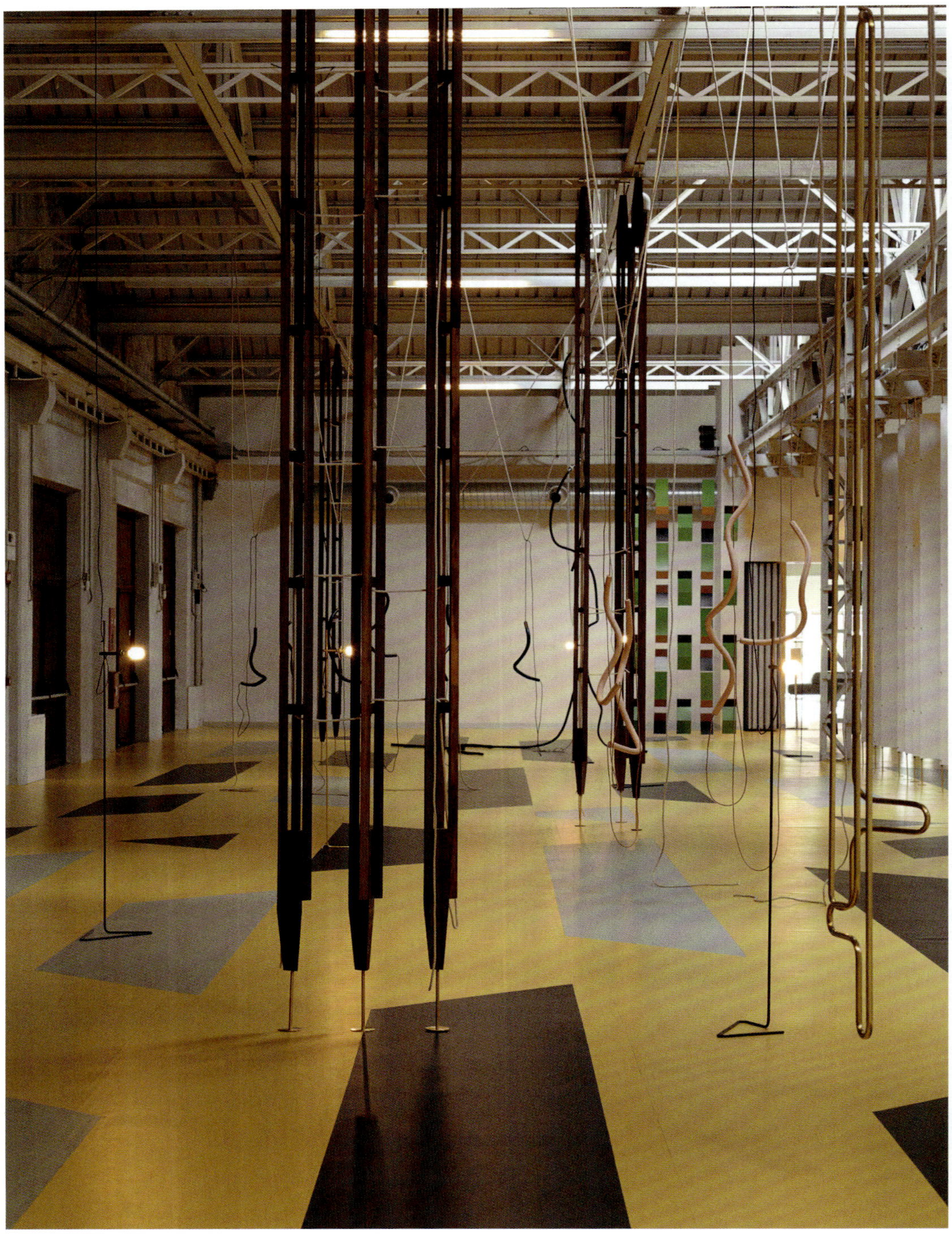

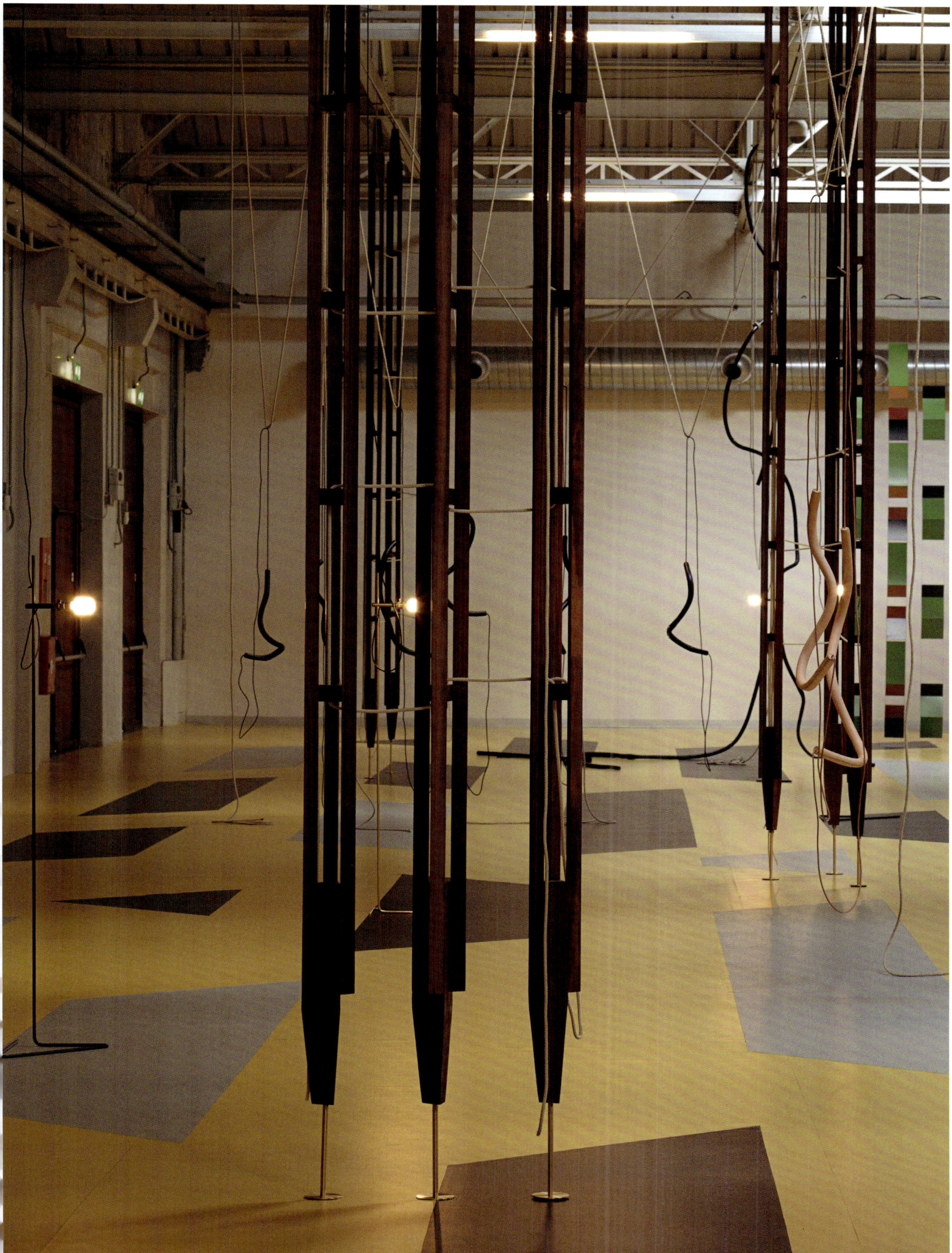

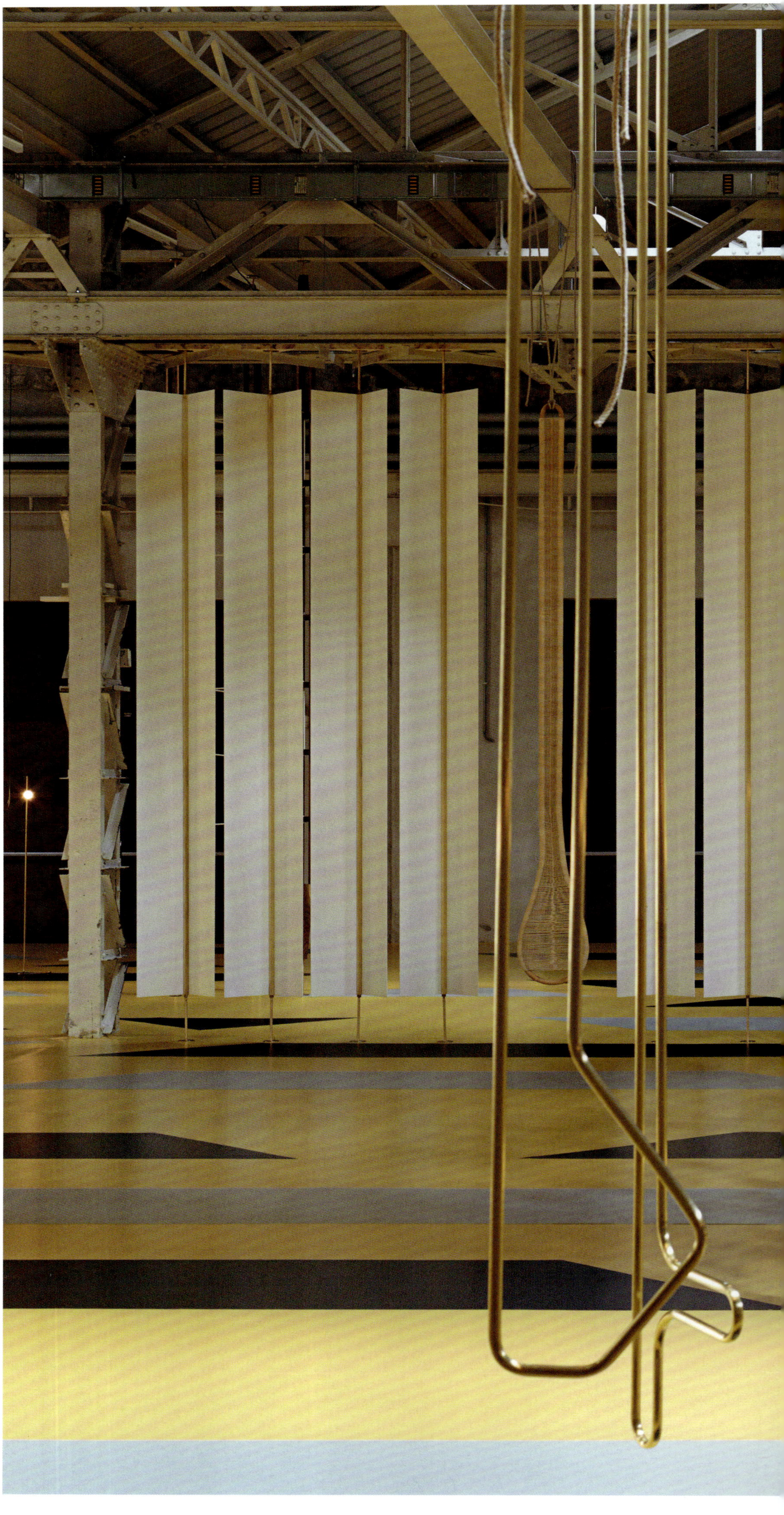

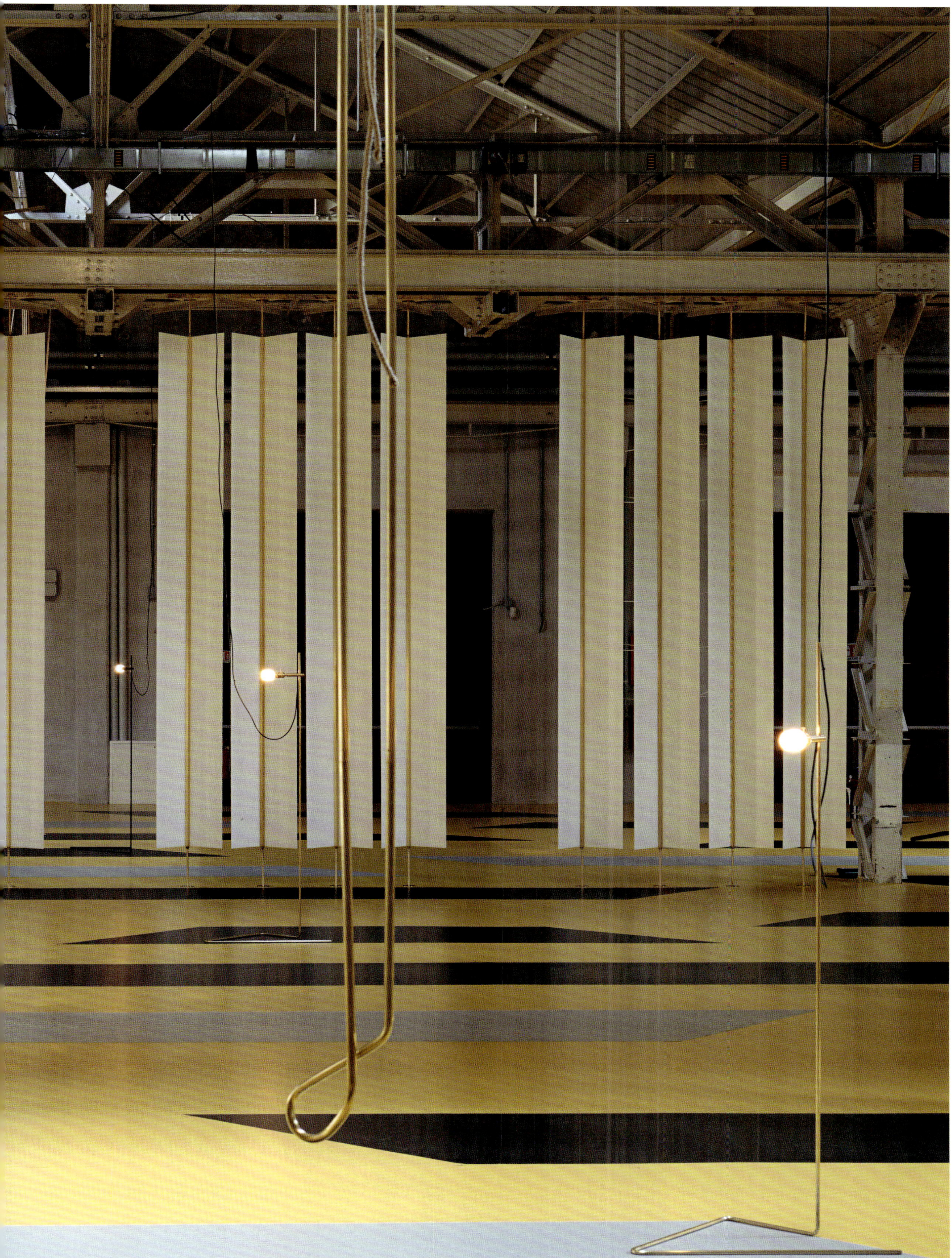

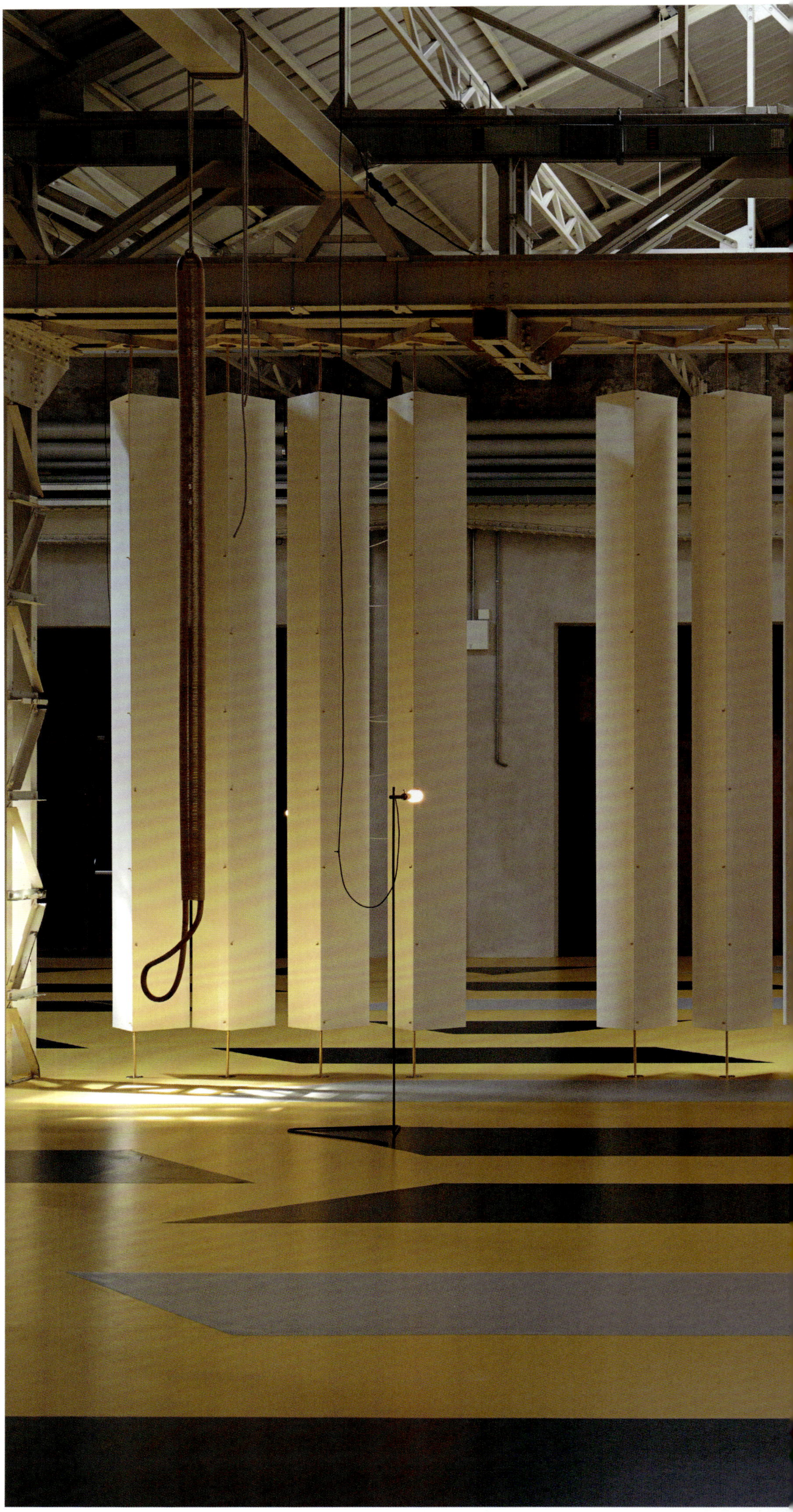

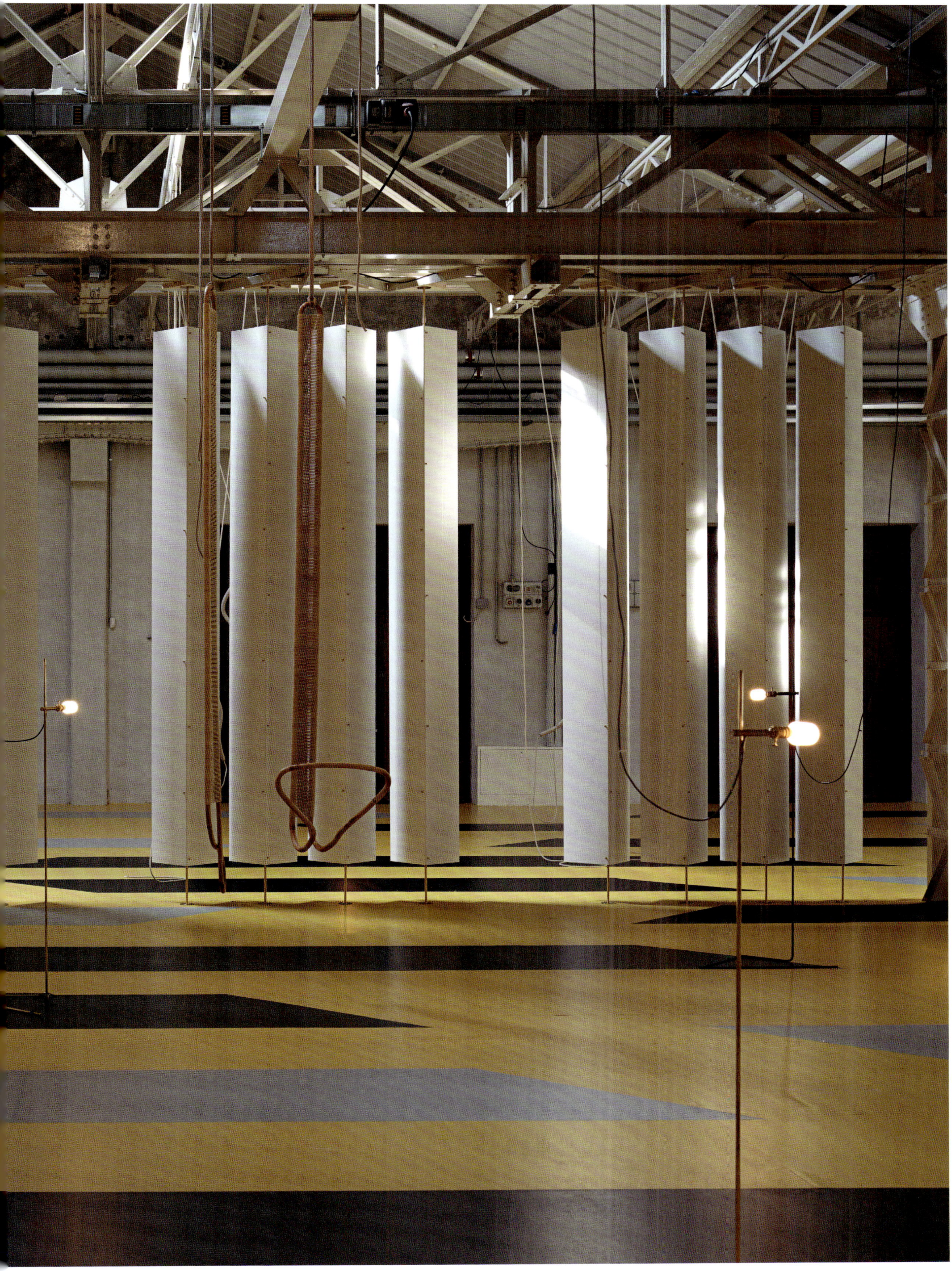

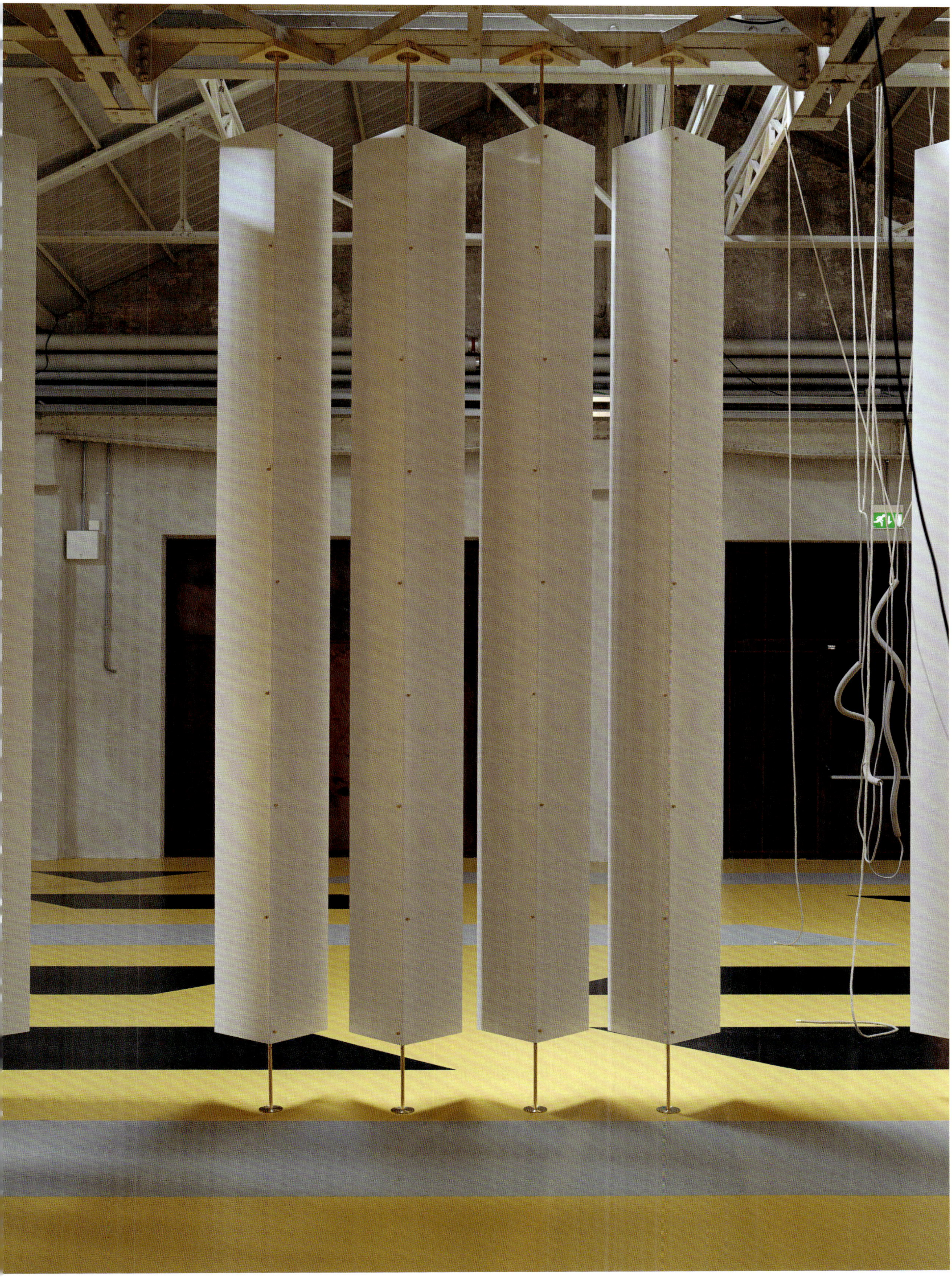

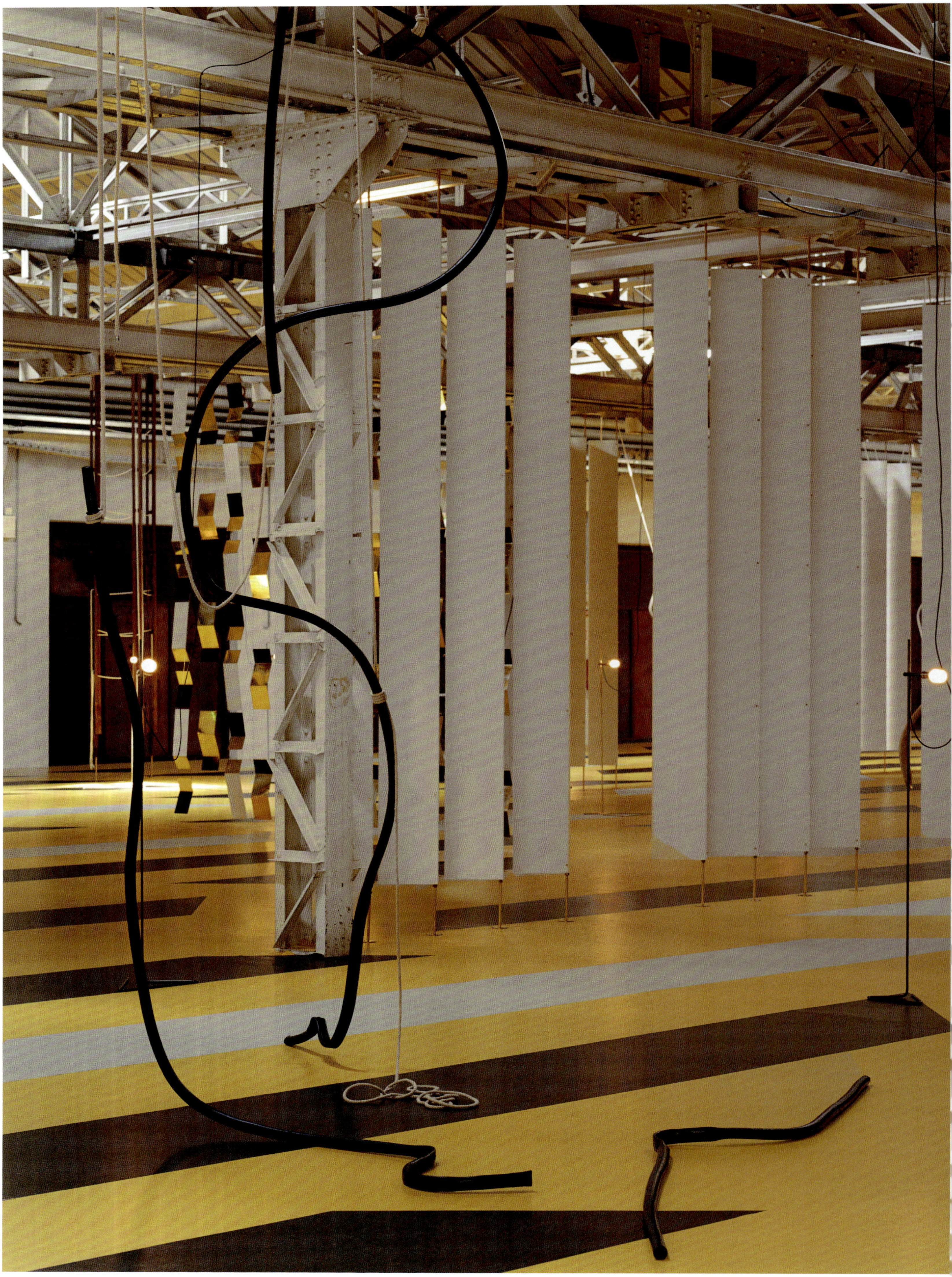

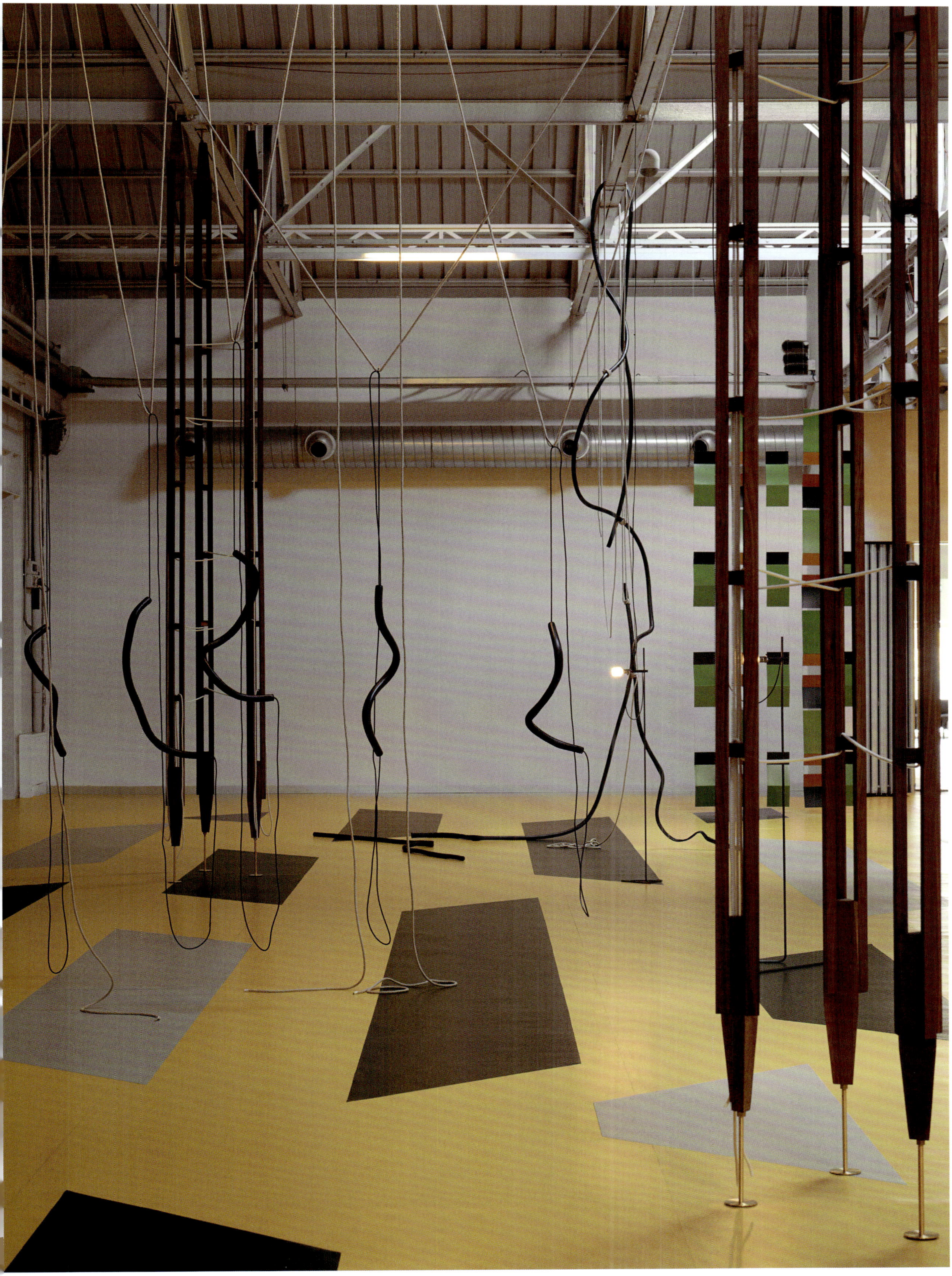

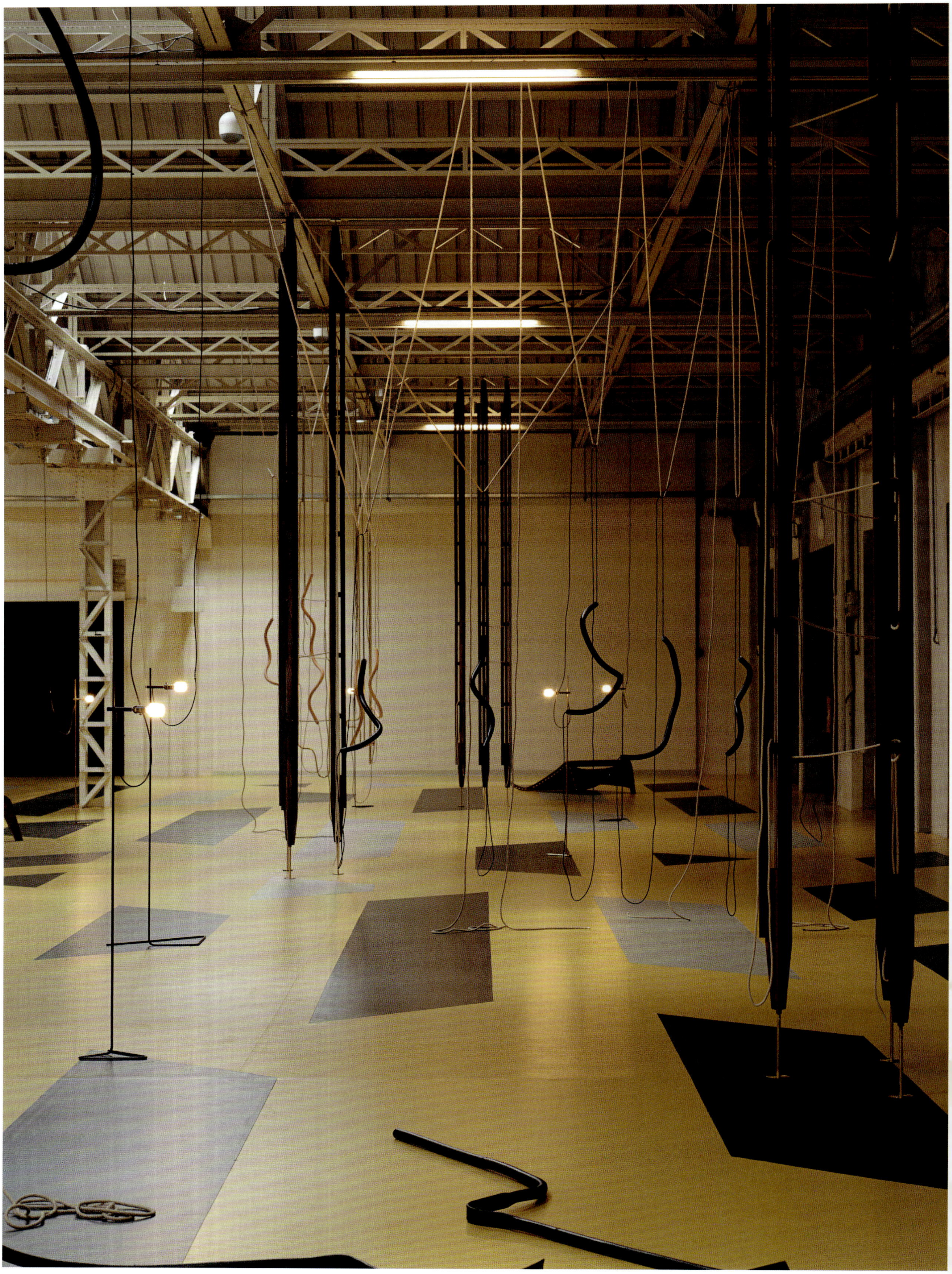

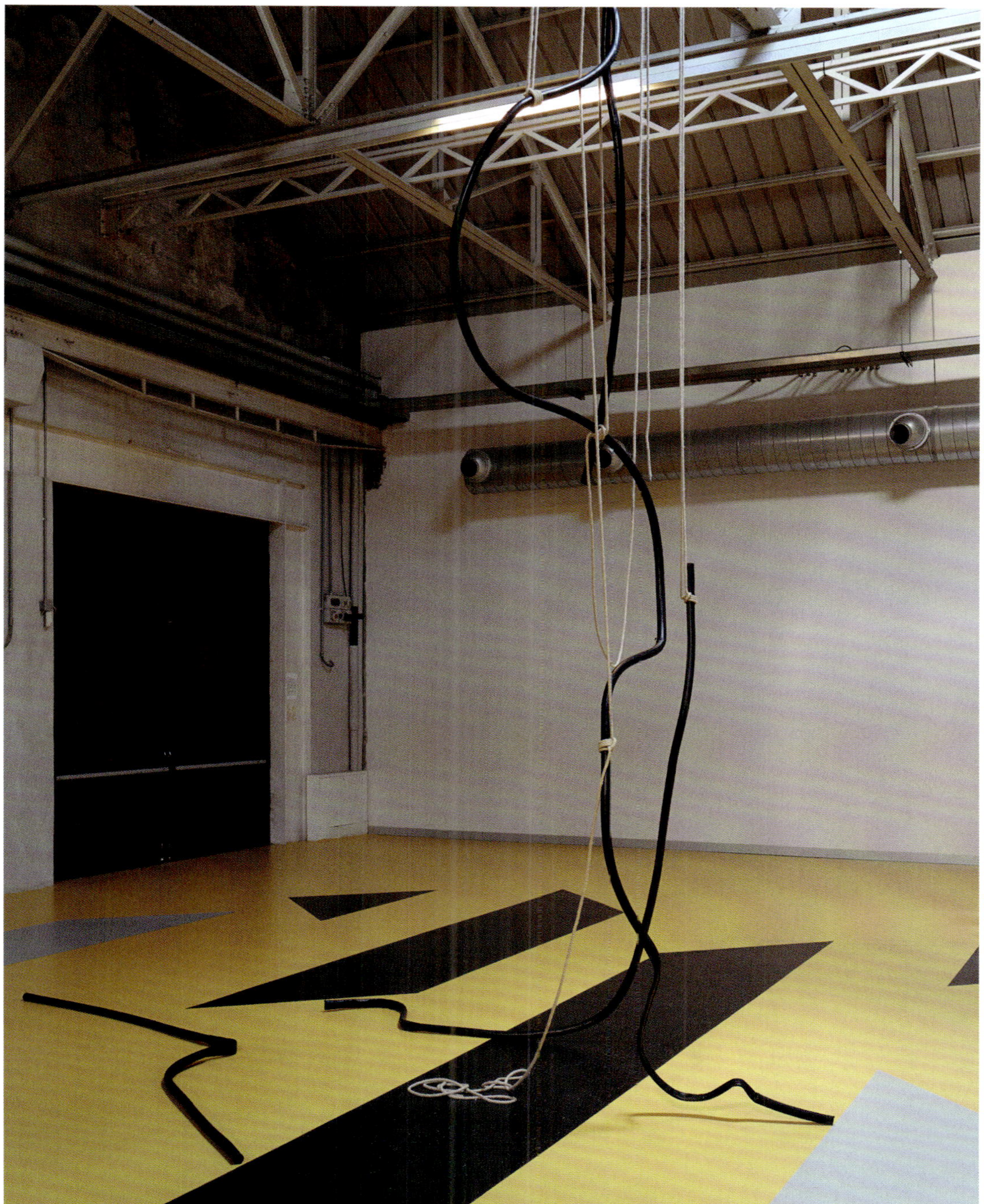

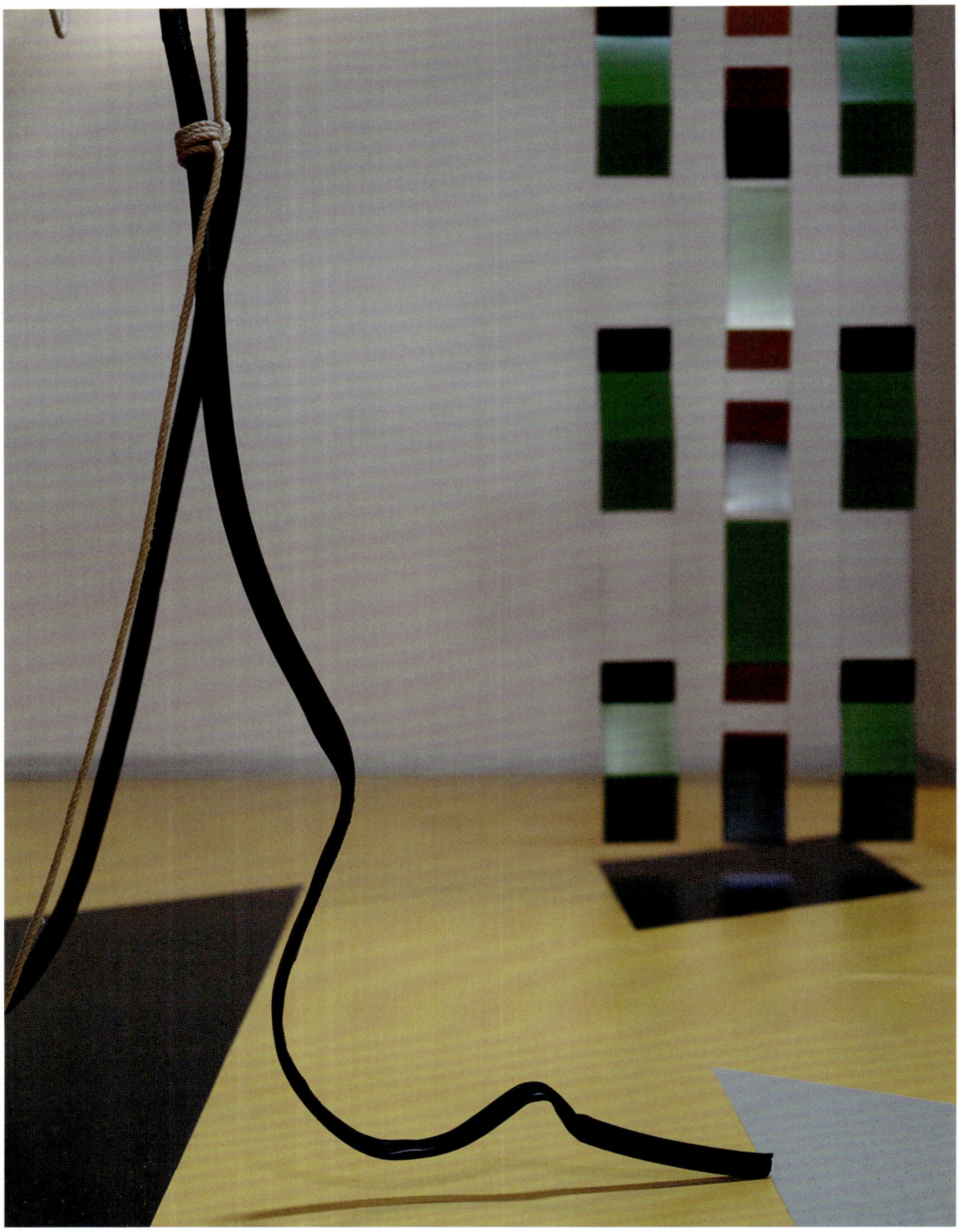

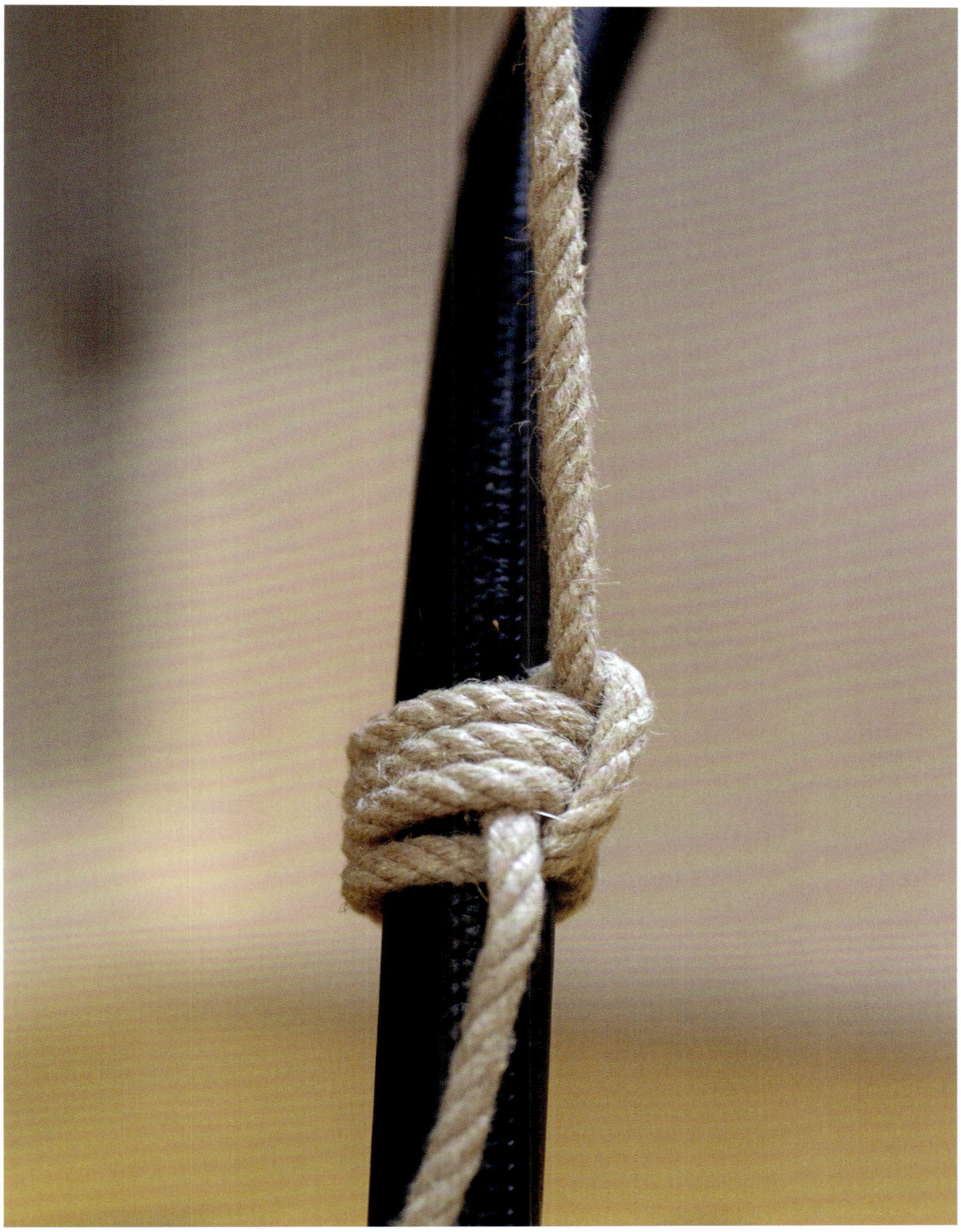

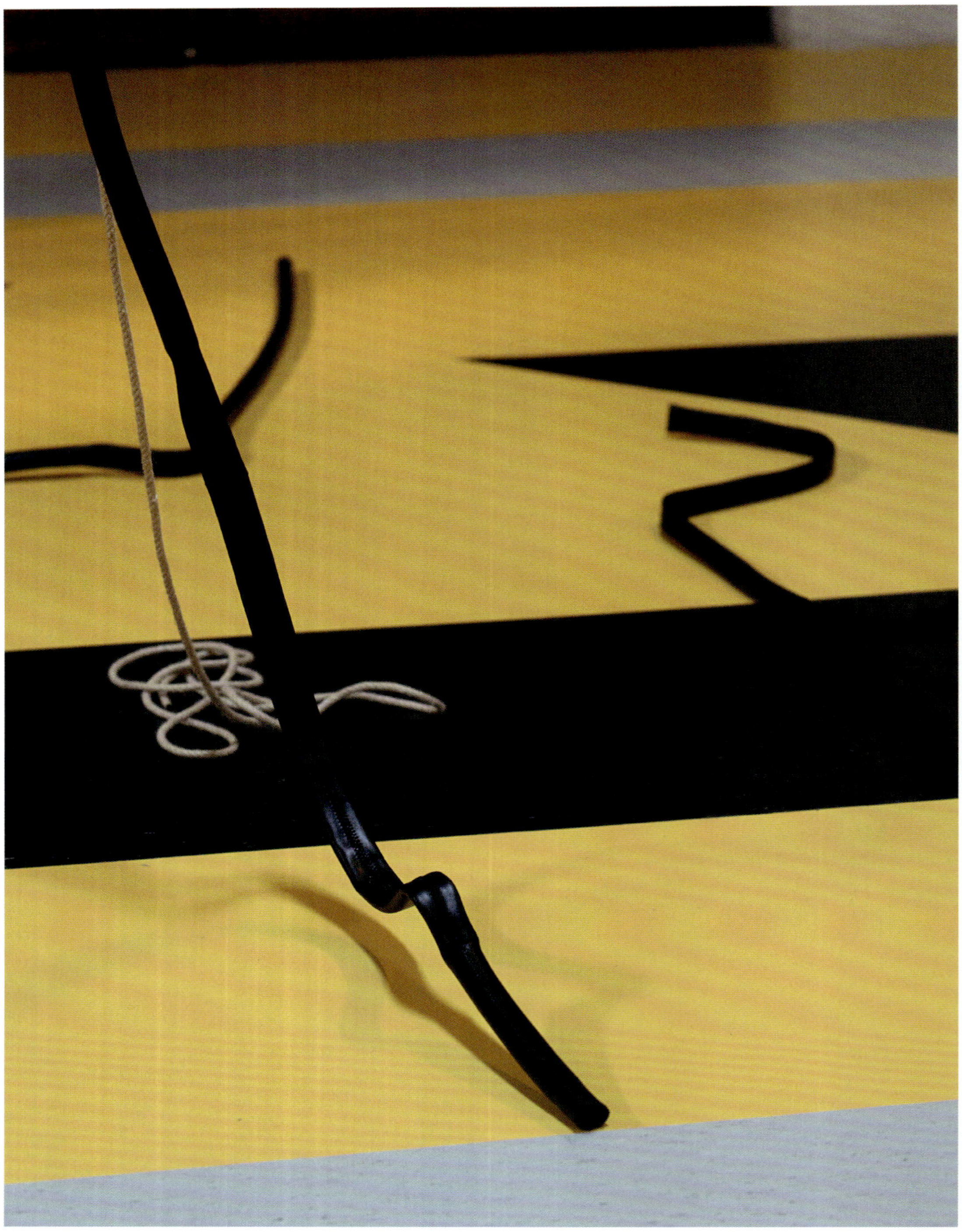

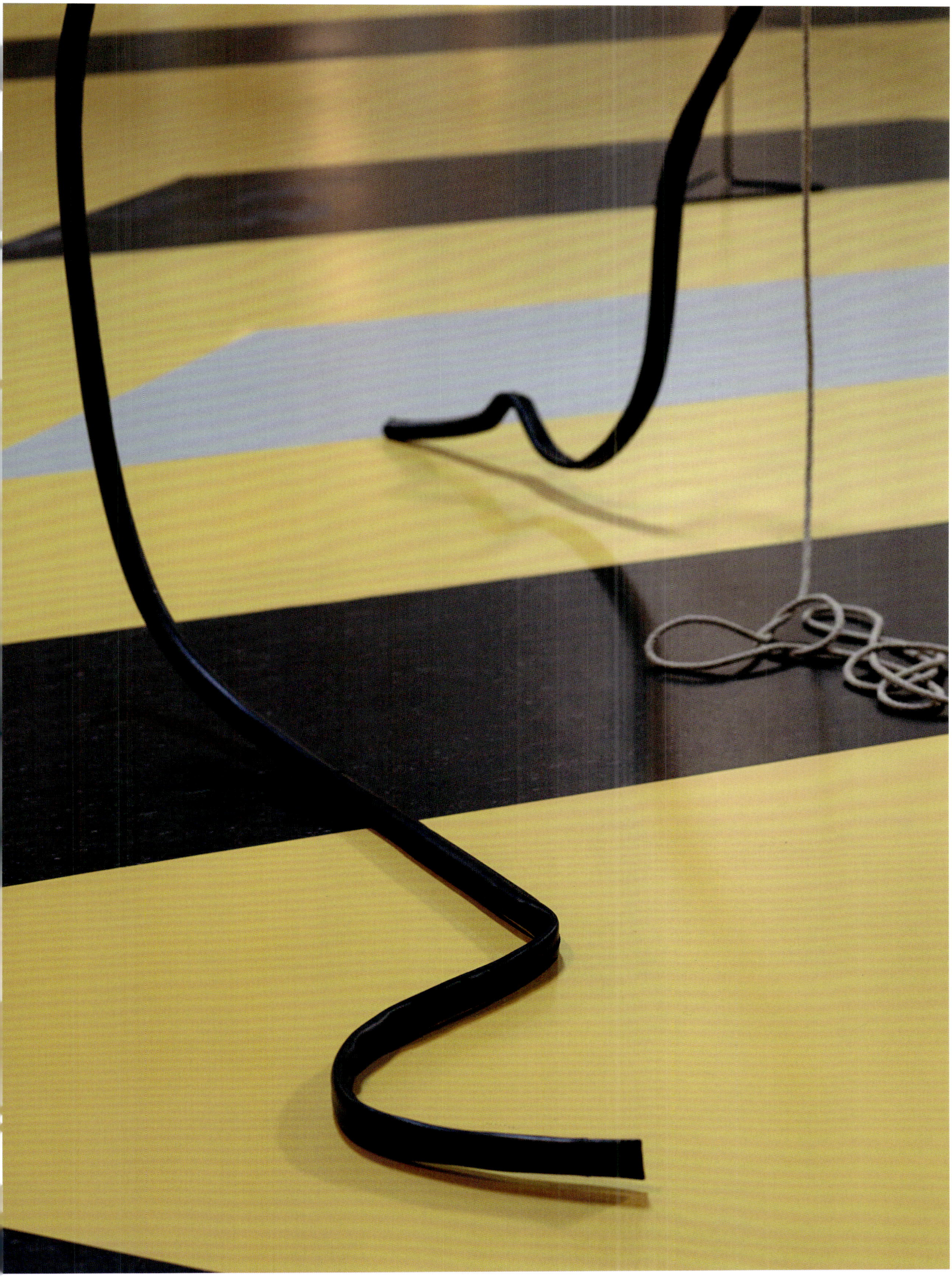

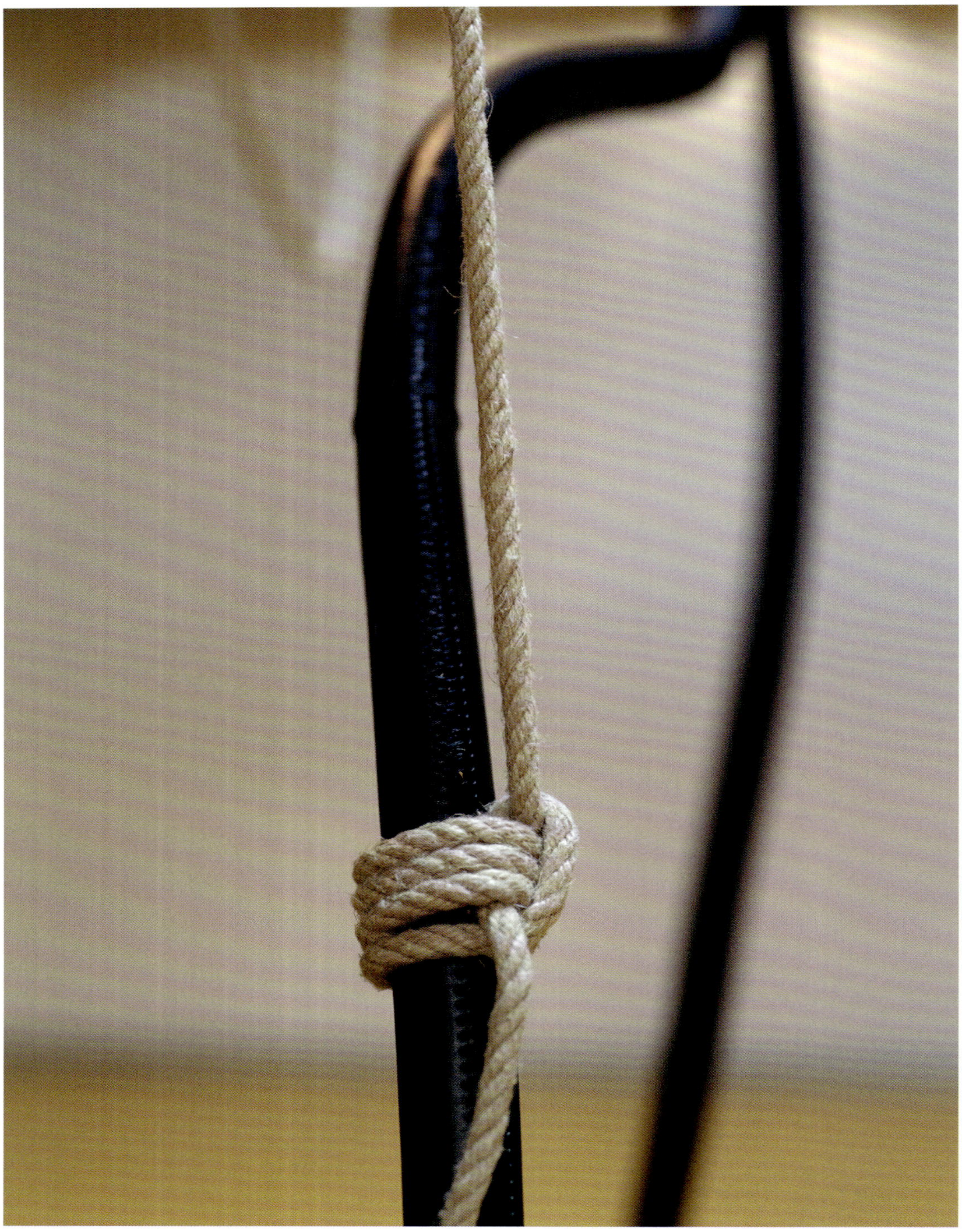

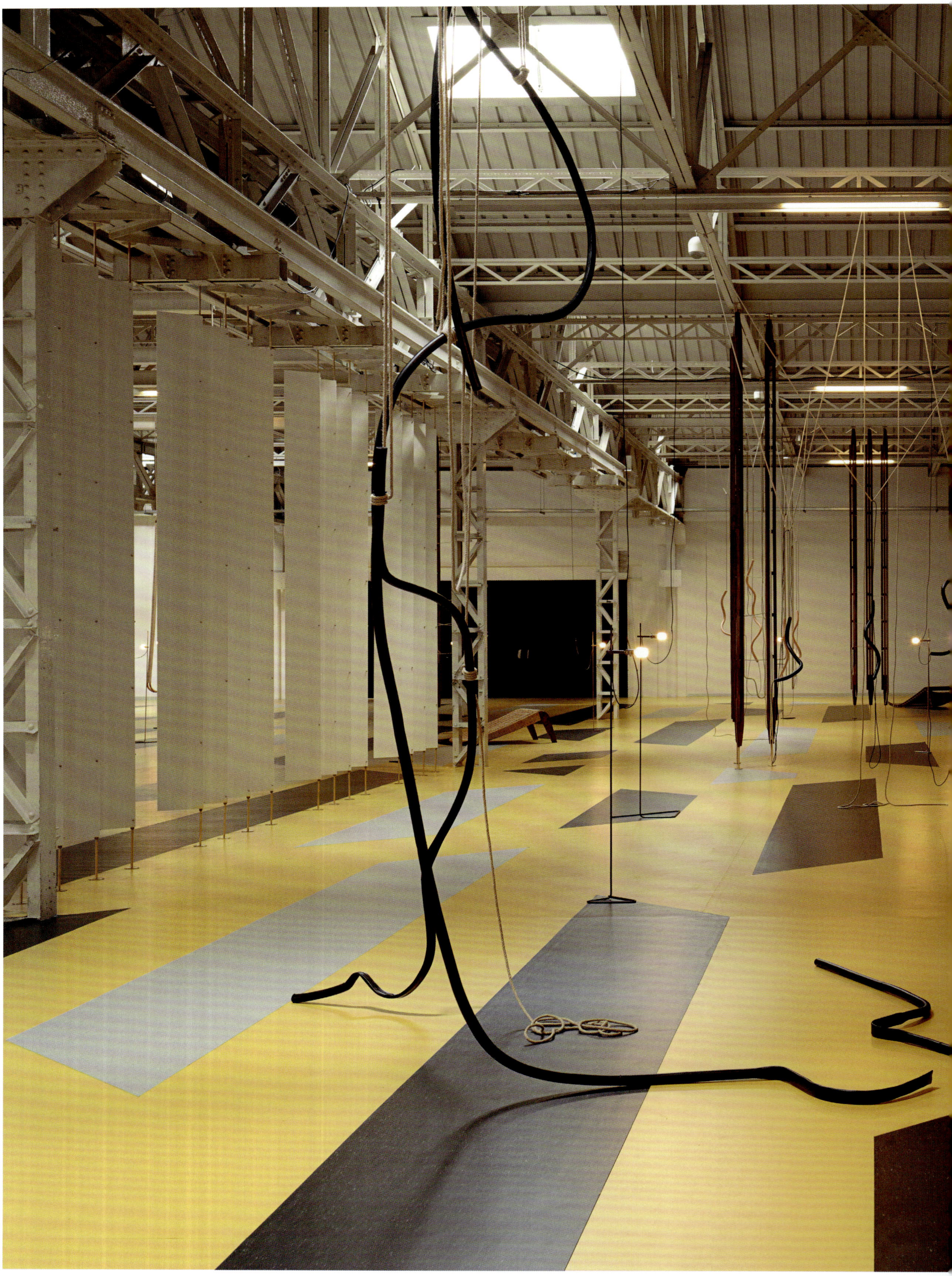

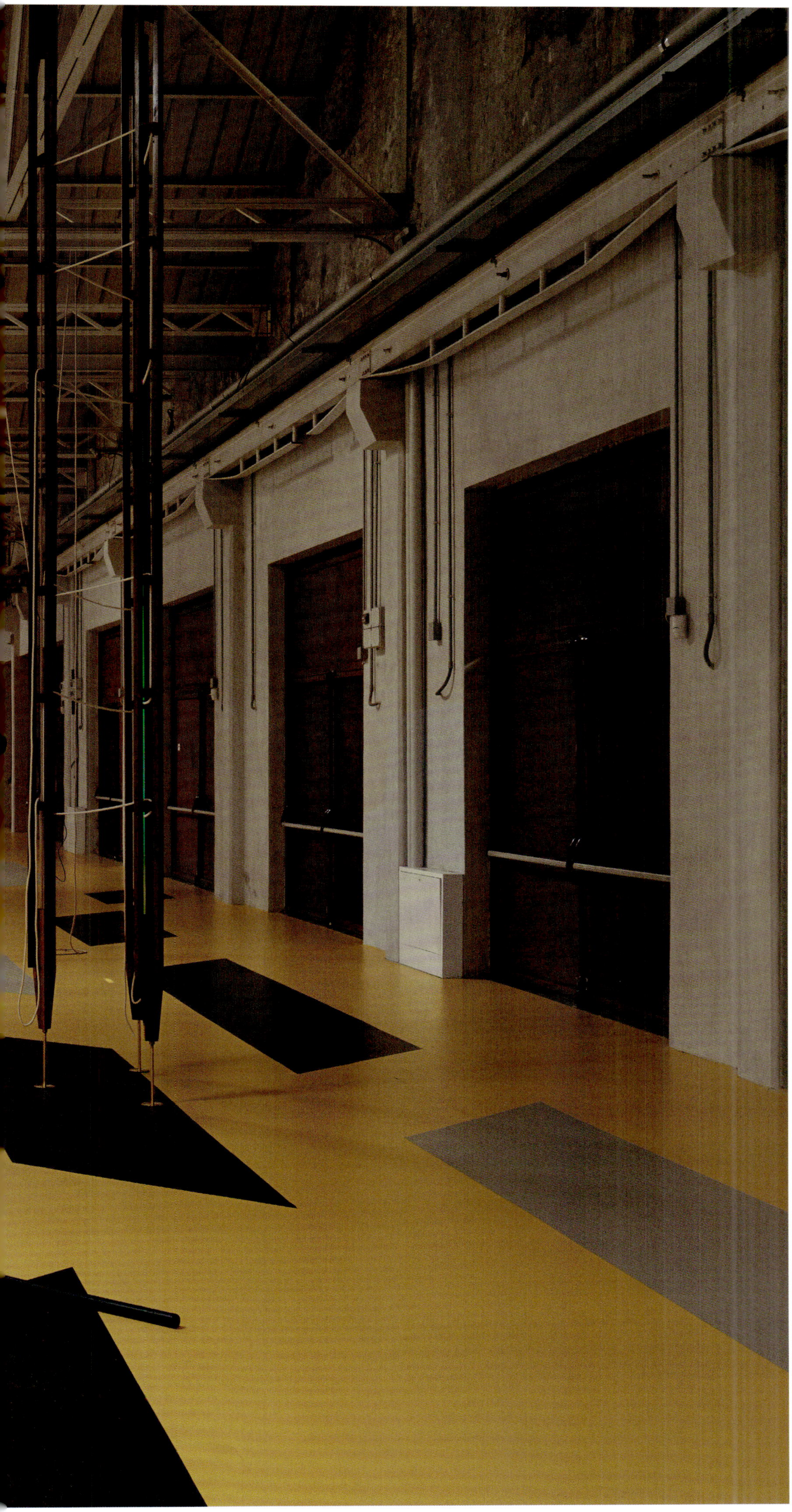

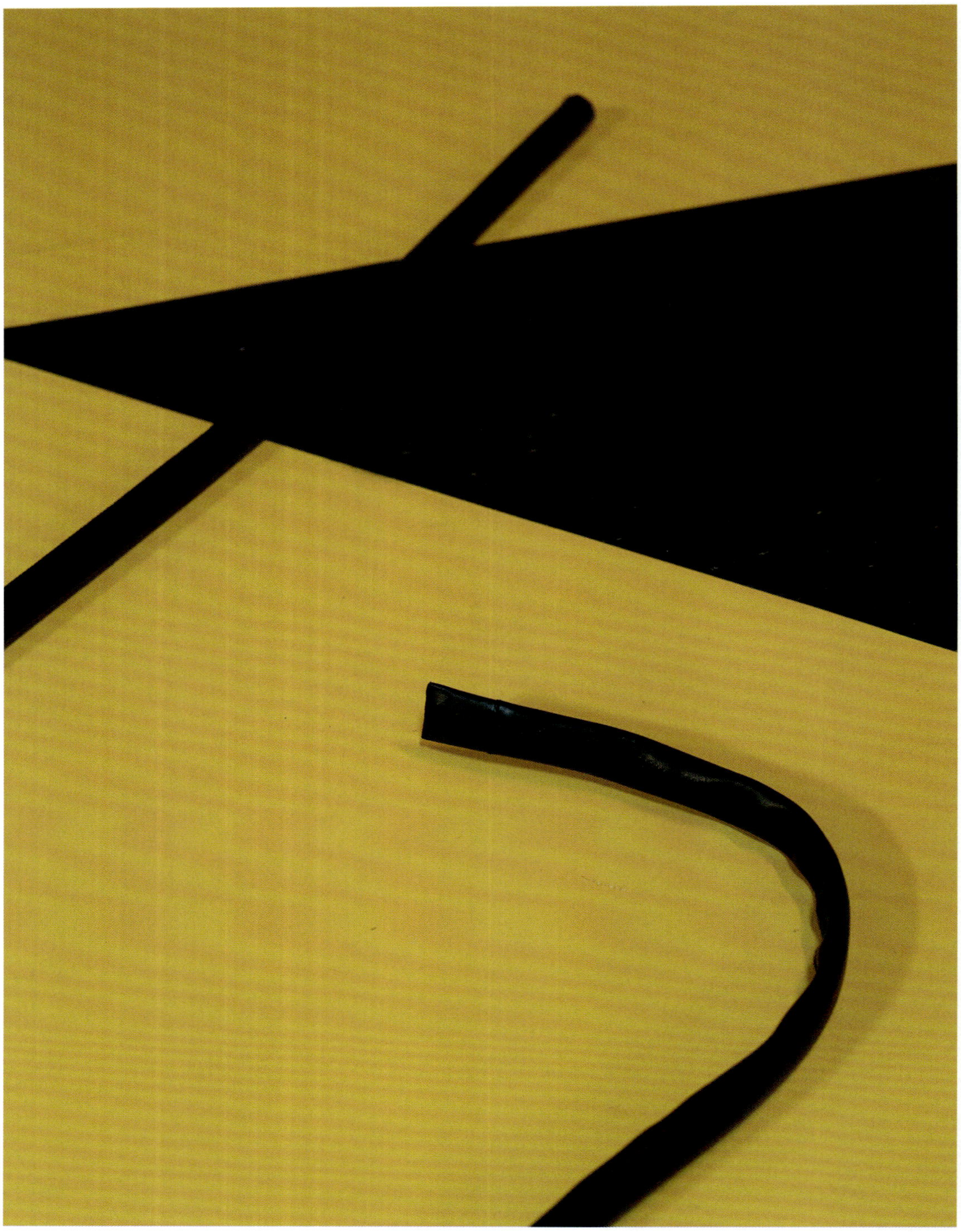

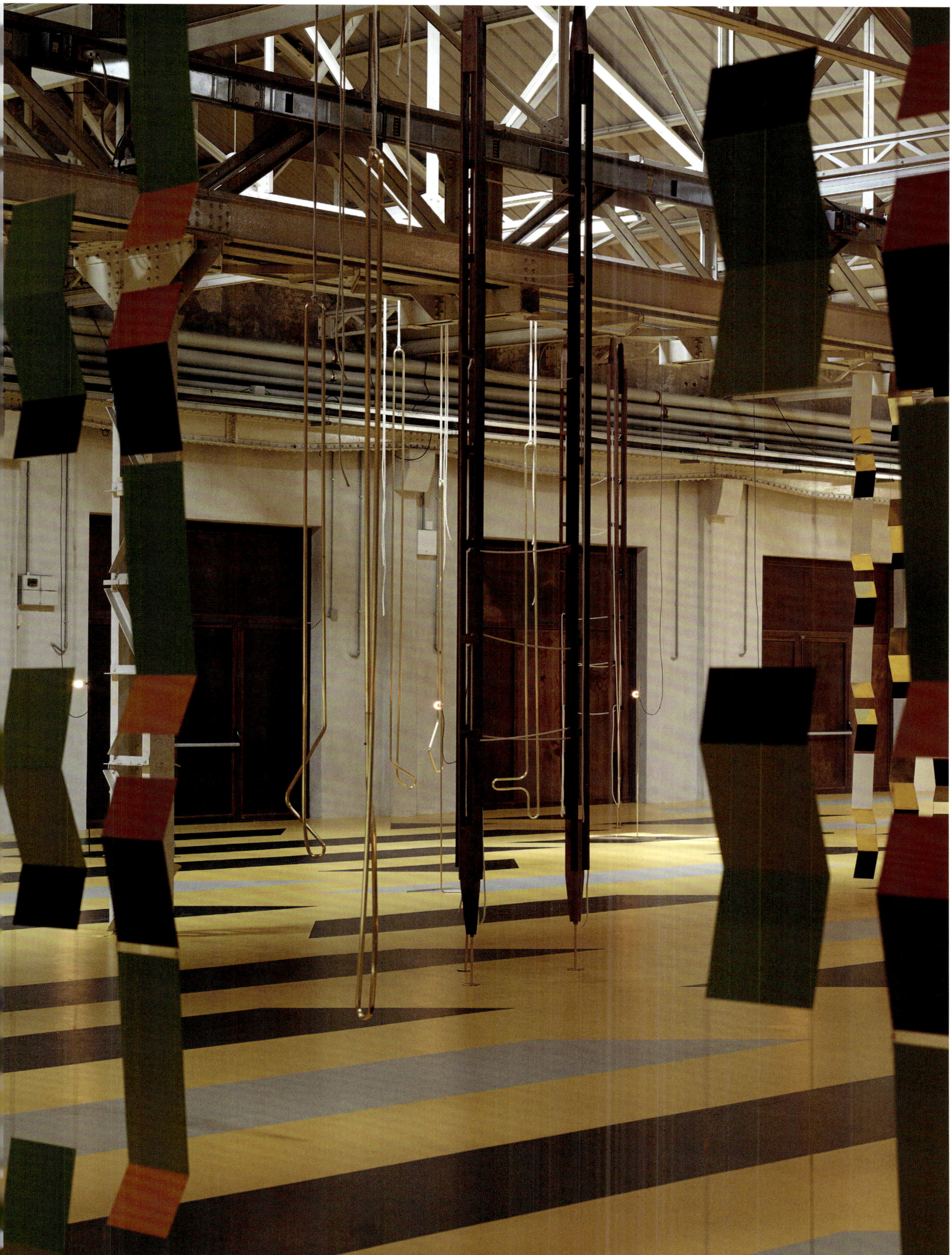

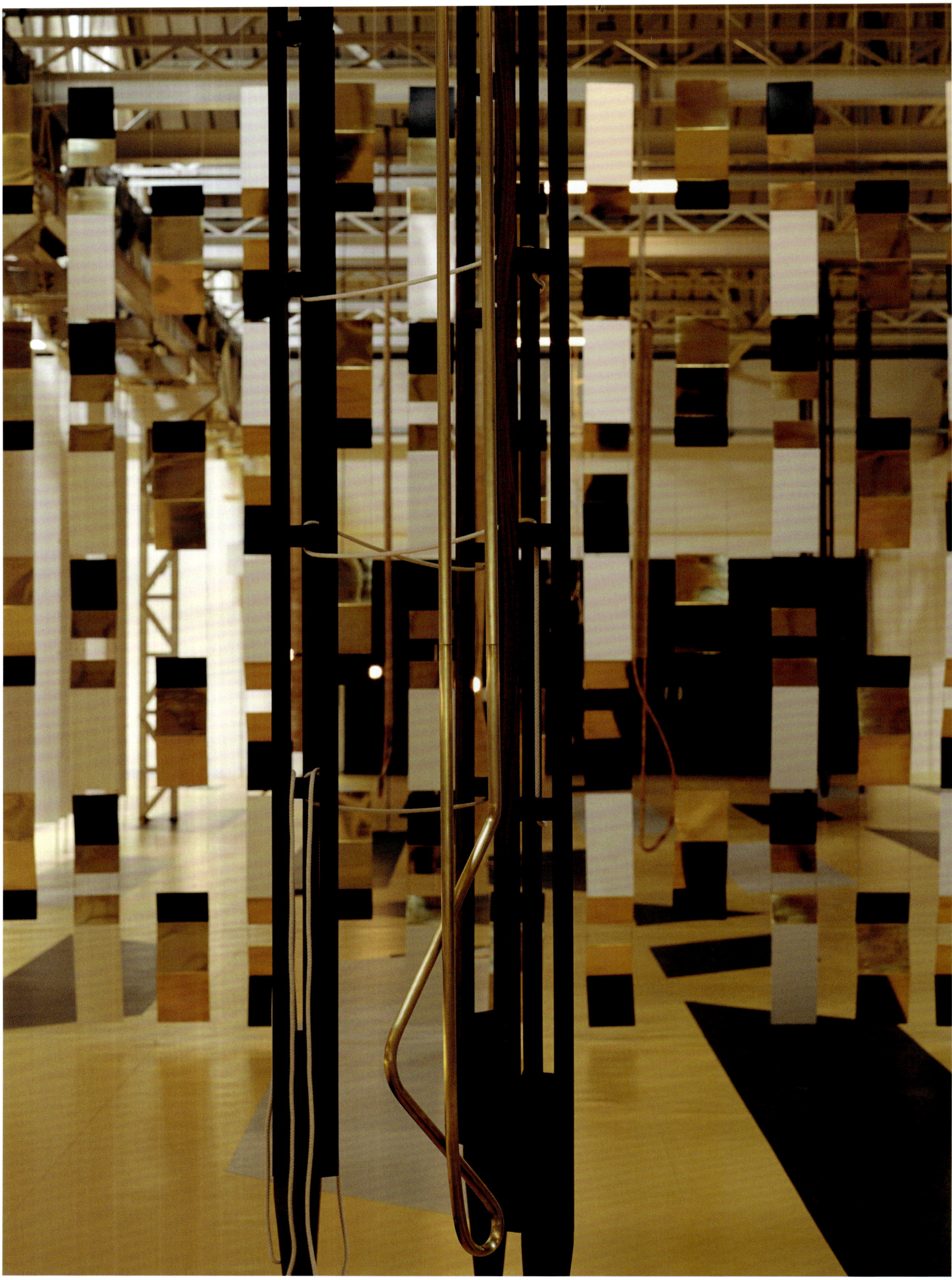

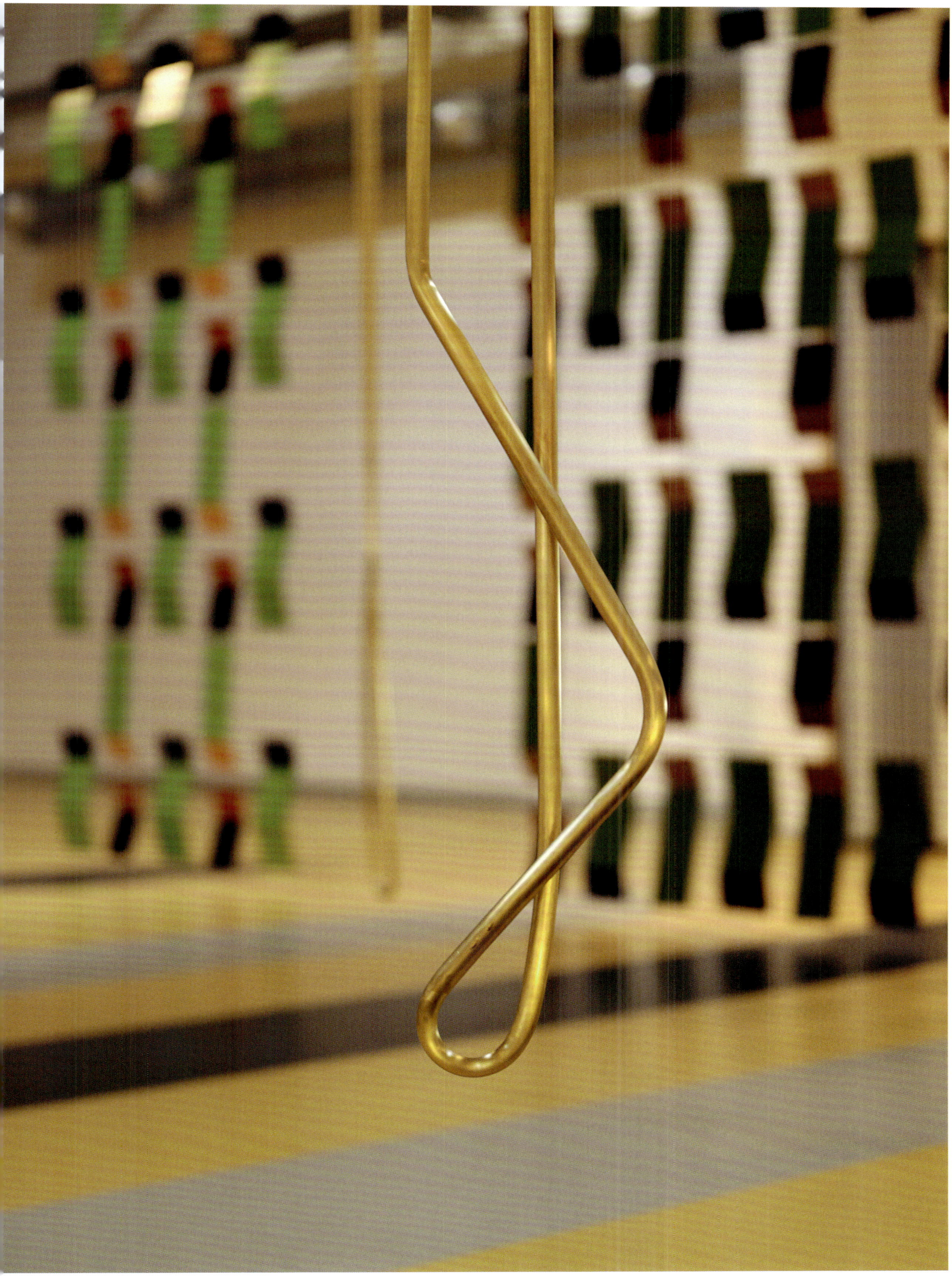

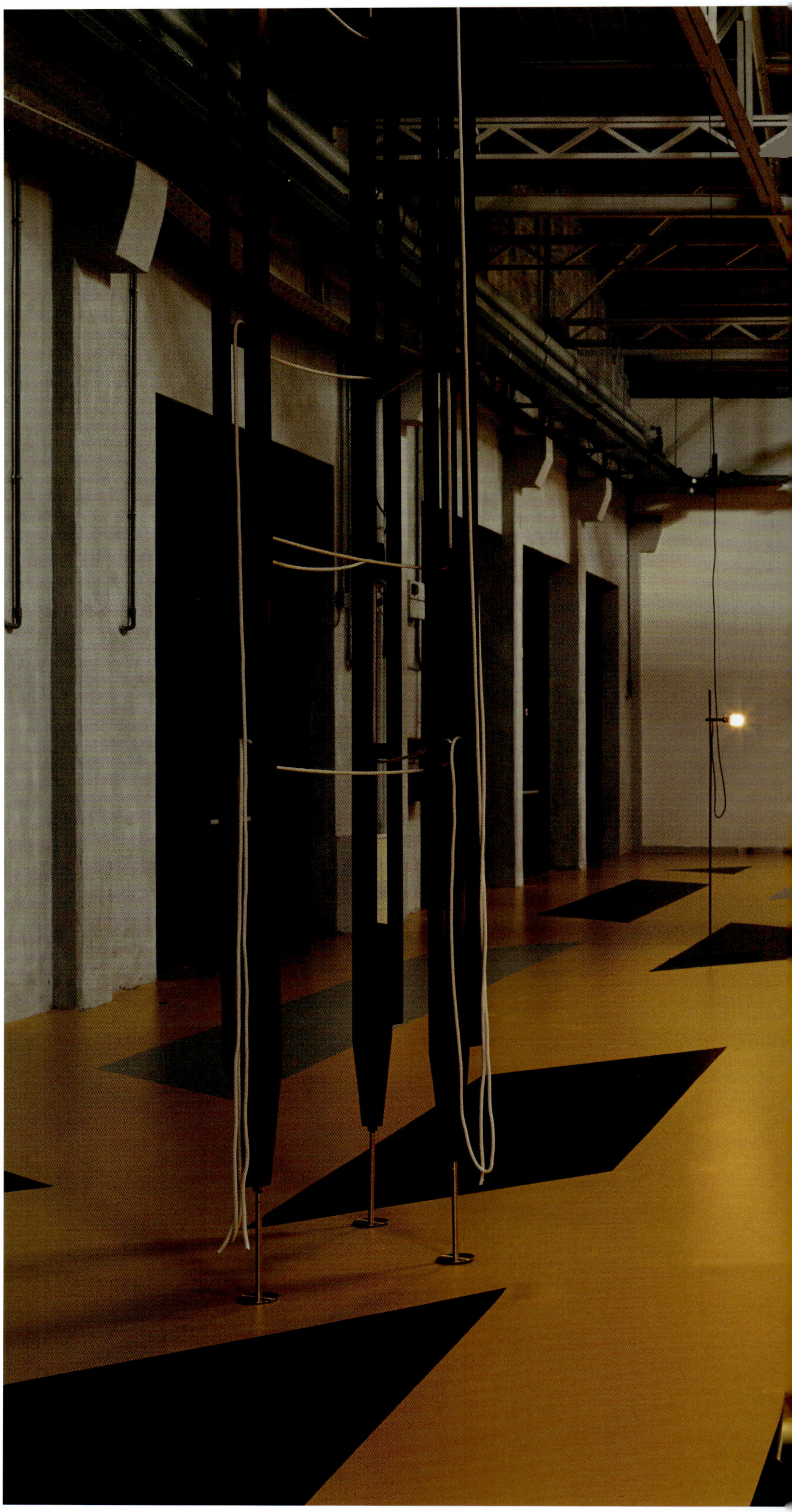

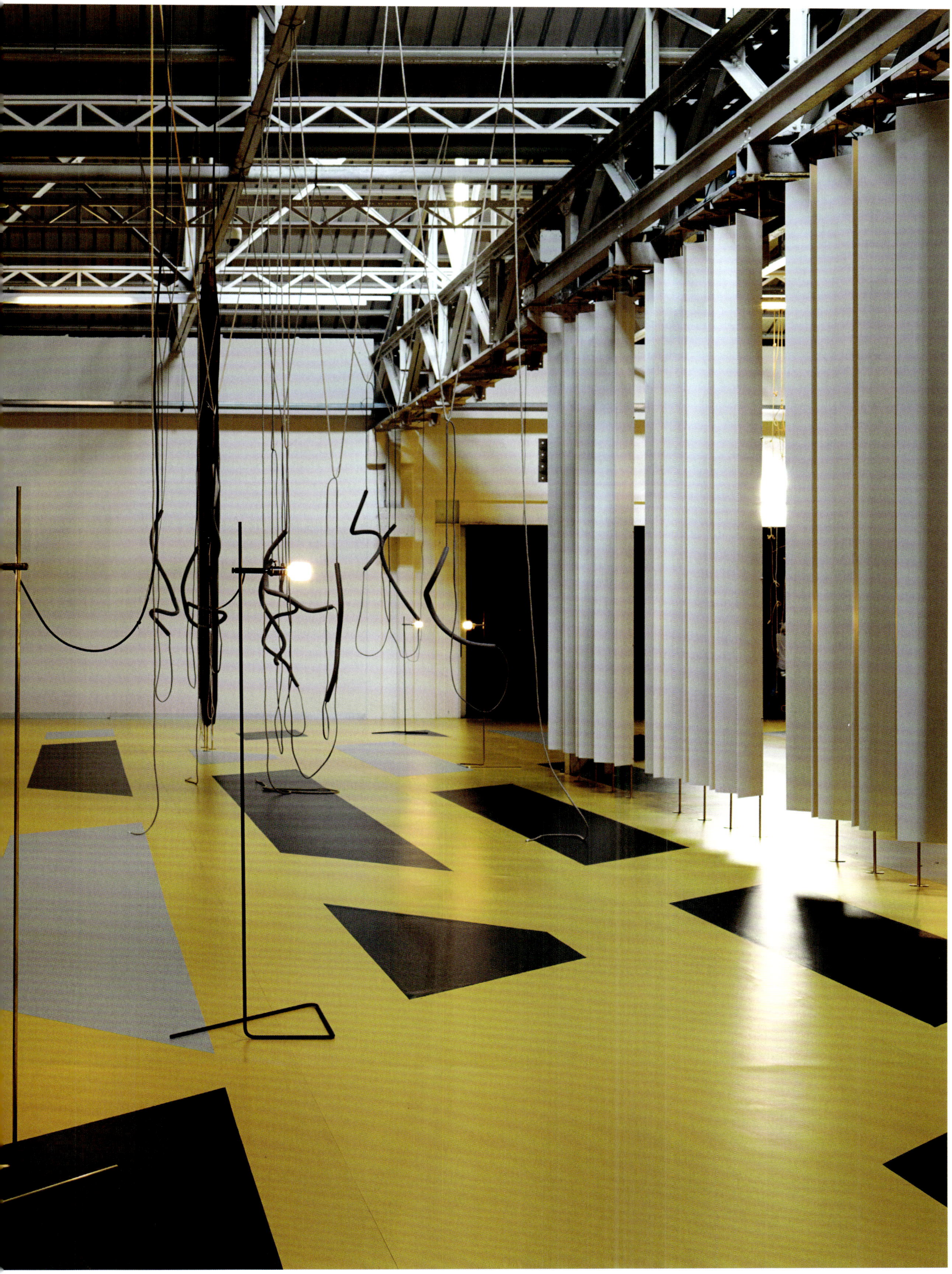

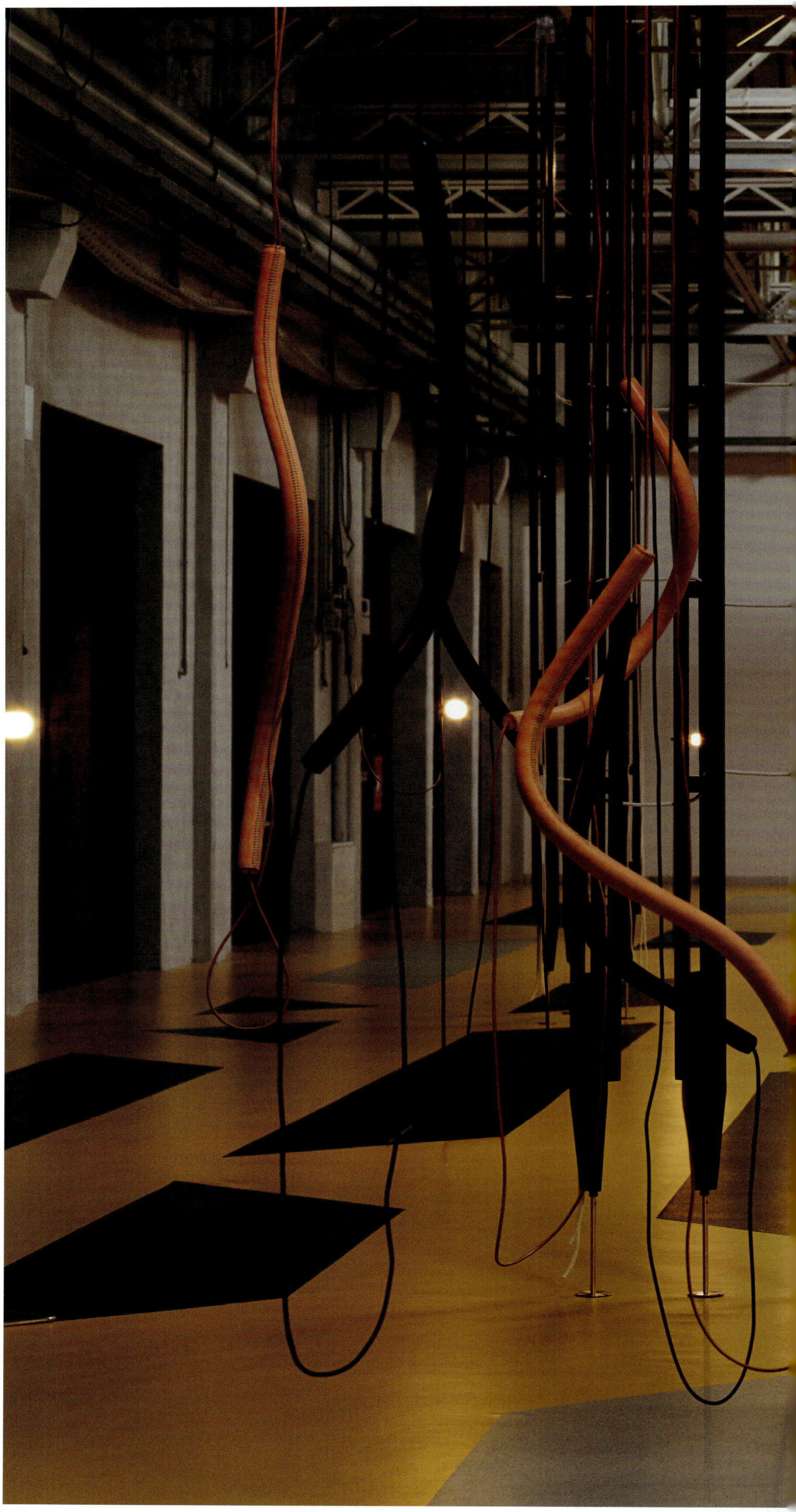

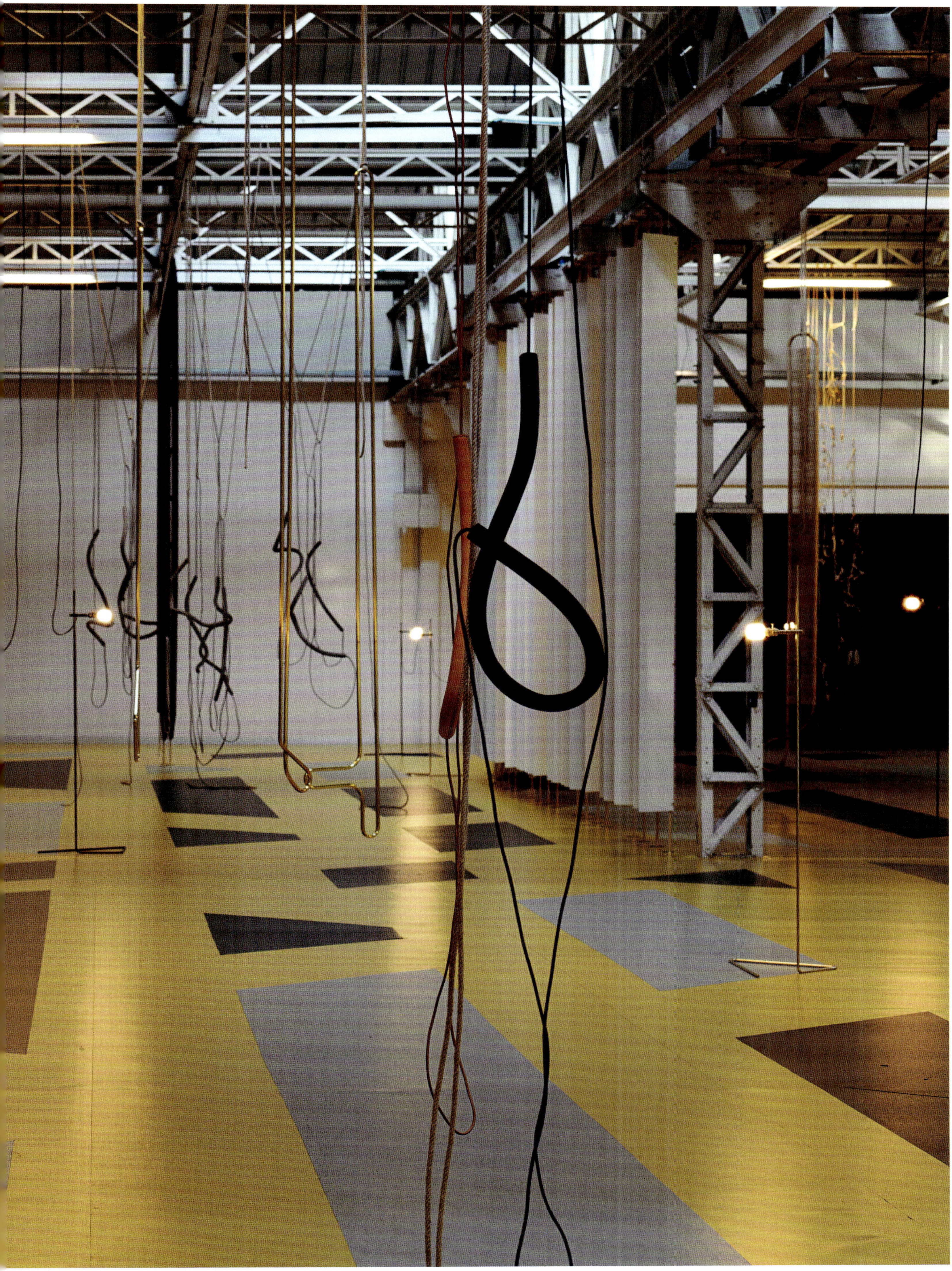

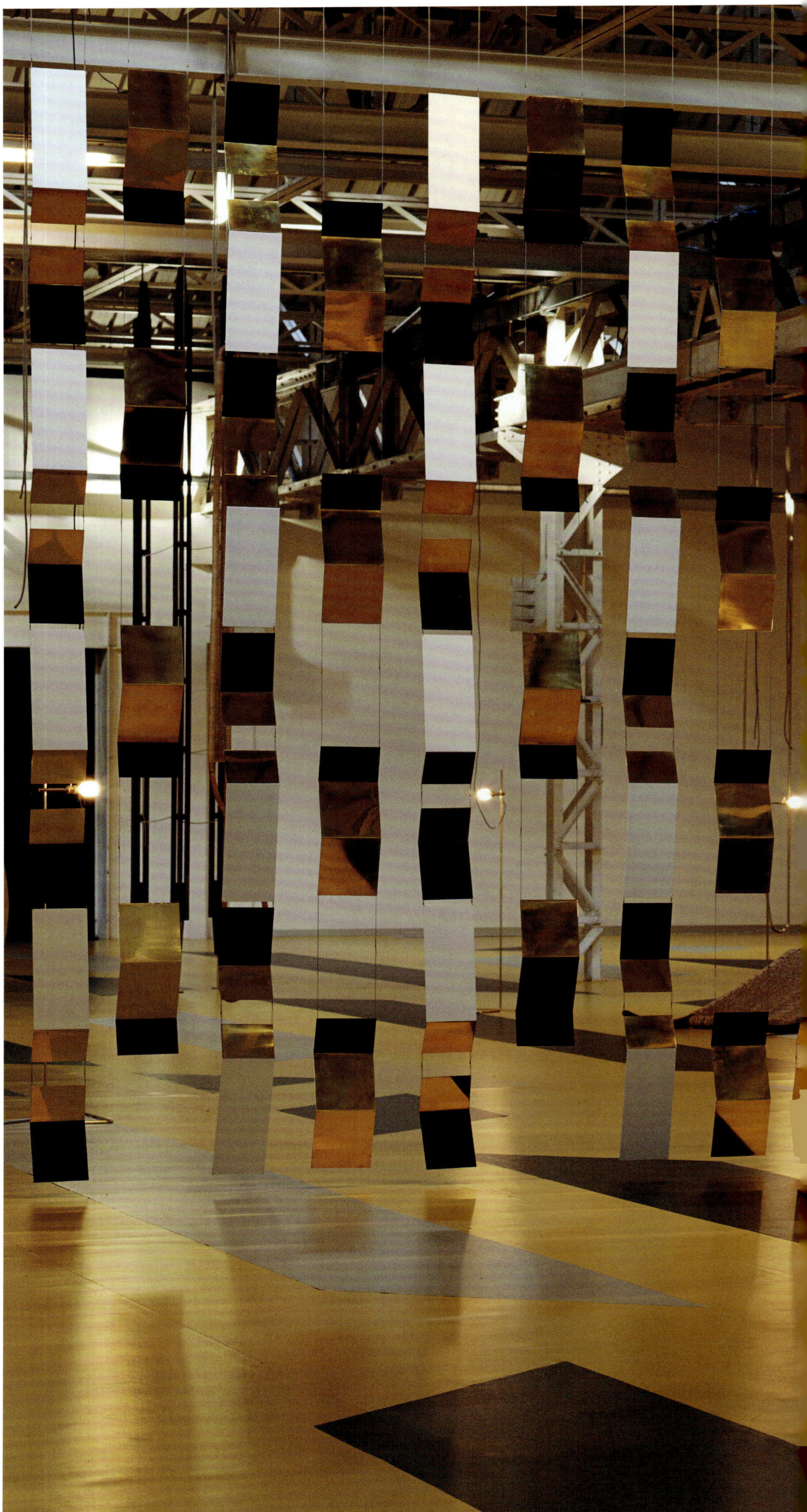

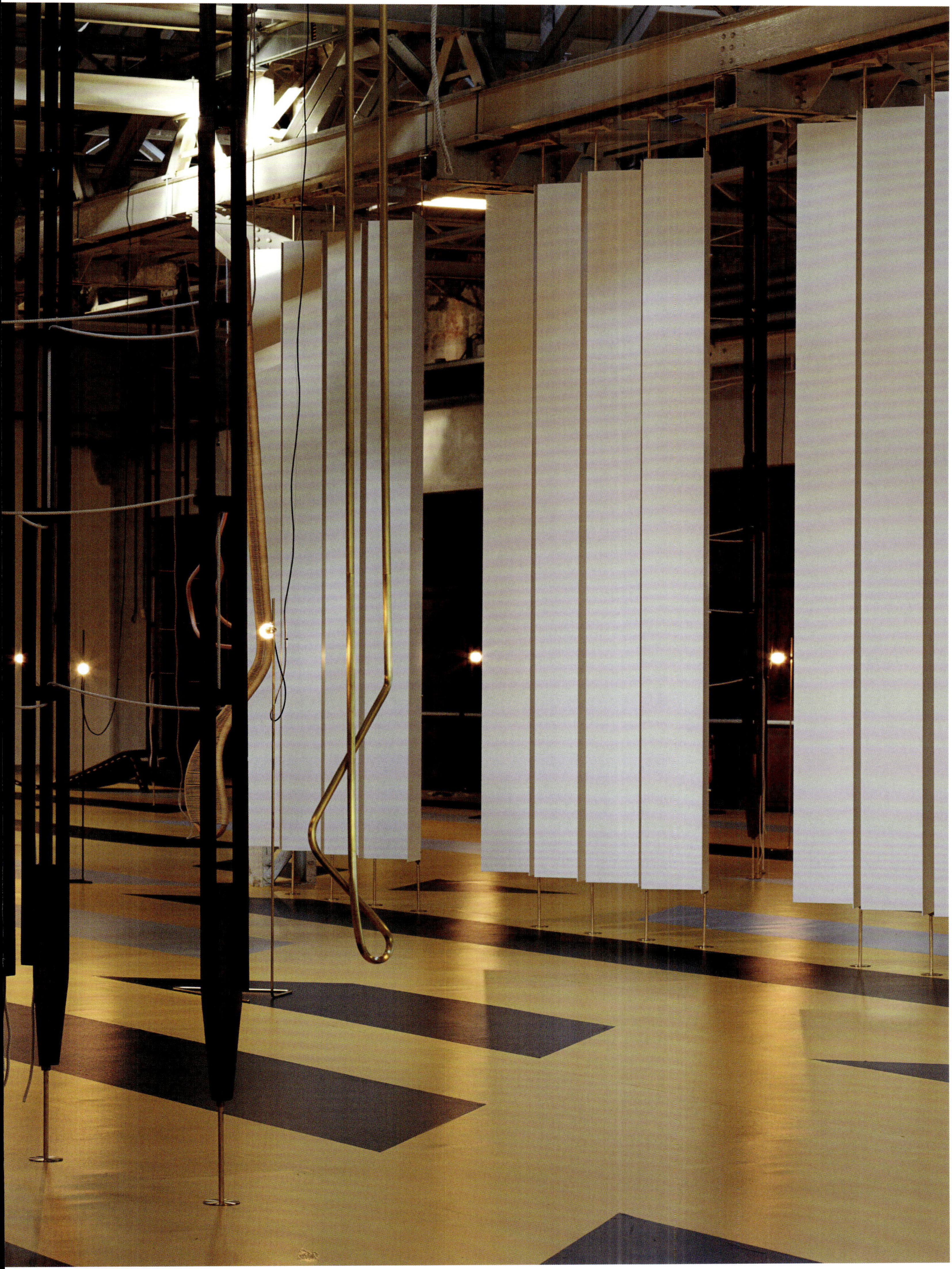

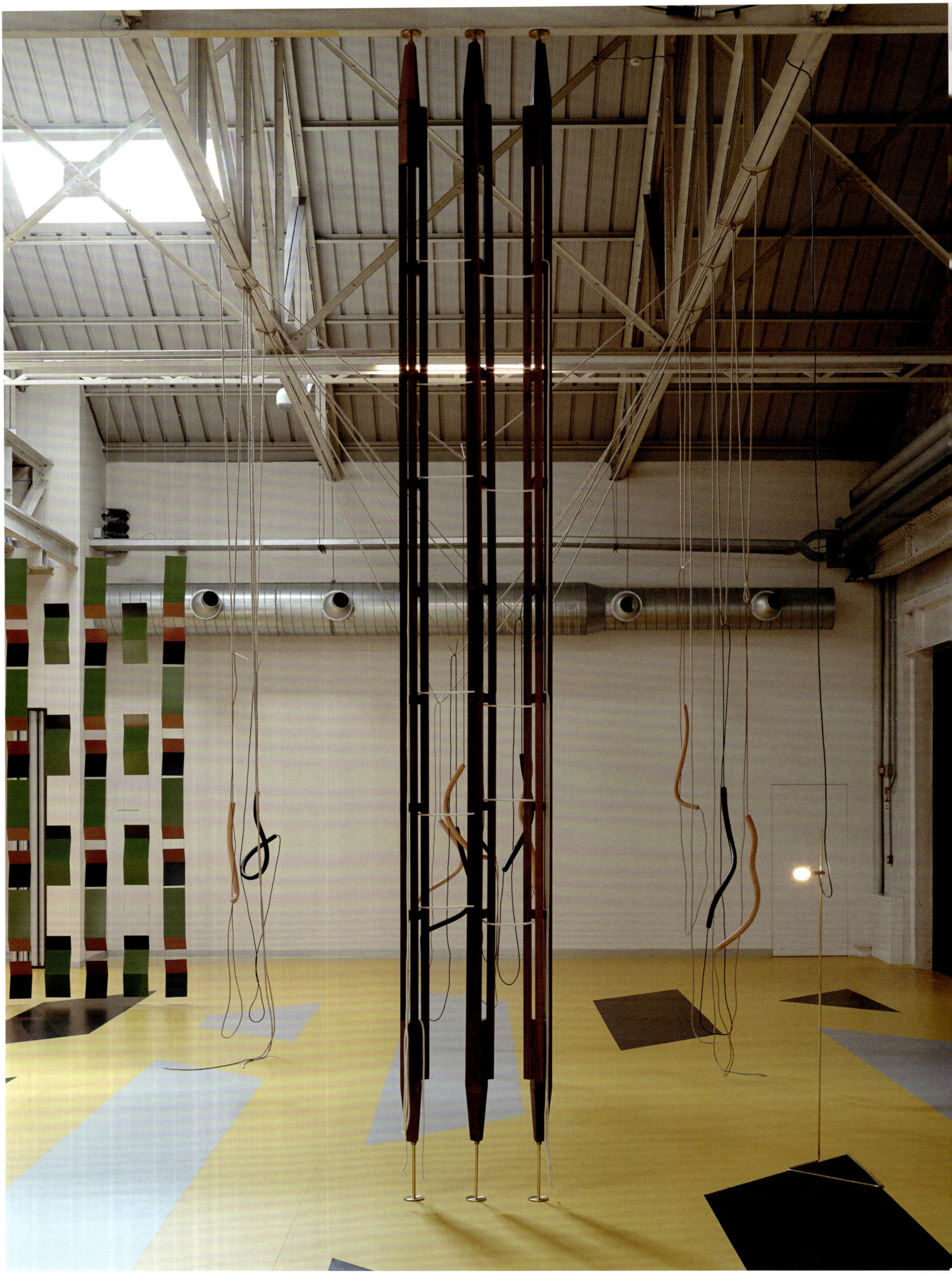

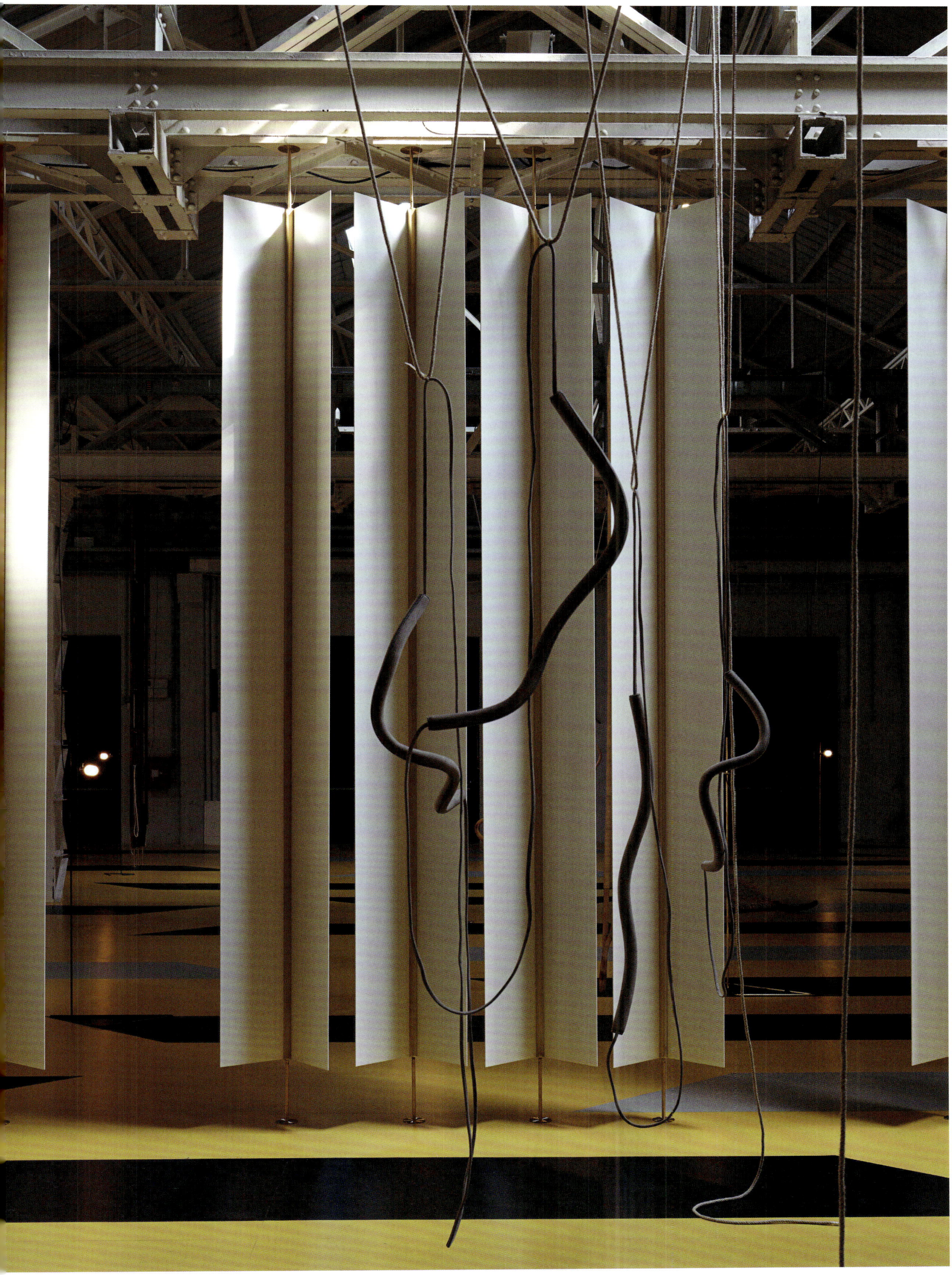

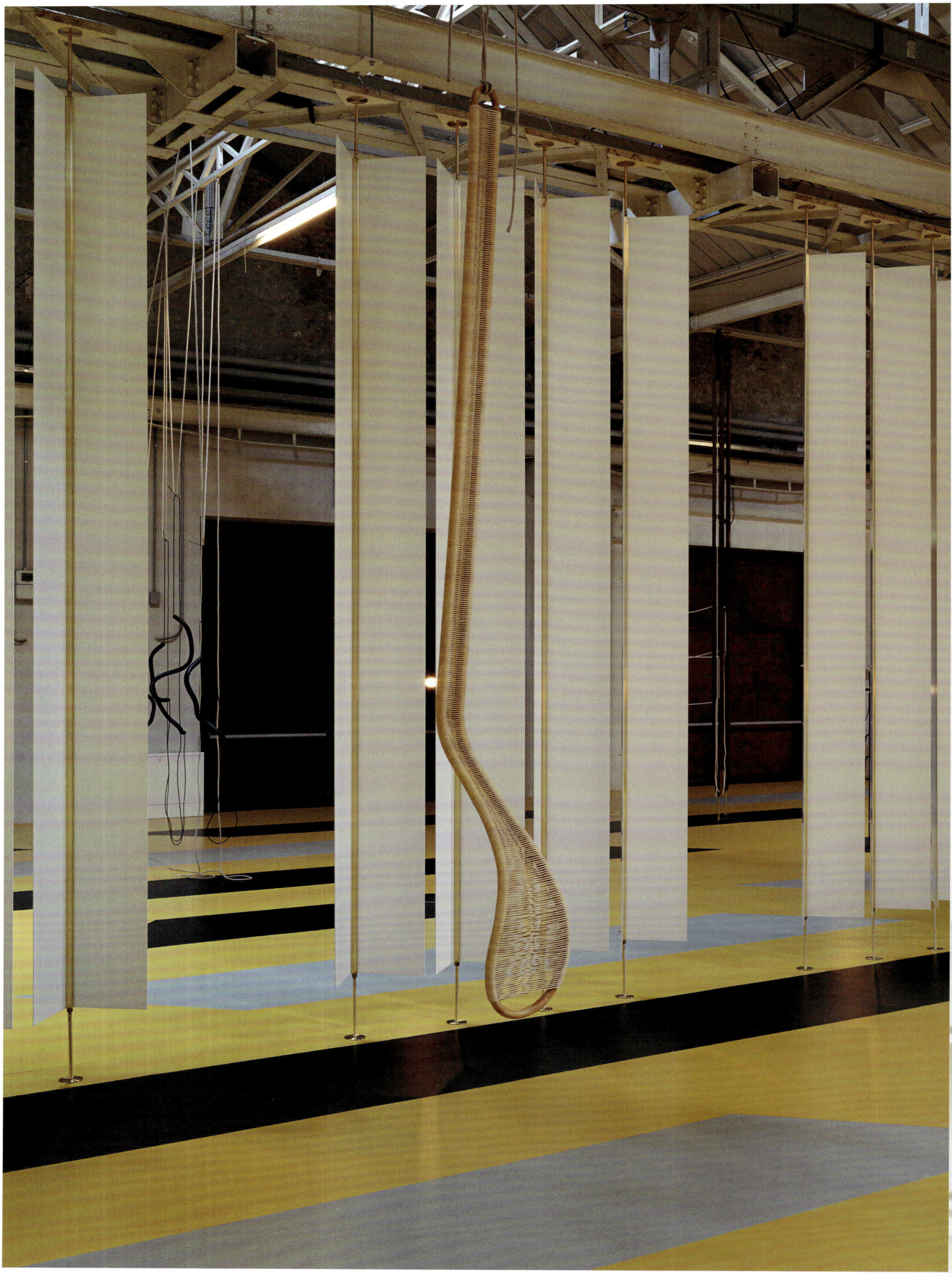

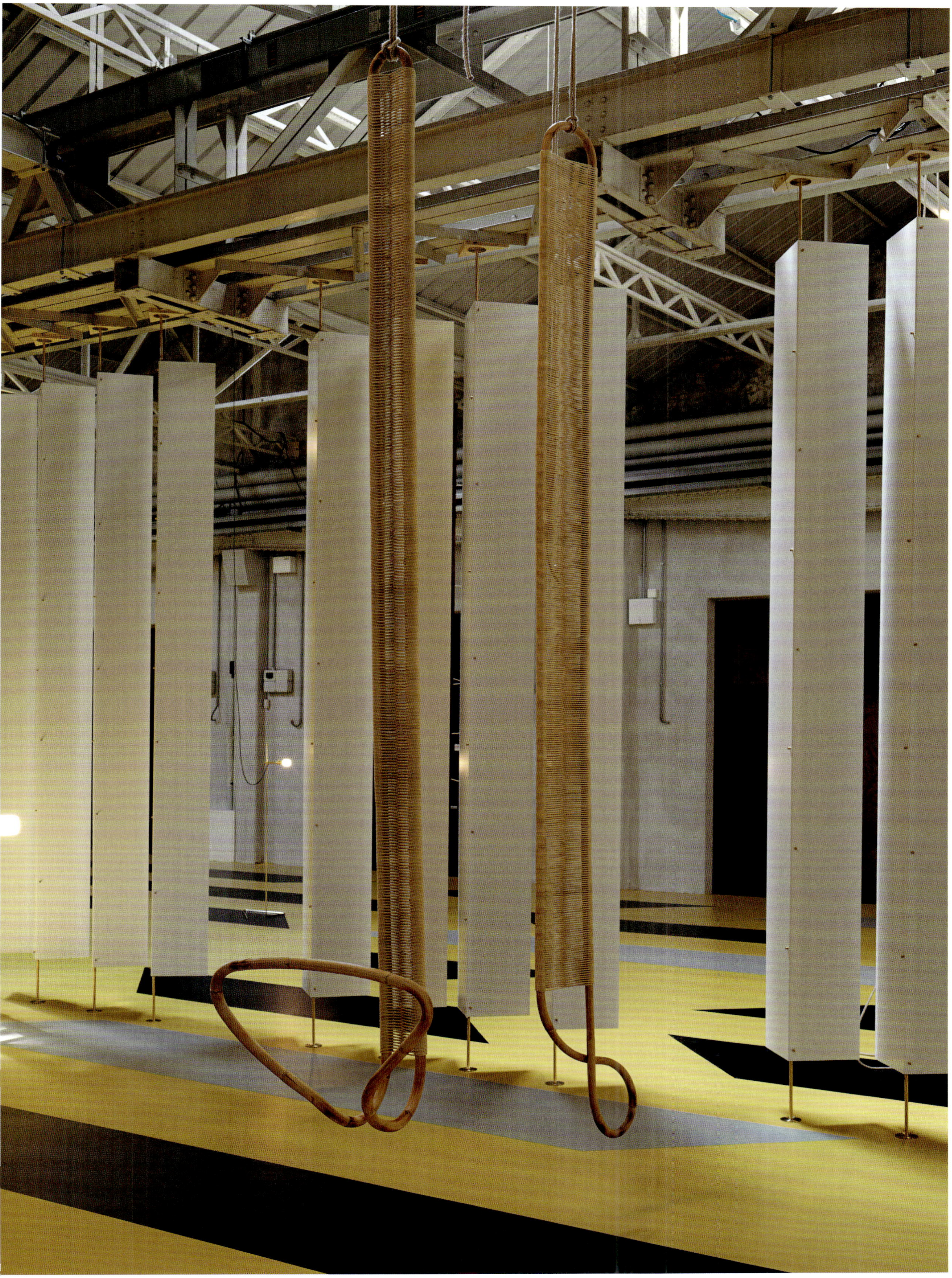

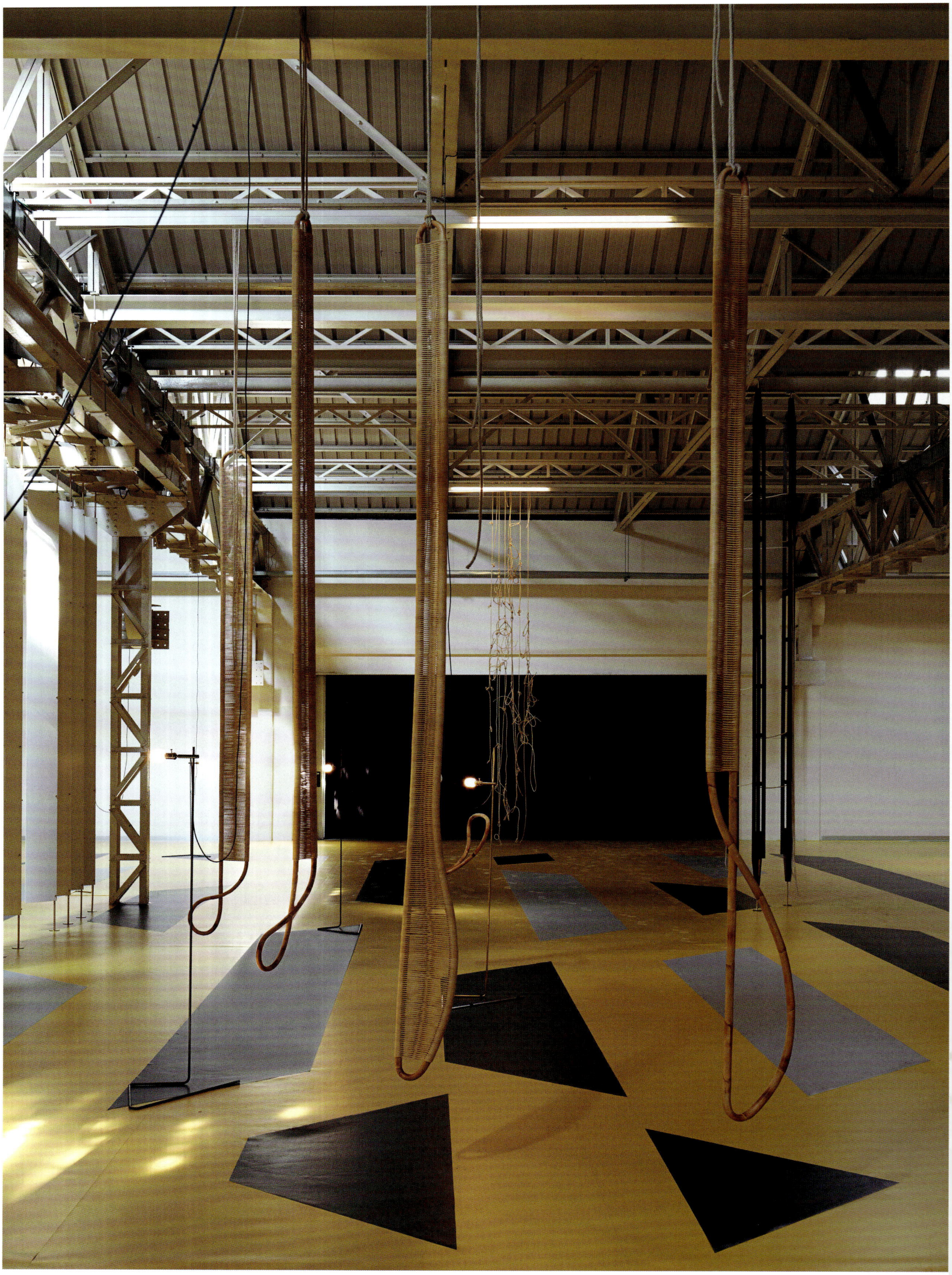

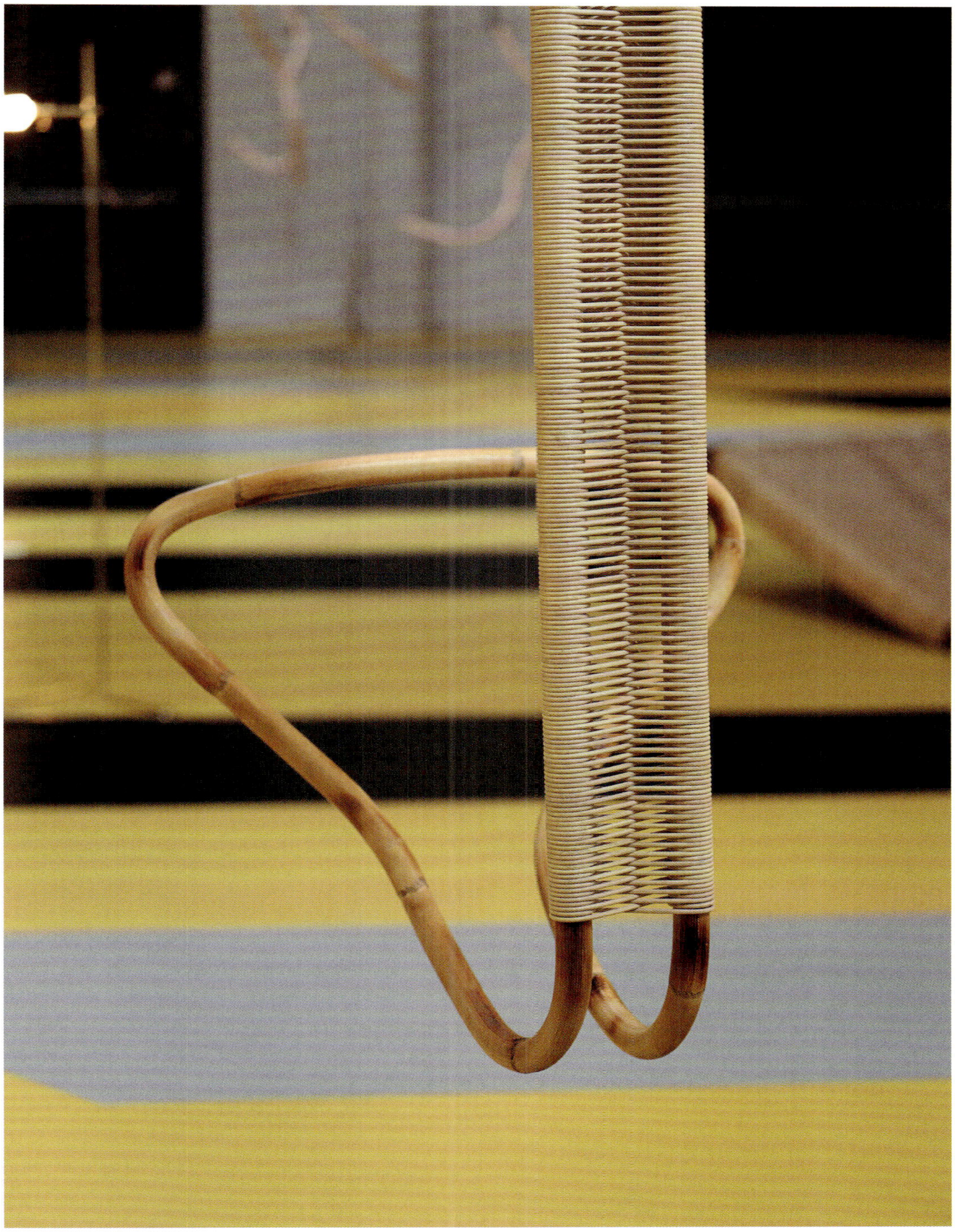

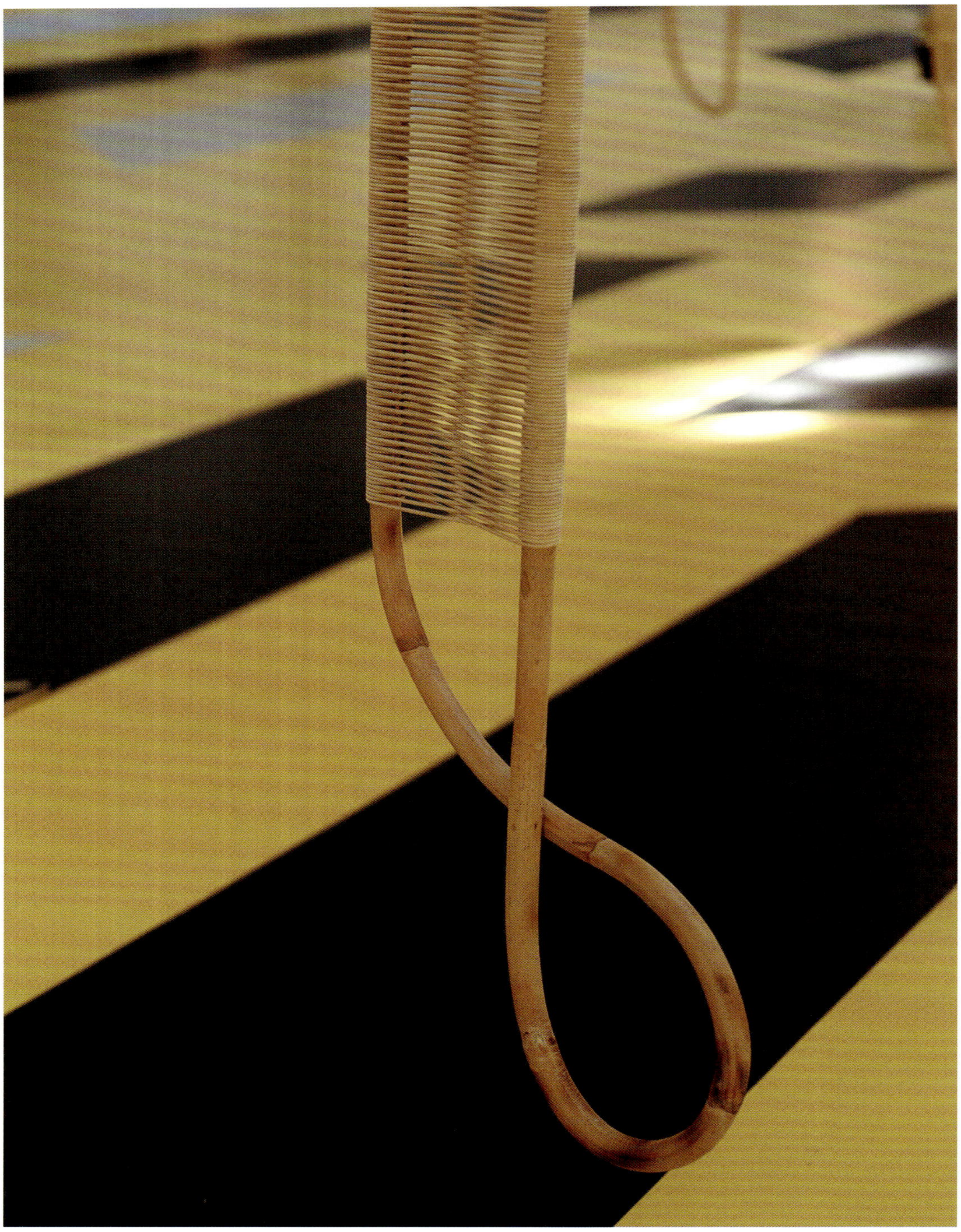

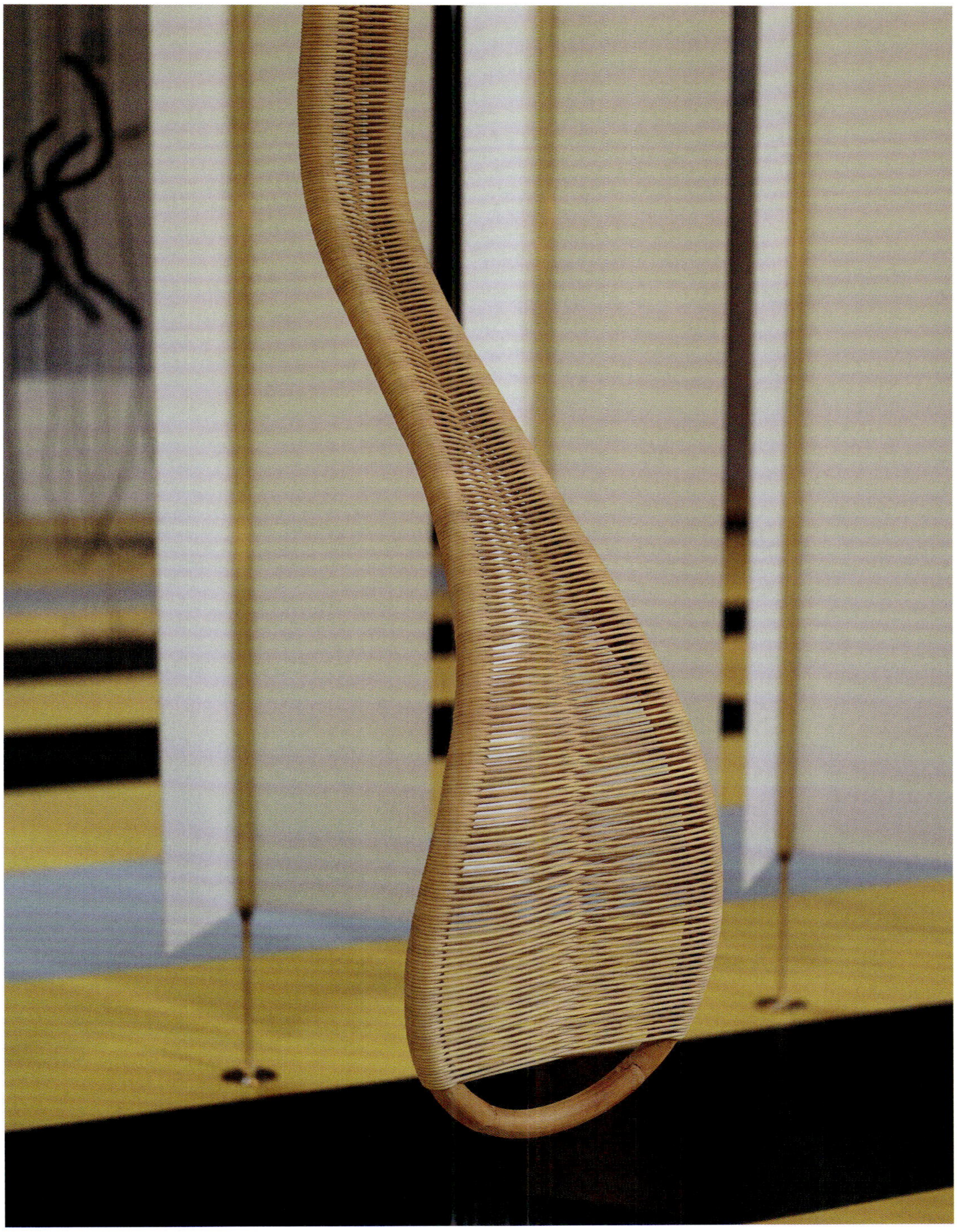

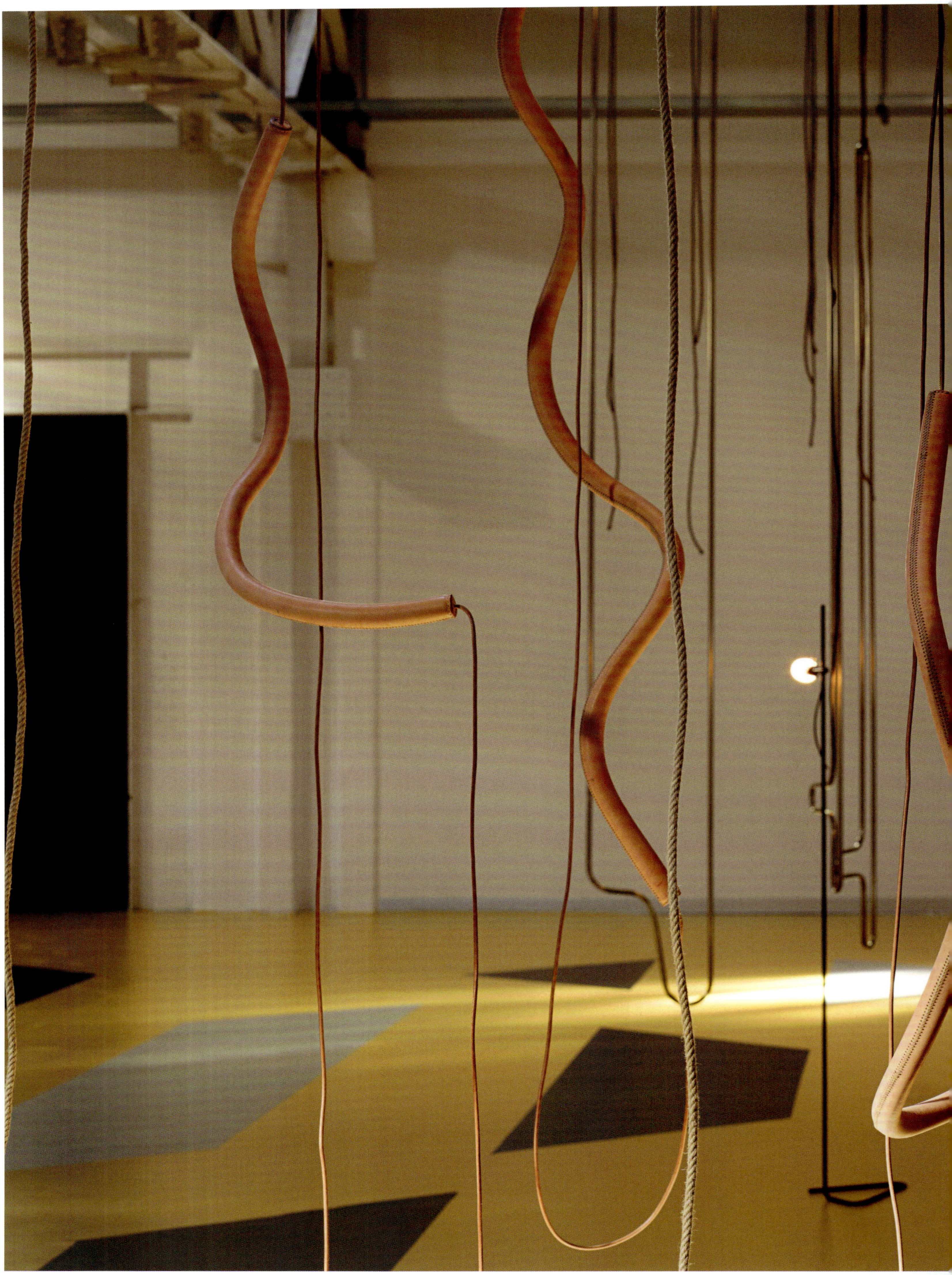

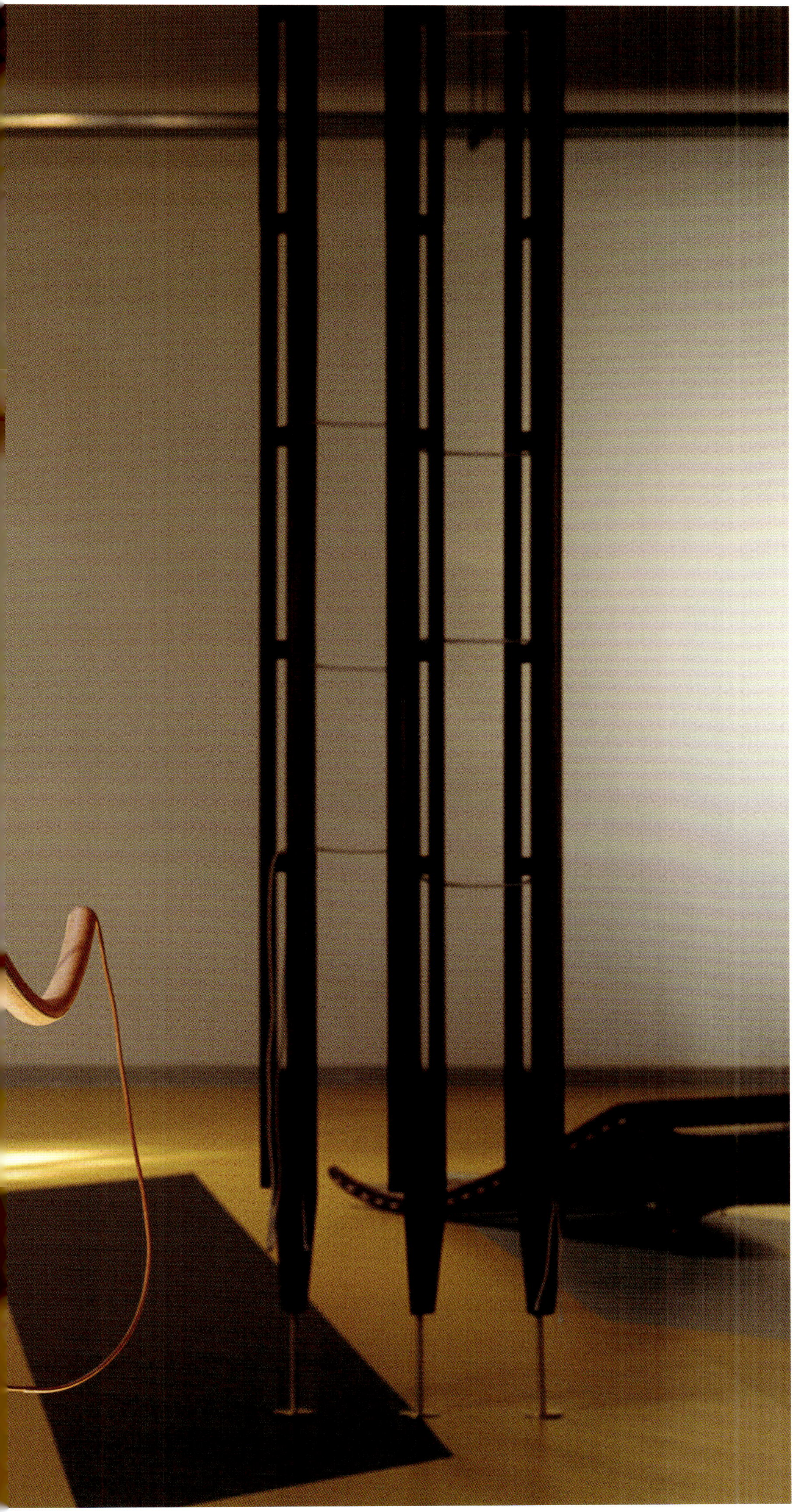

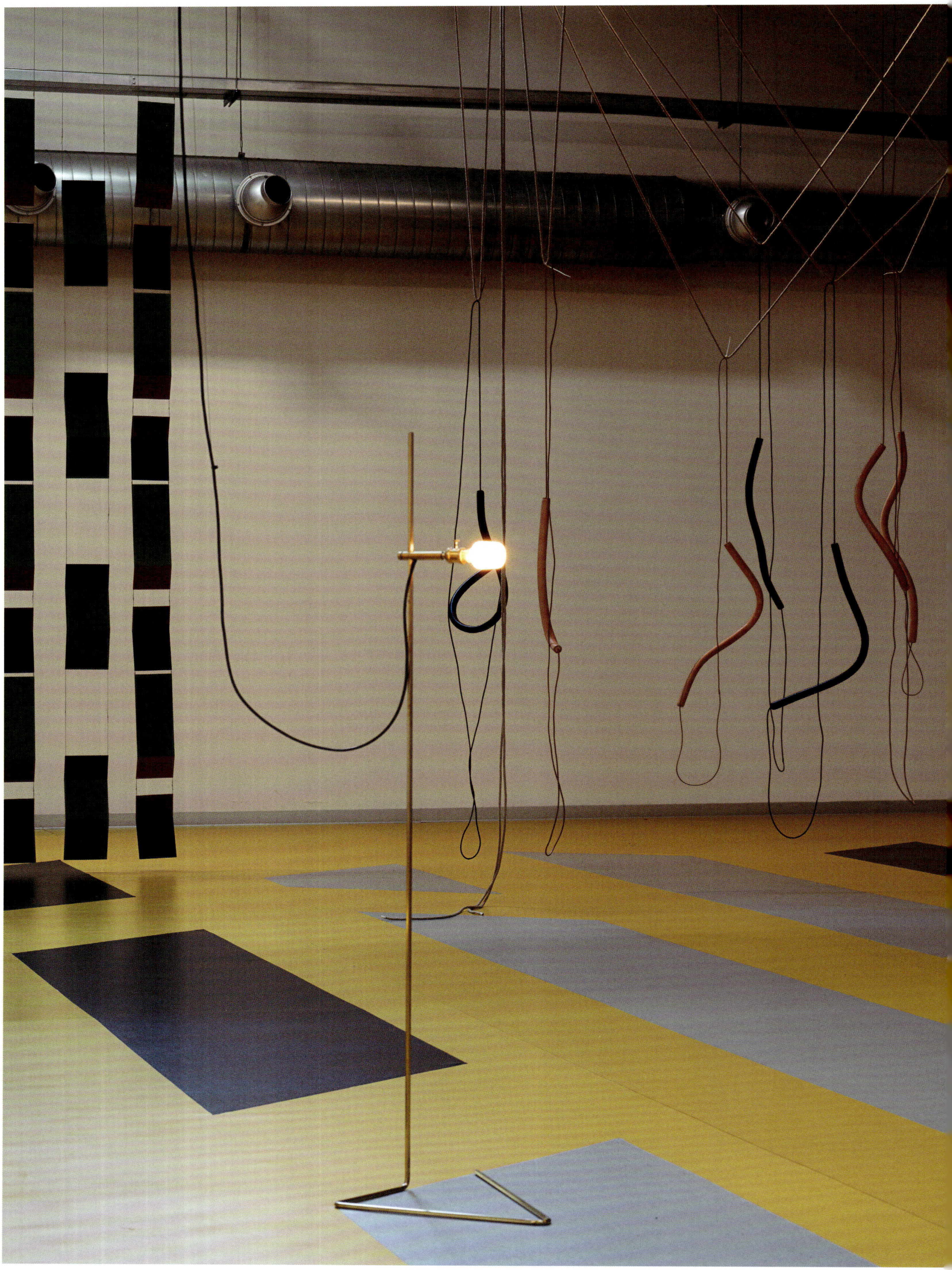

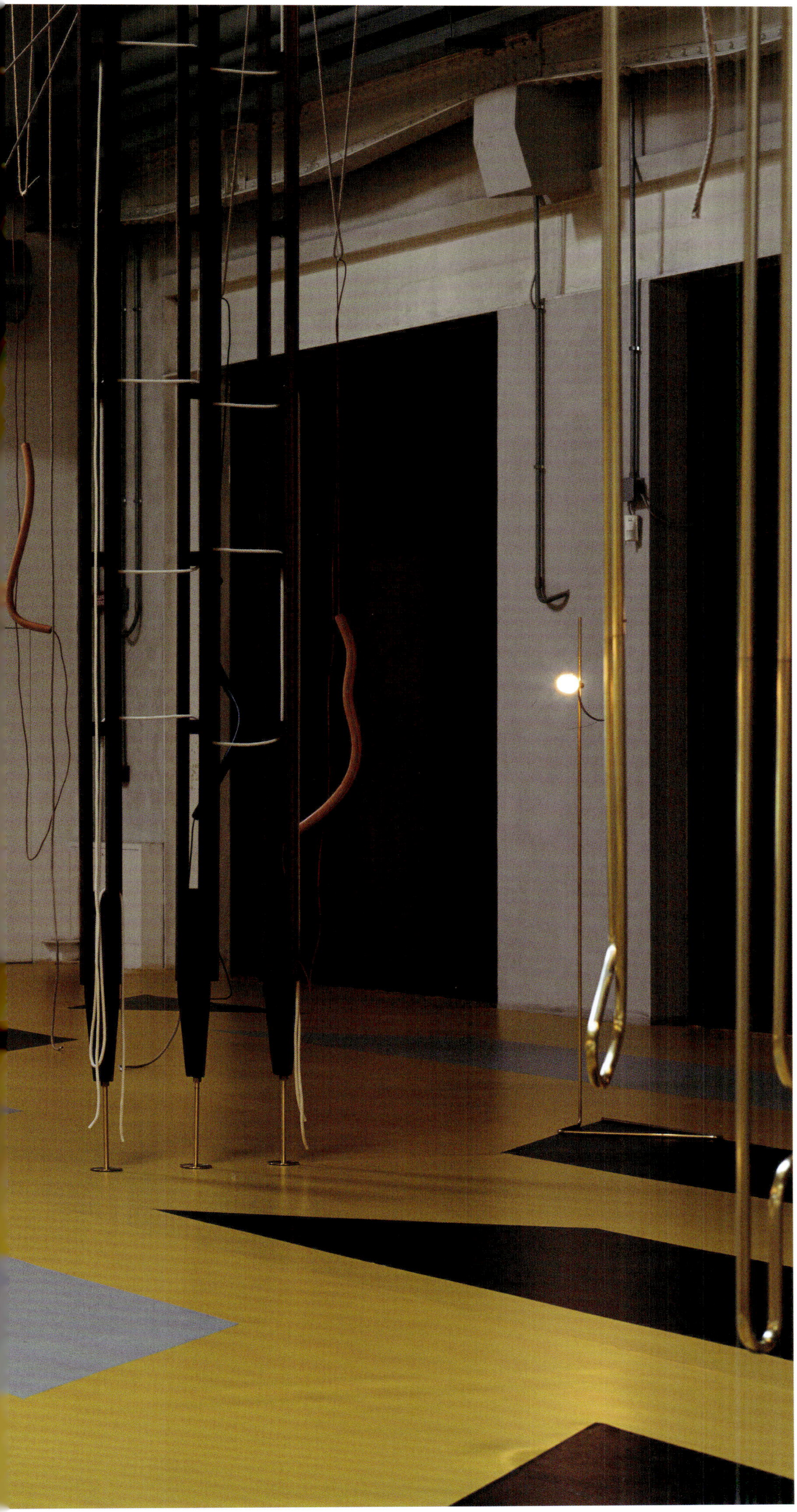

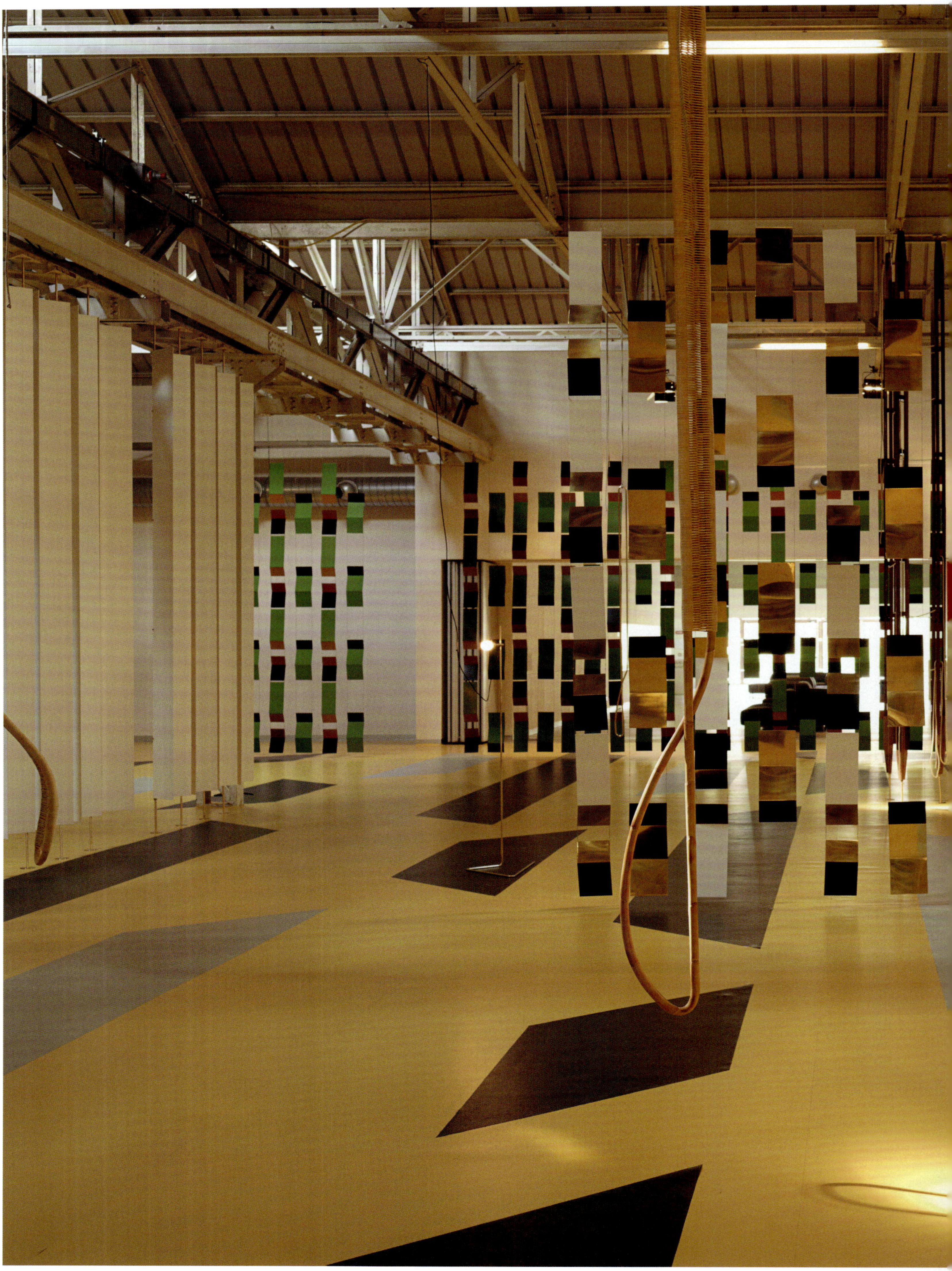

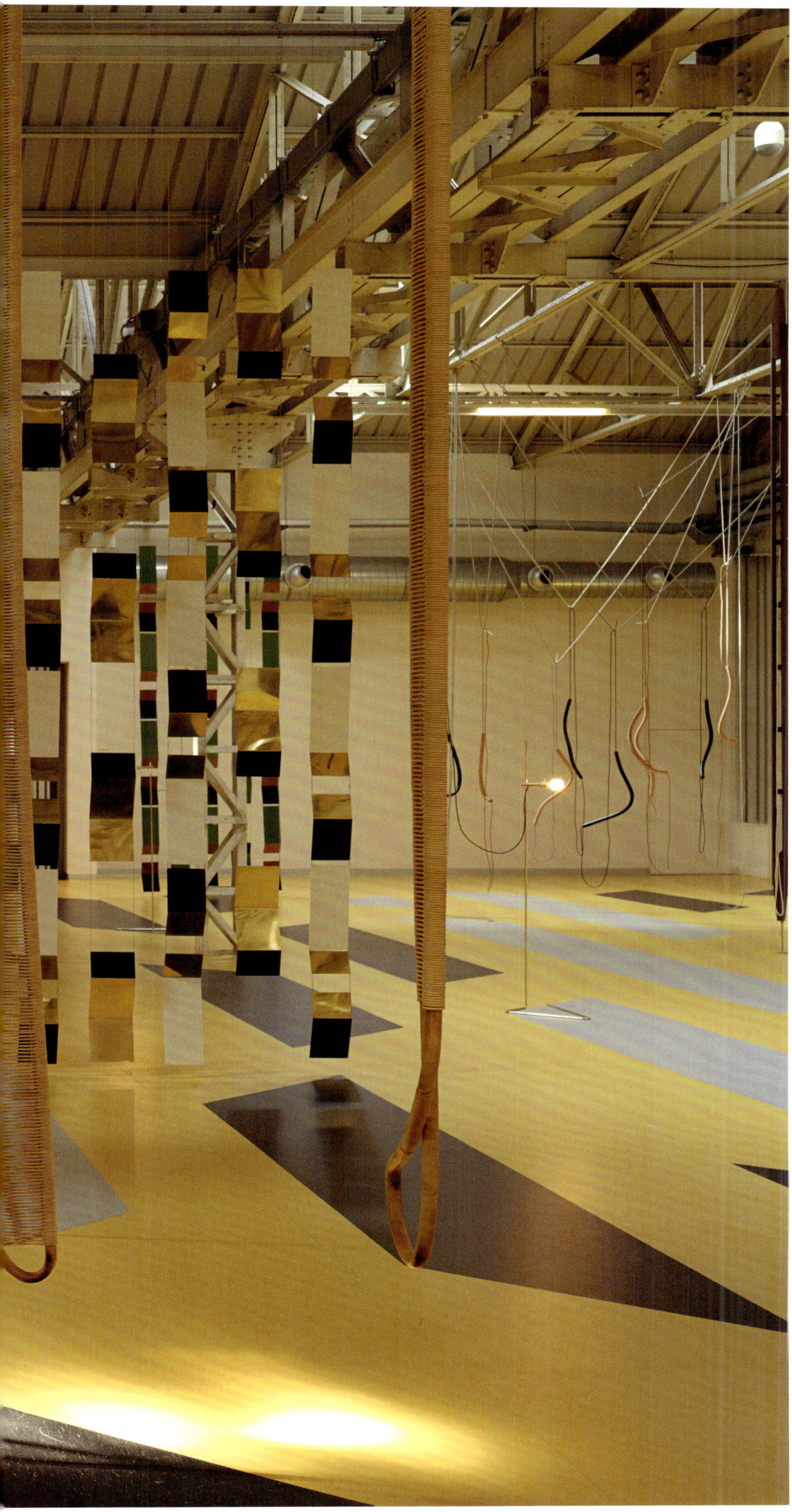

> Most of all I am interested in the idea of sculpture per se, which still operates as a very specific medium. The space it generates, between the viewer and the object, and vice versa—but then this is just a beginning…
> —Leonor Antunes, 2012[1]

In a recent interview, published on the occasion of her spring-summer 2018 exhibition at Marian Goodman's London gallery, Leonor Antunes describes how she is "interested in a lot of craftsmanship, in how people work with particular materials, and in ancient ways of doing things. I'm not fascinated by the material per se," she cautions, "but rather the idea of craftsmanship itself, and of knowledge."[2] Such a statement, of course, simply reiterates what is perhaps the most widely recognized aspect of this artist's practice: her deep research into, and dialogue with, a feminine tradition of craft that has frequently been marginalized within histories of art and architecture that remain, all too often, stubbornly masculinist in their biases. To take only her recent work into account, Antunes has referenced the German-born textile designer Anni Albers, Danish furniture designer Nanna Ditzel, Cuban-born interior designer Clara Porset, and British architect Alison Smithson. Such examples could be multiplied, and indeed critics and curators have been assiduous in following up such citations, acknowledging these frequently under-known figures and annotating their appearances in Antunes's art.[3] Yet what has not been sufficiently addressed is the use to which these antecedents have been put, the *function* served by allusions to "craftsmanship" and "how people work with particular materials" in what is, after all, an ambitious and formally complex sculptural practice that far exceeds a merely archival aesthetic.

So rather than once again excavating the specificities of her references from a history of modernist design, we might more productively ask after the broader role that craft has been understood to have in the space-shaping arts. The hierarchical segregation of the lowly realm of craft apart from that of architecture's higher aspiration—a segregation itself dependent upon a gendered distinction between hand and mind—has not always been enforced as stringently it would be during the height of international modernism. In the mid-nineteenth century, German architect and writer Gottfried Semper developed a materialist theory of architecture, or what we could more accurately term a historical anthropology of architecture, that located its origins precisely in craft and design. Such a theory was already sketched out in a book of 1851, in which he described how the art of building was born from the handicrafts: those who, early in human history, wove mats and those who made carpets gave us the first walls, the first sense of spatial enclosure. In a famous footnote, Semper drew attention to the common derivation of the German terms *Wand*—meaning wall, partition, or screen—and *Gewand*—dress, garments, or clothing—from the Proto-Indo-European root *wend^h*, that is, to wind, to turn. Enclosure was a matter of hanging or stretching such woven material, whether wickerwork, carpet, or the like, between structural posts. A decade later, in the first volume of his monumental *Der Stil in den technischen und tektonischen Künsten*, 1860, entirely devoted to textiles, he brought these traditional domestic crafts, coded as feminine, into the heart of his story of architecture's foundation and evolution, insisting that what had previously been considered purely secondary and supplemental to the structural task of building was, in fact, primary.[4]

At the heart of those ancient ways of doing things, for Semper, was the knot, the interlacing of flexible fibers that he once again, through a creative etymology, linked to tectonic form. As Joseph Rykwert has pointed out, Semper connected the terms *Naht*, a seam or join, with *Knoten*, knot, through their elusive relation to the Greek *anánke*, force, constraint, necessity.[5] The joint or knot was thus elevated to the fundamental tectonic component of building art. This was more than a rejection of the bare structural frame of Enlightenment architectural theory's primitive hut, with its static idealism, but a wholesale revision of the essence of building. "Architecture," Mark Wigley comments, "is no longer seen to originate in the construction of material protection, a simple wooden shelter that is later supplemented and represented by successive ornamental traditions—such that ornament is always representative of, and subordinate to, the original structure."[6] No, in Semper's model, "ornament" or "decoration" is itself structural: "it is decoration that builds," or rather, we might say, construction begins in the humble act of knotting. Such woven fabrics, moreover, did not simply subdivide a preexistent space by demarcating an interior from an exterior, but actively *generated* space, producing the very concept of dwelling. Wigley puts it this way:

> It is not that the fabrics are arranged in a way that provides physical shelter. Rather, their texture, their sensuous play, their textuality, like that of the languages that Semper studied, opens up a space of exchange… The interior is not defined by a continuous enclosure of walls but by

the folds, twists, and turns in an often discontinuous ornamental surface.[7]

Or, as anthropologist Tim Ingold would say, "the world of our experience is, indeed, continually and endlessly coming into being around us as we weave."[8]

Weaving has long been a constitutive element of Antunes's sculptural vocabulary. Important early work—the small clay models of *the space of the window* (2004), produced during a residency in Paris—resembled tiny props of some sort of abstract theater.[9] But they of course also recalled the "theatricality" of the minimalist object itself and its triangulation of sculpture, body, and space; those lessons have remained with Antunes, and we can hear their echoes in her insistence that her art only exists in context, that her sculptures be in the closest relationship with the spaces for which they are conceived, that her work is linked "with the idea of the body measuring space."[10] Just as significant, however, is the sense of her "domestication" of this industrial, masculine mode of sculptural production, a move already suggested by her choice of "Dwelling Place" as the title of a 2007–2008 exhibition.[11] But this assimilation of minimalism is almost immediately tempered or inflected by the countervailing stimulus of Eva Hesse, an impact certainly felt in individual works—such as *1969* (2008), which takes up the forms of *Vinculum II* (1969)—but is even more evident in sculptural ensembles like *a part considered in relation to the hole (détail)* (2007/2008), with its recollections of the photographs Gretchen Lambert took in Hesse's Bowery studio in winter 1966.[12] Yet Hesse's lesson for Antunes would extend beyond simple morphological cues to a properly structural lesson: beyond modeling, or carving, or even welding, one might *weave* sculpture.

This can be traced as a rather direct development, from, say, a Hesse-inflected work such as *folded back against the pillars* (2008) to the nylon nets of her 2013 Kunsthalle Basel exhibition. *folded back* exists in two parts, one an oblong, perforated piece of leather strung with rubber threads that fall to the floor where they lay tangled, the other in which the leather piece is positioned vertically on the wall and the same rubber thread hangs in two long strands down either side. The reference to Hesse, to, say, a work like her *Addendum* (1967), with its horizontal bar and chaotic cascades of rope, its combination of the serial and the handmade, is clear. But so, too, is the sense, conveyed in Antunes's title, of sculpture working *against* architecture, of something soft and pliable that contrasts with the structural—what succumbs to gravity as opposed to what resists its pull. The leather form sags, the rubber falls, and we intuit their formal antagonism to the wall on which *folded back* hangs. Weaving had appeared, but its tectonic principle is not yet evident, as it will be five years later: at Basel, Antunes exhibited three versions of *assembled, moved, re-arranged and scrapped continuously* (2013), nylon nets hung off wooden frames. Here the lightweight fabric grids, draped casually over the suspended oak superstructures, assume a properly Semperian function, producing a space in their weave.[13] They are at once fishing nets, as if hung out to dry, and an intimation of enclosure, both *Knoten* and *Naht*, we might say. Between these two moments, it was her encounter with the work of Anni Albers that had, perhaps, revealed the tectonic possibilities of the weave—an encounter that, not coincidentally, had intensified precisely around 2011, as Antunes began preparing the Basel exhibition.[14] In this reading, the mediating role played by Albers would have opened up precisely the space-generating role of these fabric-like grids.

The tectonic has, of course, already been claimed for sculpture; such is the argument Hal Foster makes regarding Richard Serra, who has deployed it as a means at once of resisting "the becoming-image of the work" and of reasserting "the rights of the body." For Foster, this becomes a critical maneuver in relation to architecture, to the "scenographic kitsch" of 1980s post-modernism as much as the "capitalist technologies of the simulacral and the virtual" of contemporary design.[15] He does so with reference to Kenneth Frampton's reading of the tectonic, with its exaltation of the joint as a not merely constructive but well-nigh ontological element of architecture; tellingly, this is a reading that, while reliant of Semper's historical anthropology, elides the role of weaving to instead focus on those more masculine elements of compressive mass and structural frame. What is metaphysical in Frampton's architectural theory is rendered materialist in Foster's exegesis of Serra, but both have recourse of a vocabulary of the muscular, the weighty, and the engineered against the perceived flimsiness of atectonic form. We may well agree that contemporary sculpture, like architecture, is caught between image and structure, surface and tectonics, while still recognizing the limits of this particular solution. Antunes provides another possibility: not the ornamental or decorative posed against the structural, but, as we have seen, the woven, the knotted, the coiled as itself tectonic, generative of space.

The weave begins with a thread, and critics have rightly called attention to the significance of line and measurement in Antunes's practice.[16] But what has become evident over the last decade or so is the primacy of what that line produces in the weave, and that it is here that the artist has proposed a new model for sculptural production. Traditionally, as we have seen, sculpture has been an art form in which form and substance, design and raw material, are clearly distinguished: the *making* of sculpture happens precisely where that brute matter "meets the space of action of those forces that impinge upon it" as a surface to be transformed—the sculptor chipping away at a block of marble, or applying manual pressure to the lump of clay, or even welding together pieces of metal.[17] Even within minimalist and post-minimalist practice, this distinction was largely maintained. Those relations of surface, force, and the generation of form are, however, fundamentally reconfigured in Antunes's objects. Her art does not, generally, entail the alteration of the surface of her materials, which are not so much transformed as built up through knotting, twisting, draping, suspending, and the like. Artistic labor resides instead in something like a pattern of skilled movement, of its rhythmic repetition through which the form of the work arises. This is Tim Ingold's great insight into the challenge weaving poses to conventional notions of making, an insight Antunes herself arrived at through careful study of the culture of textiles and the world of traditional craft. Form does not issue from a preexistent idea that she would impose upon her material, it instead results from "the gradual unfolding of that field of forces set up through the active and sensuous engagement of practitioner and material. The field is neither internal to the material nor internal to the practitioner…; rather, it cuts across the emergent interface between them."[18] Antunes's engagement with craftspeople, with those who work leather or wood or fiber, is of course a matter of preserving these traditional ways of doing, but it is also, then, a recognition of their implications for contemporary sculptural practice.

This essay began by insisting on the sculptural specificity of Antunes's work, and on a cordoning-off of the usual critical strategy of engaging with her "sources" in design history. But can textile and text be so neatly separated? Doesn't fabric have a textuality all its own, and vice versa? We draw out our stories, or cut them short; narratives are woven, too, tales embroidered. The personification of *anánke*—of that realm of force, constraint, or necessity that for the Greeks undergirded tectonic joint and fibrous knot alike—was commonly depicted as holding a spindle. Like the ornamental realm to which weaving was most often consigned, we may wish to see her references as merely supplemental to the real work of the sculpture, but the two are tied closely together. To make a world through weaving, as Antunes does, is also to make meaning, to shape our sense of space through shaping the sensuous experience of it. Her knot of female practitioners and anonymous craftspeople, in their diverse ways, attempted to do the same. In the end, we will need to bind them back into this story, not simply as influence or archive but as premonitory ways of doing, a repository of muscle memories—the mind in the weave itself.

TOM MCDONOUGH

1 Leonor Antunes, quoted in Jennifer Higgie, "Sculptors Discuss Sculpture," *Frieze*, 147, May 2012, p. 206.
2 Antunes, quoted in Joe Lloyd, "Leonor Antunes: 'I'm interested in ancient ways of doing things,'" *Studio International*, July 30, 2018, accessible at https://www.studiointernational.com/index.php/leonor-antunes-interview-i-am-interested-in-ancient-ways-of-doing-things.
3 For a recent example, see the essays collected in Lydia Yee and Habda Rashid (eds.), *Leonor Antunes: The Frisson of the Togetherness* (London: Whitechapel Gallery, 2017).
4 See Mary McLeod, "Undressing Architecture: Fashion, Gender, and Modernity," in Deborah Fausch et al., *Architecture: In Fashion* (New York: Princeton Architectural Press, 1994), pp. 47-48.
5 Joseph Rykwert, "Semper and the Conception of Style," in Adolf Max Vogt, Christina Reble, and Martin Fröhlich (eds.), *Gottfried Semper und die Mitte des 19.Jahrhunderts* (Basel and Stuttgart: Birkhäuser, Coll. "Geschichte und Theorie der Architektur, Eidgenössische Technische Hochschule Zürich," 18, 1976), p. 72. For more on the significance of these etymological ruminations, see Kenneth Frampton, *Studies in Tectonic Culture*, ed. John Cava (Chicago: Graham Foundation for Advanced Studies in the Fine Arts and Cambridge, MA and London: The MIT Press, 1995), p. 86.
6 Mark Wigley, *White Walls, Designer Dresses* (Cambridge, MA and London: The MIT Press, 1995), p. 11.
7 Ibid., p. 12.
8 Tim Ingold, "Making Culture and Weaving the World," in Paul Graves-Brown (ed.), *Matter, Materiality and Modern Culture* (London and New York: Routledge, 2000), p. 69.
9 This moment had been preceded by a series of site-specific interventions in museums, including a work in *7 artistas ao 10.° mês*, Museu Calouste Gulbenkian (PT) (1999) and a solo exhibition at the Museu Nacional de Arte Antiga (PT) (2002), that should undoubtedly be seen as precursors to her better-known works, although they remain beyond the scope of this essay. For a brief account, see Bruno Leitão, "On Leonore Antunes," *Revista Atlántica*, 58 (2017).
10 Antunes, quoted in "RRS Museo Reina Sofía Radio," accessible at https://www.museoreinasofia.es/en/exhibitions/leonor-antunes-walk-around-there-look-through-here.

Indeed, we could say that by the mid-2000s, Antunes had assimilated the three fundamental principles motivating post-minimalist sculptural practice: the "constructivist" principle of structuring materials; the "phenomenological" principle of motivating the body; and the "situational" principle of demarcating place. See Hal Foster, "Sculpture Remade," in *The Art-Architecture Complex* (London and New York: Verso, 2011), pp. 140–141.

11 As noted by Dieter Roelstraete, who however reads such references in terms of what he calls a "melancholy fantasy of homeliness away from home" on the part of contemporary, peripatetic artists. See his "Home Is Where the Art Is: Apropos and Around the Work of Leonor Antunes," *Les Cahiers Purple*, 1 (2009): pp. 122–124.

12 For a discussion of Hesse's work with significant relevance for an understanding of Antunes, see Mark Godfrey, "A String of Nots: Eva Hesse's Hanging Sculpture," in Elisabeth Sussman and Fred Wasserman, *Eva Hesse: Sculpture* (New York: The Jewish Museum and New Haven and London: Yale University Press, 2006), pp. 29-51.

13 Adam Szymczyk, "Thinking Objects," in Szymczyk (ed.), *Leonor Antunes: the last days in chimalistac*, (Basel: Kunsthalle Basel and Berlin: BOM DIA BOA TARDE BOA NOITE, 2016), pp. 3-6. A similar imperative may be seen in her contemporaneous exhibition at the Kunsthalle Lissabon, *the thread is so tiny that the eye, though armed with a magnifying-glass, suspects it rather than sees it* (2013), with its elegant Agba wood standing frames inside which nylon grids were suspended; the title is derived from a sentence describing the Pine Processionary caterpillar in a 1916 essay by French entomologist Jean Henri Fabre.

14 See Antunes, "Connecting with Anni Albers," *Tate Etc*, 44 (autumn 2018). For more on Albers see Ann Coxon, Briony Fer, and Maria Müller-Schareck (eds.), *Anni Albers* (London: Tate, 2018) and, on Bauhaus textile design more broadly, T'ai Smith, *Bauhaus Weaving Theory: From Feminine Craft to Mode of Design* (Minneapolis and London: University of Minnesota Press, 2014).

15 Hal Foster, "Sculpture Remade," Op. cit., pp. 148, 150.

16 See Doris von Drathen, "Of 'World Lines' and Other Forgotten Voices," *Afterall*, 24 (summer 2010): pp. 91-97.

17 Tim Ingold, "Making Culture," Op. cit., p. 51.

18 Ibid., p. 57.

> Soprattutto mi interessa l'idea della scultura in sé, che agisce ancora come mezzo molto specifico. Lo spazio che essa genera tra l'osservatore e l'oggetto e viceversa, ma, d'altra parte, questo è soltanto l'inizio...
> —Leonor Antunes, 2012[1]

In una recente intervista, pubblicata in occasione della mostra presso la galleria Marian Goodman di Londra nella primavera-estate del 2018, Leonor Antunes spiega di essere "interessata a molte forme di artigianato, a come le persone lavorino con particolari materiali e a certi metodi antichi di fare le cose. Non sono affascinata dal materiale in sé", precisa, "ma piuttosto dall'idea dell'artigianato e della conoscenza"[2]. Una simile affermazione, naturalmente, non fa altro che ribadire quello che forse è l'aspetto più riconosciuto della pratica di questa artista: la sua approfondita ricerca e dialogo con una tradizione artigianale femminile spesso rimasta ai margini della storia dell'arte e dell'architettura, che il più delle volte restano ostinatamente maschiliste nei loro pregiudizi. Per prendere in considerazione soltanto la sua produzione più recente, Antunes si è riferita alla designer tessile tedesca Anni Albers, alla designer di mobili danese Nanna Ditzel, alla designer d'interni cubana Clara Porset e all'architetto britannico Alison Smithson. Gli esempi potrebbero moltiplicarsi all'infinito e, in effetti, critici e curatori non hanno esitato a indagare simili citazioni, riconoscendo queste figure spesso poco note e commentando le loro apparizioni nell'arte di Antunes[3]. Ciò che non è stato esaminato a sufficienza, tuttavia, è l'uso di questi antecedenti, la *funzione* assolta dalle allusioni all'"artigianato" e a "come le persone lavorino con particolari materiali", in quella che, dopotutto, è una pratica scultorea ambiziosa e formalmente complessa, capace di andare ben oltre un'estetica puramente archivistica.

Così, anziché sviscerare di nuovo le specificità dei rimandi di Antunes a una storia del design modernista, sarebbe più proficuo interrogarsi sul ruolo più ampio che è stato assegnato alle capacità manuali nelle arti deputate a plasmare lo spazio. La segregazione gerarchica dell'umile dimensione dell'artigianato da quella della più nobile aspirazione dell'architettura — segregazione che dipende a sua volta da una distinzione di genere tra mano e mente — non è sempre stata applicata con il rigore che sarebbe stato adottato all'apice del modernismo internazionale. Alla metà del XIX secolo, l'architetto e scrittore tedesco Gottfried Semper propose una teoria materialista dell'architettura — o di quella che, più accuratamente, potremmo definire un'antropologia storica dell'architettura — che individuava le sue origini proprio nell'artigianato e nel design. L'autore aveva già tratteggiato un'ipotesi di questo tipo in un libro del 1851, dove spiega come l'arte della costruzione sia nata dalle attività manuali: coloro che, agli albori della storia umana, intrecciavano stuoie e creavano tappeti ci regalarono le prime pareti, la prima idea di delimitazione spaziale. In una famosa nota, Semper evidenzia la derivazione comune dei vocaboli tedeschi *Wand* (parete, divisorio o schermo) e *Gewand* (vestito, indumento o abbigliamento) dalla radice protoindoeuropea *wend^h*, cioè girare, voltare. La delimitazione consisteva nell'appendere o nell'allungare i materiali tessuti — fossero essi vimini, tappeti ecc. — tra sostegni strutturali. Dieci anni dopo, nel primo volume del monumentale *Der Stil in den technischen und tektonischen Künsten* (1860), interamente dedicato ai tessuti, Semper collocò queste arti domestiche tradizionali, codificate come femminili, al cuore della sua storia della nascita e dell'evoluzione dell'architettura. A suo parere, ciò che in passato era stato considerato puramente secondario e complementare per il compito strutturale della costruzione era, in realtà, primario[4].

Al centro di questi antichi modi di fare le cose c'è, secondo Semper, il nodo, l'intreccio di fibre flessibili, che, tramite un'etimologia creativa, egli lega ancora una volta alla forma tettonica. Come sottolinea Joseph Rykwert, Semper associa i termini *Naht* (cucitura o giuntura) e *Knoten* (nodo) attraverso il loro rapporto elusivo con il greco *anánke*, ossia forza, costrizione, necessità[5]. Così il giunto o nodo fu elevato a componente tettonico fondamentale dell'arte della costruzione. Non si trattava soltanto di rifiutare la nuda impalcatura strutturale della capanna primitiva della teoria architettonica illuminista, con il suo idealismo statico, bensì di effettuare un'ampia revisione dell'essenza della costruzione. "Non si ritiene più", commenta Mark Wigley, "che l'architettura abbia origine dalla costruzione della protezione materiale, un semplice riparo di legno che in seguito viene completato e rappresentato da tradizioni ornamentali consecutive. Un simile ornamento è sempre rappresentativo della struttura originale, e subordinato ad essa."[6] No, nel modello di Semper l'"ornamento" o la "decorazione" è di per sé strutturale: "È la decorazione a costruire", o meglio, potremmo dire che la costruzione comincia dall'umile atto di annodare. Questi tessuti, inoltre, non si limitano a suddividere uno spazio preesistente segnando i confini tra interno ed esterno, ma *generano* attivamente lo spazio, producendo il concetto di abitazione. Nelle parole di Wigley:

> Non è che i tessuti siano disposti in modo da creare un riparo fisico. Piuttosto, la loro consistenza, il loro gioco sensuale, la loro testualità, come quella dei linguaggi studiati da Semper, aprono uno spazio di scambio [...] L'interno non è definito da un involucro continuo di pareti, ma dalle pieghe, dagli intrecci e dagli avvolgimenti in una superficie ornamentale spesso discontinua.[7]

Oppure, come direbbe l'antropologo Tim Ingold, "in verità, il mondo dell'esperienza prende forma continuamente e infinitamente intorno a noi mentre tessiamo"[8].

La tessitura è da tempo un elemento costitutivo del vocabolario scultoreo di Antunes. Alcune importanti opere iniziali — i piccoli modelli d'argilla di *the space of the window* [lo spazio della finestra, 2004], realizzati durante un soggiorno a Parigi — sembrano i minuscoli arredi scenici di un teatro astratto[9], ma naturalmente ricordano anche la "teatralità" dell'oggetto minimalista e la sua triangolazione di scultura, corpo e spazio; Antunes non ha dimenticato queste lezioni, di cui udiamo l'eco quando l'artista afferma che la sua arte esiste solo nel contesto, che le sue sculture sono in strettissimo rapporto con gli spazi per i quali sono state concepite, che la sua produzione è legata "all'idea del corpo che misura lo spazio"[10]. Altrettanto significativa, però, è la sensazione dell'"addomesticamento" di questo metodo industriale e maschile di produzione scultorea, una mossa già suggerita dalla scelta di "Dwelling Place" come titolo di una mostra del 2007-2008[11]. Questa assimilazione del minimalismo, tuttavia, è mitigata o modulata quasi immediatamente dall'influsso contrapposto di Eva Hesse, impatto che senza dubbio si avverte nelle singole opere — come *1969* (2008), che riprende le forme di *Vinculum II* (1969) — ma che è ancora più evidente in complessi scultorei come *a part considered in relation to the whole (detail)* [una parte considerata in relazione al tutto (dettaglio), 2007-2008], con i suoi rimandi alle fotografie scattate nell'inverno del 1966 da Gretchen Lambert nell'atelier di Hesse in Bowery Street a New York[12]. L'insegnamento di Hesse, tuttavia, era destinato a estendersi al di là dei semplici spunti morfologici, diventando, per Antunes, una vera e propria lezione strutturale: oltre a modellare, intagliare o addirittura saldare, la scultura si poteva *tessere*.

Questo processo si può considerare una transizione abbastanza diretta da un'opera influenzata da Hesse come *folded back against the pillars* [ripiegato contro i pilastri, 2008] alle reti di nylon della mostra del 2013 alla Kunsthalle Basel. *Folded back* consiste di due parti, una striscia di cuoio oblunga perforata, cui sono fissati fili di gomma che cadono sul pavimento aggrovigliandosi, e un altro pezzo di cuoio posizionato verticalmente sulla parete, con lo stesso filo di gomma che pende su ciascun lato in due lunghi nastri. Il riferimento a Hesse — per esempio a un'opera come *Addendum* (1967), con la sua barra orizzontale e le sue caotiche cascate di corda, nonché il suo accostamento di produzione in serie e a mano — è lampante. Lo stesso vale, però, per l'impressione, trasmessa dal titolo di Antunes, di una scultura che opera *contro* l'architettura, di qualcosa di morbido e duttile che si oppone allo strutturale, di ciò che soccombe alla gravità in contrasto a ciò che resiste alla sua attrazione. La forma di cuoio si incurva, la gomma cade, e intuiamo il loro antagonismo formale rispetto alla parete cui è appeso *folded back*. La tessitura è presente, ma il suo principio tettonico non è ancora visibile, come invece lo sarà cinque anni dopo: a Basilea, Antunes ha esposto tre versioni di *assembled, moved, re-arranged and scrapped continuously* [assemblato, spostato, ridisposto e gettato via continuamente, 2013], composte da reti di nylon che pendono da telai di legno. Qui le griglie di tessuto leggero, drappeggiate con noncuranza sulle sovrastrutture di quercia sospese, assumono una forma tipicamente semperiana, generando uno spazio con la loro trama[13]. Sono insieme reti da pesca stese ad asciugare e un presagio di delimitazione, insieme *Knoten* e *Naht*, potremmo dire. Tra questi due momenti, è stato l'incontro dell'artista con la produzione di Anni Albers a rivelarle, forse, le possibilità tettoniche della tessitura, incontro che, non a caso, si era intensificato proprio intorno al 2011, quando Antunes aveva iniziato a preparare la mostra di Basilea[14]. In questa lettura, il ruolo di mediatrice svolto da Albers avrebbe inaugurato esattamente il compito di generazione spaziale di queste griglie simili a tessuti.

La tettonica, naturalmente, era già stata rivendicata per la scultura; è questa l'osservazione che Hal Foster fa riguardo a Richard Serra, che ha usato la tettonica come mezzo sia per resistere al "divenire immagine dell'opera" sia per riaffermare "i diritti del corpo". Per Foster, questa diventa una manovra fondamentale rispetto all'architettura, al "kitsch scenografico" del postmodernismo degli anni ottanta e alle "tecnologie capitaliste del simulacrale e del virtuale" del design contemporaneo[15]. Foster si riallaccia all'interpretazione della tettonica da parte di Kenneth Frampton, con la sua esaltazione del giunto non come elemento architettonico puramente costruttivo, ma quasi ontologico; significativamente, questa è una lettura che, pur facendo affidamento sull'antropologia storica di Semper, elide il ruolo della tessitura per concentrarsi invece sui fattori più maschili della massa compressiva e dell'impalcatura strutturale. Ciò che è metafisico nella teoria architettonica di Frampton è reso materialista nell'esegesi fosteriana di Serra, ma entrambe ricorrono al vocabolario del muscolare, del pesante e del costruito, rispetto alla presunta inconsistenza della forma atettonica. Possiamo concordare che la scultura contemporanea, come l'architettura, è in bilico tra immagine e struttura, tra superficie e tettonica, pur riconoscendo tuttora i limiti di questa soluzione particolare. Antunes offre un'altra possibilità: non l'ornamentale o il decorativo contrapposto allo strutturale ma, come abbiamo visto, il tessuto, l'annodato, l'attorcigliato, inteso come tettonico, come capace di generare spazio.

La tessitura comincia con un filo e i critici hanno giustamente attirato l'attenzione sull'importanza della linea e della misurazione nella pratica di Antunes[16]. Negli ultimi dieci anni circa, tuttavia, è diventata evidente la supremazia dell'effetto della linea sulla tessitura, oltre al fatto che qui l'artista ha proposto un nuovo modello di produzione scultorea. Di solito, come abbiamo accennato, la scultura è un'espressione artistica in cui la forma e la sostanza, il design e la materia prima sono chiaramente distinti. La *creazione* della scultura accade proprio dove la materia grezza "incontra lo spazio d'azione delle forze che la influenzano" come superficie da trasformare: l'intaglio del blocco di marmo da parte dello scultore, l'applicazione della pressione manuale al grumo di argilla o persino la saldatura di pezzi di metallo[17]. Questa distinzione si è perlopiù conservata persino nella pratica minimalista e postminimalista. Questi rapporti di superficie, forza e generazione di forma, però, si riconfigurano radicalmente negli oggetti di Antunes. In generale, la sua arte non implica l'alterazione della superficie dei materiali, che non vengono tanto trasformati quanto costruiti progressivamente, annodando, attorcigliando, drappeggiando, sospendendo e così via. Il lavoro artistico risiede piuttosto in qualcosa di simile a uno schema di movimento specializzato, della sua ripetizione ritmica, da cui nasce la forma dell'opera. Questa è la grande intuizione di Tim Ingold riguardo alla sfida che la tessitura lancia alle concezioni convenzionali di creazione, un'intuizione cui Antunes è arrivata studiando attentamente la cultura dei tessuti e il mondo dell'artigianato tradizionale. La forma non scaturisce da un'idea preesistente da imporre al materiale, bensì deriva dal "dispiegamento graduale del campo di forze prodotto dall'impegno attivo e sensuale del professionista e del materiale. Il campo non è interno al materiale né al professionista [...]; piuttosto, trascende l'interfaccia emergente tra loro"[18]. Naturalmente, l'interesse di Antunes per gli artigiani, per coloro che lavorano il cuoio, il legno o la fibra, mira a conservare questi modi di fare tradizionali, ma allora è anche un riconoscimento delle loro implicazioni per la pratica scultorea contemporanea.

All'inizio di questo saggio ho messo l'accento sulla specificità scultorea della produzione di Antunes e sull'individuazione dell'approccio critico abituale alle sue "fonti" nella storia del design. Ma il tessuto e il testo possono essere separati così chiaramente? Il tessuto non ha una testualità tutta sua, e viceversa? Allunghiamo le nostre storie, oppure le interrompiamo; anche le narrazioni vengono tessute e i racconti ricamati. La personificazione del *anánke* — della dimensione di forza, costrizione o necessità che, secondo i greci, sosteneva sia il giunto tettonico sia il nodo fibroso — era comunemente raffigurata con un fuso in mano. Come la dimensione ornamentale cui la tessitura era relegata molto spesso, potremmo essere tentati di vedere i suoi rimandi come semplici aggiunte alla vera opera della scultura, ma le due cose sono strettamente legate. Creare un mondo tramite la tessitura, come fa Antunes, equivale anche a creare un significato, a plasmare il senso dello spazio plasmandone l'esperienza sensuale. Le sue professioniste e i suoi artigiani anonimi hanno cercato in vario modo di fare la stessa cosa. Alla fine dovremo reinserirli in questa storia, non soltanto come influsso o archivio, bensì come modi premonitori del fare, un ricettacolo di ricordi muscolari, la mente nella tessitura stessa.

TOM MCDONOUGH

1 Leonor Antunes, in Jennifer Higgie, *Sculptors discuss Sculpture*, in "Frieze", 147, maggio 2012, p. 206.
2 Leonor Antunes, in Joe Lloyd, *Leonor Antunes: "I'm interested in ancient ways of doing things"*, in "Studio International", 30 luglio 2018, accessibile sulla pagina https://www.studiointernational.com/index.php/leonor-antunes-interview-i-am-interested-in-ancient-ways-of-doing-things.
3 Per un esempio recente, si vedano i saggi raccolti in *Leonor Antunes: The Frisson of the Togetherness*, a cura di Lydia Yee e Habda Rashid, Whitechapel Gallery, London 2017.
4 Si veda Mary McLeod, *Undressing Architecture: Fashion, Gender, and Modernity*, in *Architecture: In Fashion*, a cura di Deborah Fausch *et al.*, Princeton Architectural Press, New York 1994, pp. 47–48.
5 Joseph Rykwert, *Semper and the Conception of Style*, in *Gottfried Semper und die Mitte des 19.Jahrhunderts*, a cura di Adolf Max Vogt, Christina Reble e Martin Fröhlich, collezione

"Geschichte und Theorie der Architektur, Eidgenössische Technische Hochschule Zürich", 18, Birkhäuser, Basel-Stuttgart 1976, p. 72. Per ulteriori informazioni sulla rilevanza di queste riflessioni etimologiche, si veda Kenneth Frampton, *Studies in Tectonic Culture*, a cura di John Cava, Graham Foundation for Advanced Studies in the Fine Arts, Chicago-The MIT Press, Cambridge (Mass.)-London 1995, p. 86 (trad. it. *Tettonica e architettura*, a cura di Mara De Benedetti, Milano 2005).

6 Mark Wigley, *White Walls, Designer Dresses*, The MIT Press, Cambridge (Mass.)-London 1995, p. 11.

7 Ivi, p. 12.

8 Tim Ingold, *Making culture and weaving the world*, in *Matter, Materiality and Modern Culture*, a cura di Paul Graves-Brown, Routledge, London-New York 2000, p. 69.

9 Questo momento era stato preceduto da una serie di interventi site-specific nei musei, tra cui un'opera in "7 artistas ao 10.° mês" al Museu Calouste Gulbenkian di Lisbona nel 1999 e una personale al Museu Nacional de Arte Antiga di Lisbona nel 2002, che, pur non essendo trattate in questo saggio, vanno indubbiamente considerate precorritrici dei suoi lavori più famosi. Per un breve resoconto, si veda Bruno Leitão, *On Leonore Antunes*, in "Revista Atlântica", 58, 2017.

10 Leonor Antunes, in *RRS Museo Reina Sofía Radio*, accessibile sulla pagina https://www.museoreinasofia.es/en/exhibitions/leonor-antunes-walk-around-there-look-through-here. In verità, potremmo dire che, alla metà degli anni Duemila, Antunes aveva ormai assimilato i tre principi fondamentali alla base della pratica scultorea postminimalista: il principio "costruttivista" della strutturazione dei materiali; il principio "fenomenologico" della motivazione del corpo; e il principio "situazionale" della demarcazione dello spazio. Si veda Hal Foster, *Sculpture Remade*, in *The Art-Architecture Complex*, Verso, London-New York 2011, pp. 140-141.

11 Come osservato da Dieter Roelstraete, che tuttavia interpreta questi riferimenti dalla prospettiva di quella che definisce una "malinconica fantasia di casa lontano da casa" da parte degli artisti contemporanei peripatetici. Si veda *Home Is Where the Art Is: A propos and Around the Work of Leonor Antunes*, in "Les Cahiers Purple", 1, 2009, pp. 122-124.

12 Per una discussione sulla produzione di Hesse, utile per comprendere il lavoro di Antunes, si veda Mark Godfrey, *A String of Nots: Eva Hesse's Hanging Sculpture*, in Elisabeth Sussman e Fred Wasserman, *Eva Hesse: Sculpture*, The Jewish Museum, New York-Yale University Press, New Haven-London 2006, pp. 29-51.

13 Si veda Adam Szymczyk, *Thinking Objects*, in *Leonor Antunes: the last days in chimalistac*, a cura di Adam Szymczyk, catalogo della mostra, Kunsthalle Basel, Basel - BOM DIA BOA TARDE BOA NOITE, Berlin 2016, pp. 3-6. Un imperativo analogo si può osservare nella contemporanea installazione alla Kunsthalle Lissabon, *the thread is so tiny that the eye, though armed with a magnifying-glass, suspects it rather than sees it* [il filo è così minuscolo che l'occhio, seppure armato di lente d'ingrandimento, lo suppone anziché vederlo, 2013], con i suoi eleganti telai verticali in legno di agba all'interno dei quali erano sospese griglie di nylon; il titolo deriva da una frase che descrive un lepidottero, la processionaria del pino, in un saggio del 1916 dell'entomologo francese Jean-Henri Fabre.

14 Si veda Leonor Antunes, *Connecting with Anni Albers*, in "Tate Etc", 44, autunno 2018. Per ulteriori informazioni su Albers, si veda *Anni Albers*, a cura di Ann Coxon, Briony Fer e Maria Müller-Schareck, Tate, London 2018, e, per una panoramica più generale del design tessile del Bauhaus, T'ai Smith, *Bauhaus Weaving Theory: From Feminine Craft to Mode of Design*, University of Minnesota Press, Minneapolis-London 2014.

15 Hal Foster, *Sculpture Remade*, cit., pp. 148, 150.

16 Si veda Doris von Drathen, *Of "World Lines" and Other Forgotten Voices*, in "Afterall", 24, estate 2010, pp. 91-97.

17 Tim Ingold, *Making culture and weaving the world*, cit., p. 51.

18 Ivi, p. 57.

PIRELLI PLANTS
SETTIMO TORINESE
AND BOLLATE, 2018

PHOTOS BY
HEINZ PETER KNES

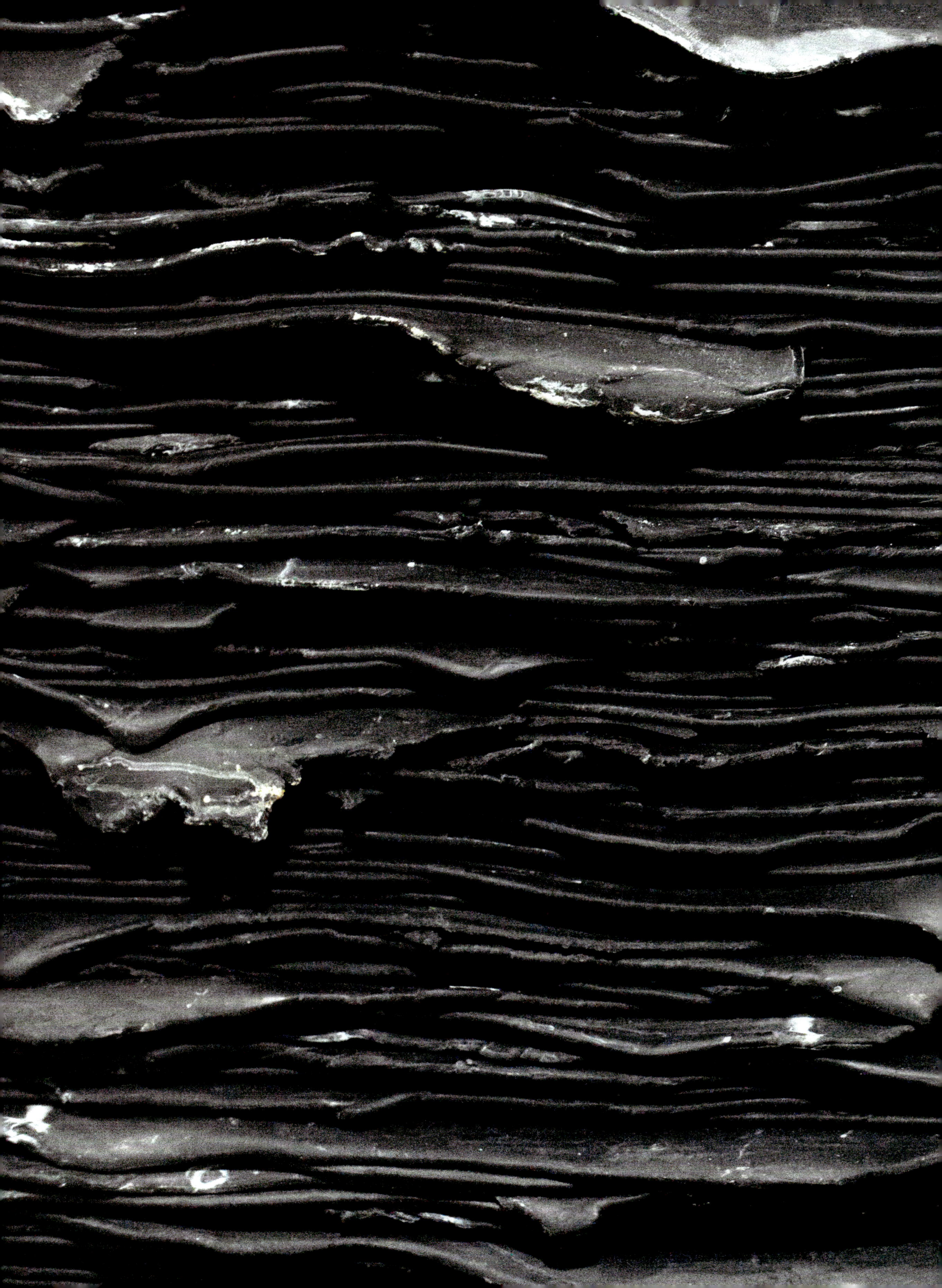

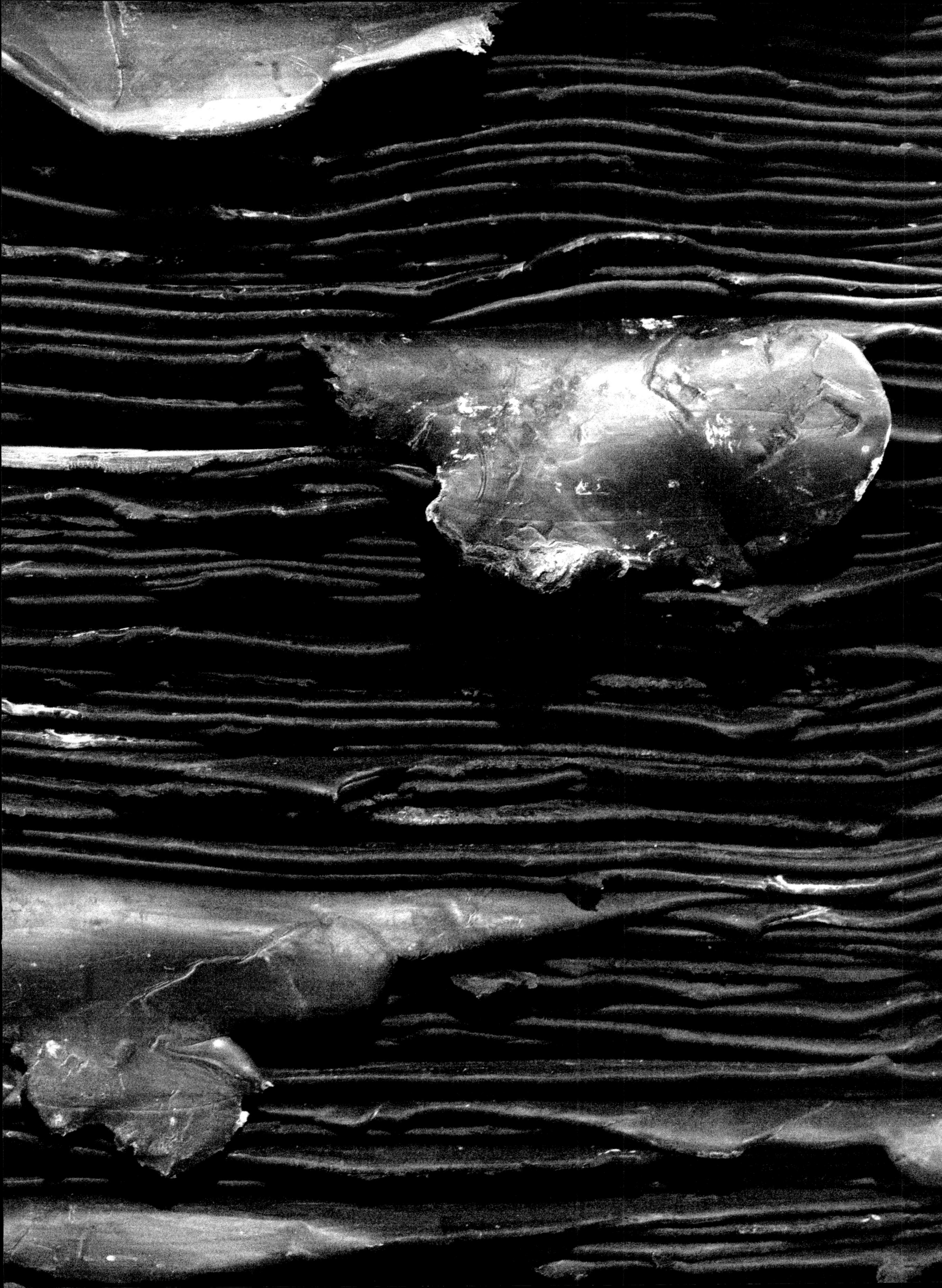

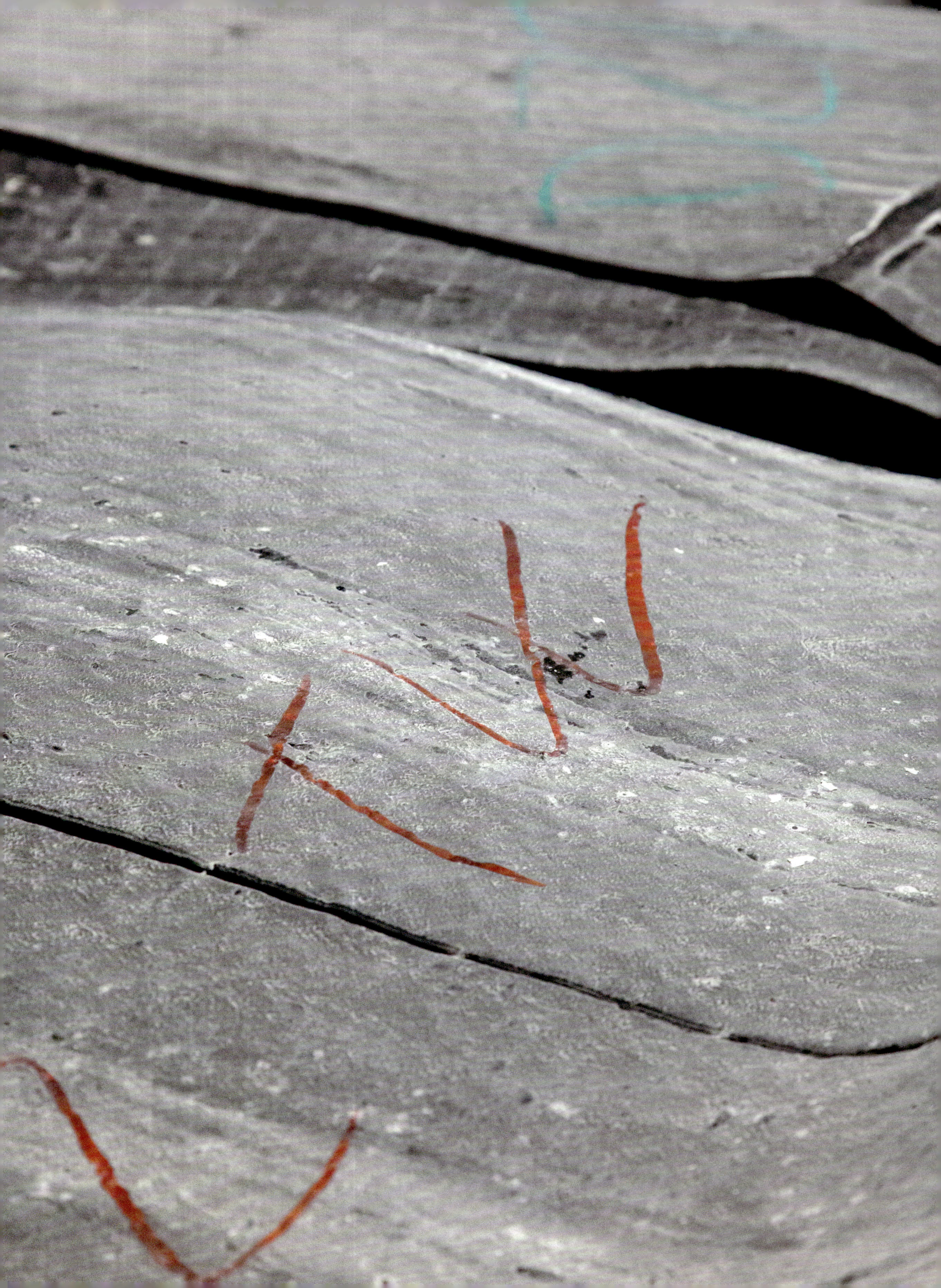

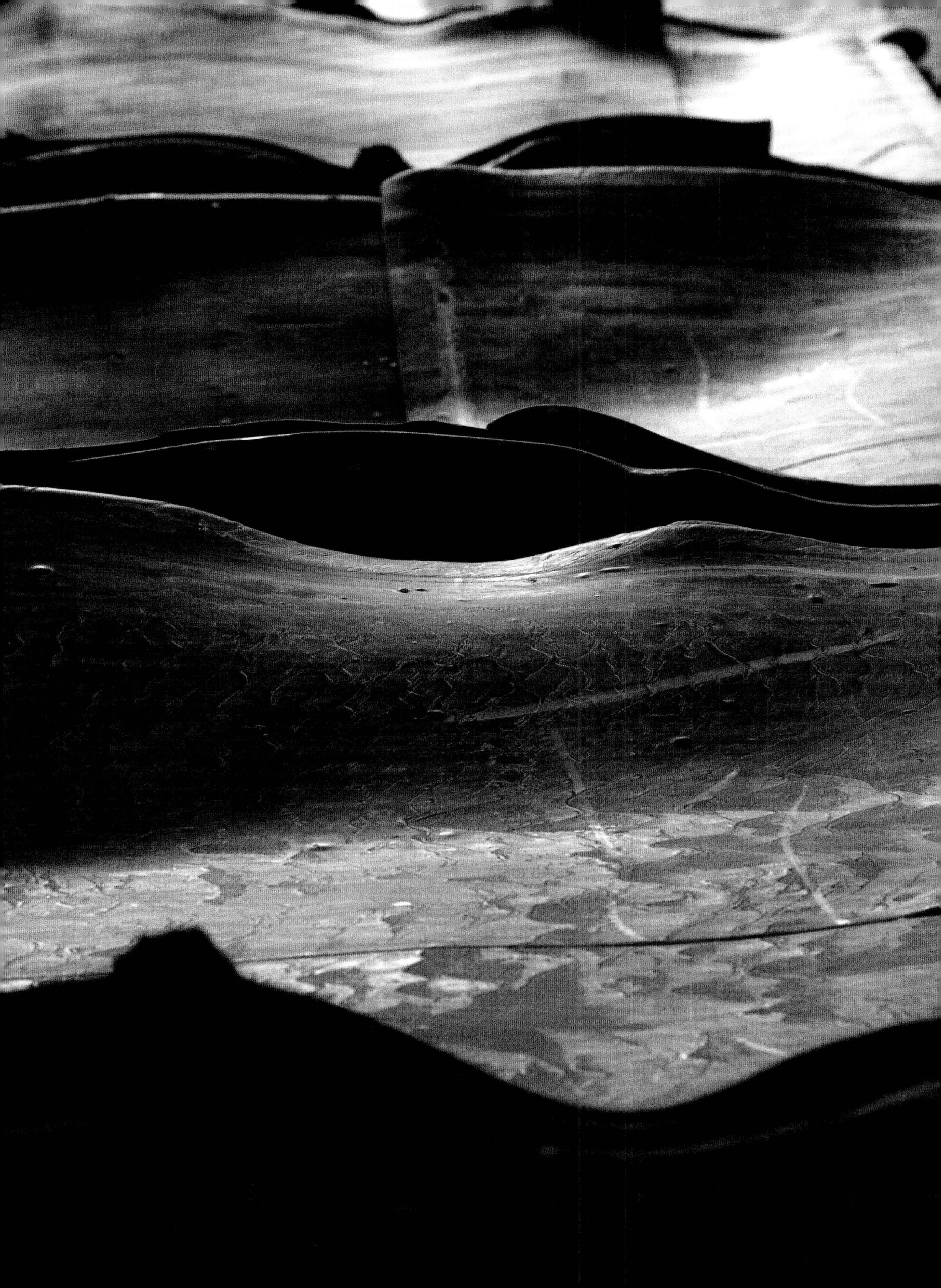

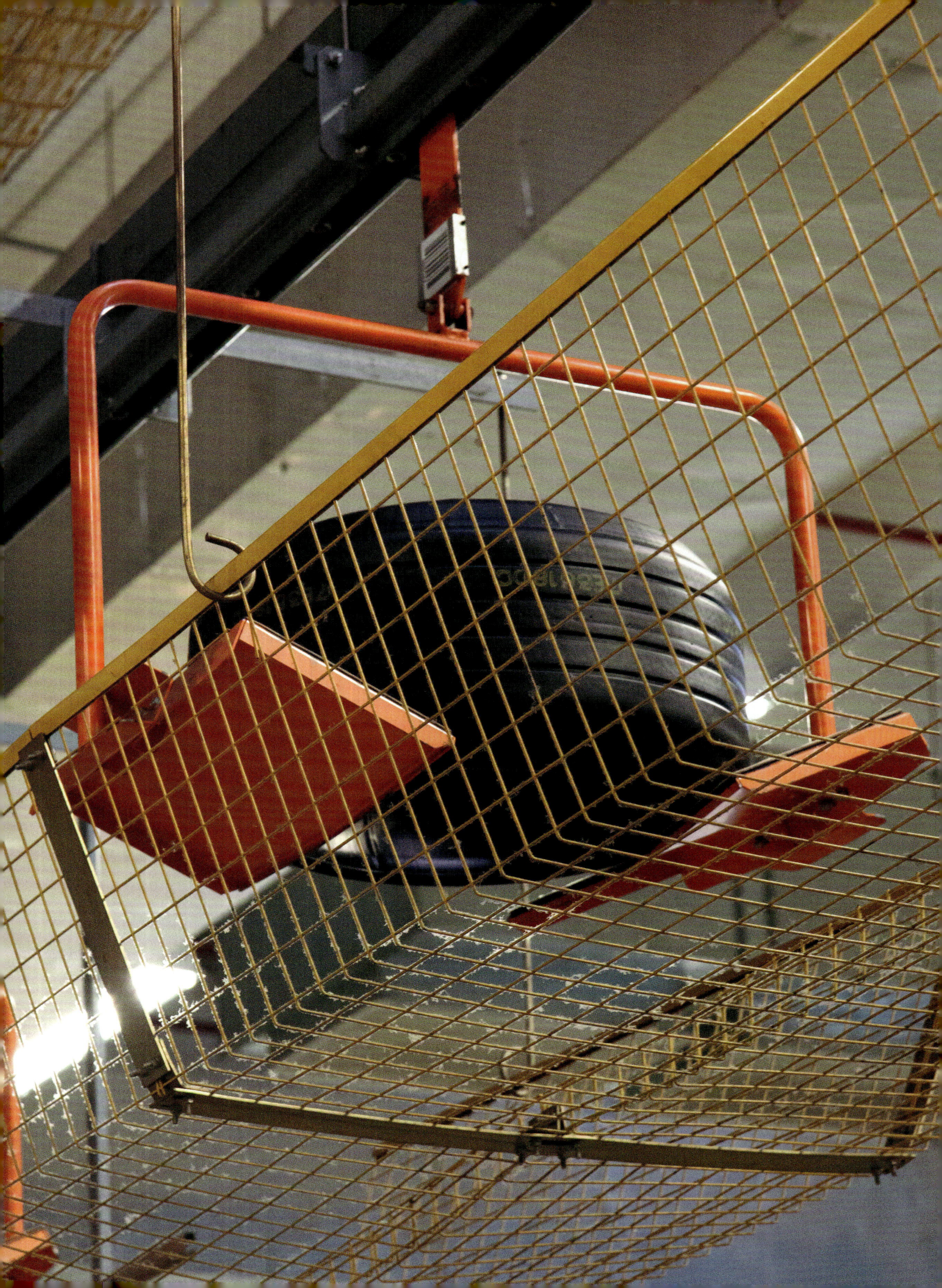

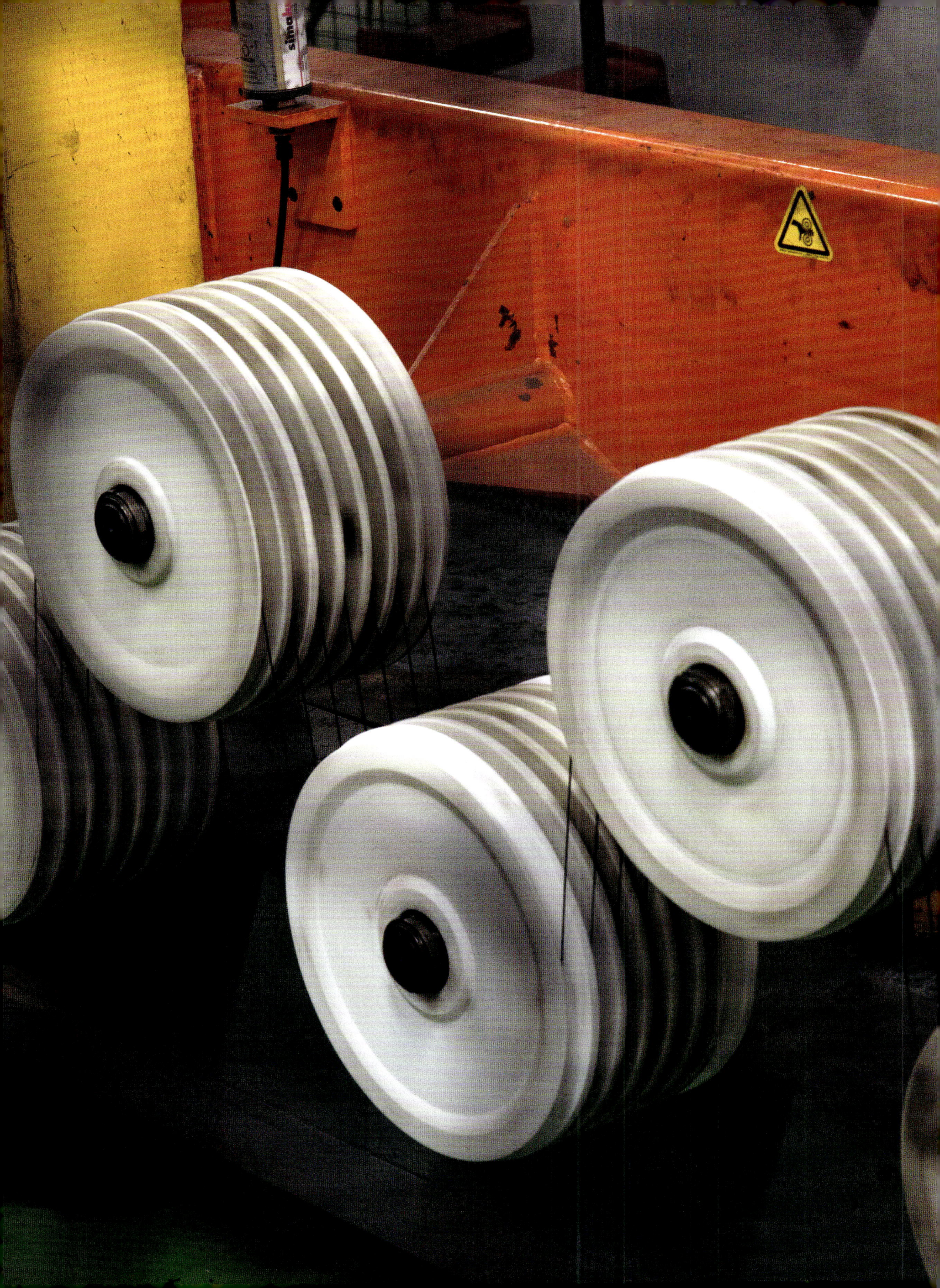

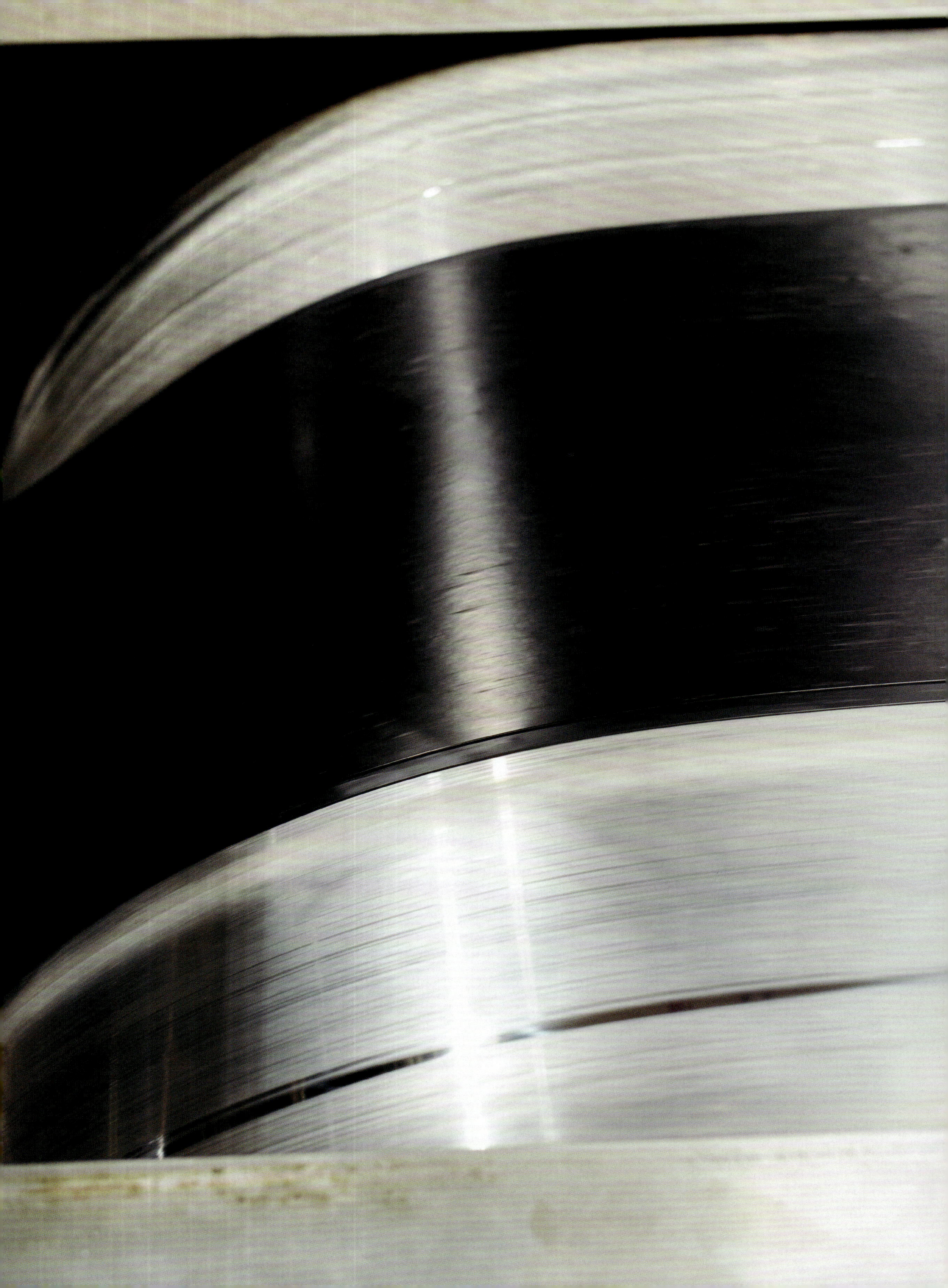

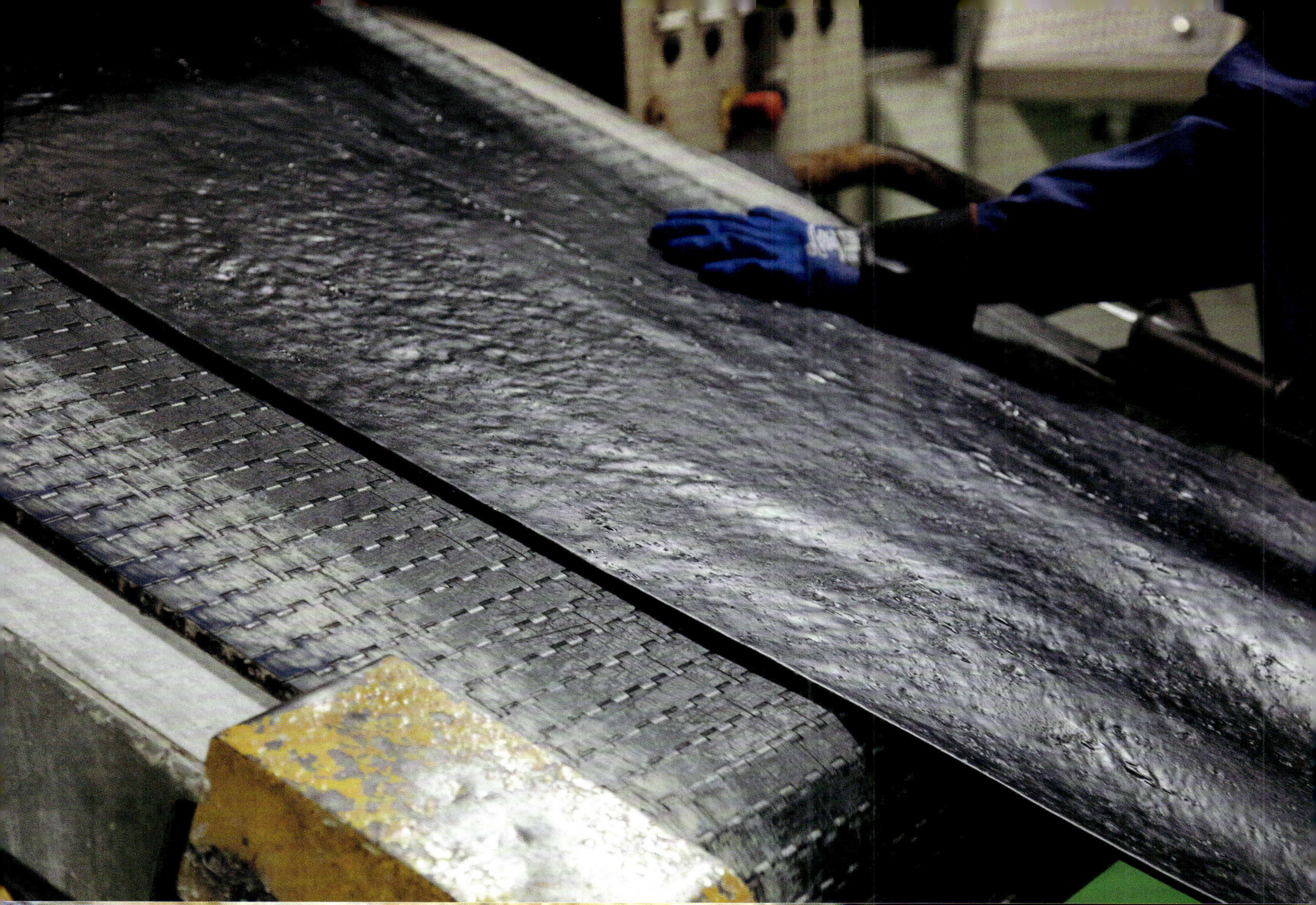
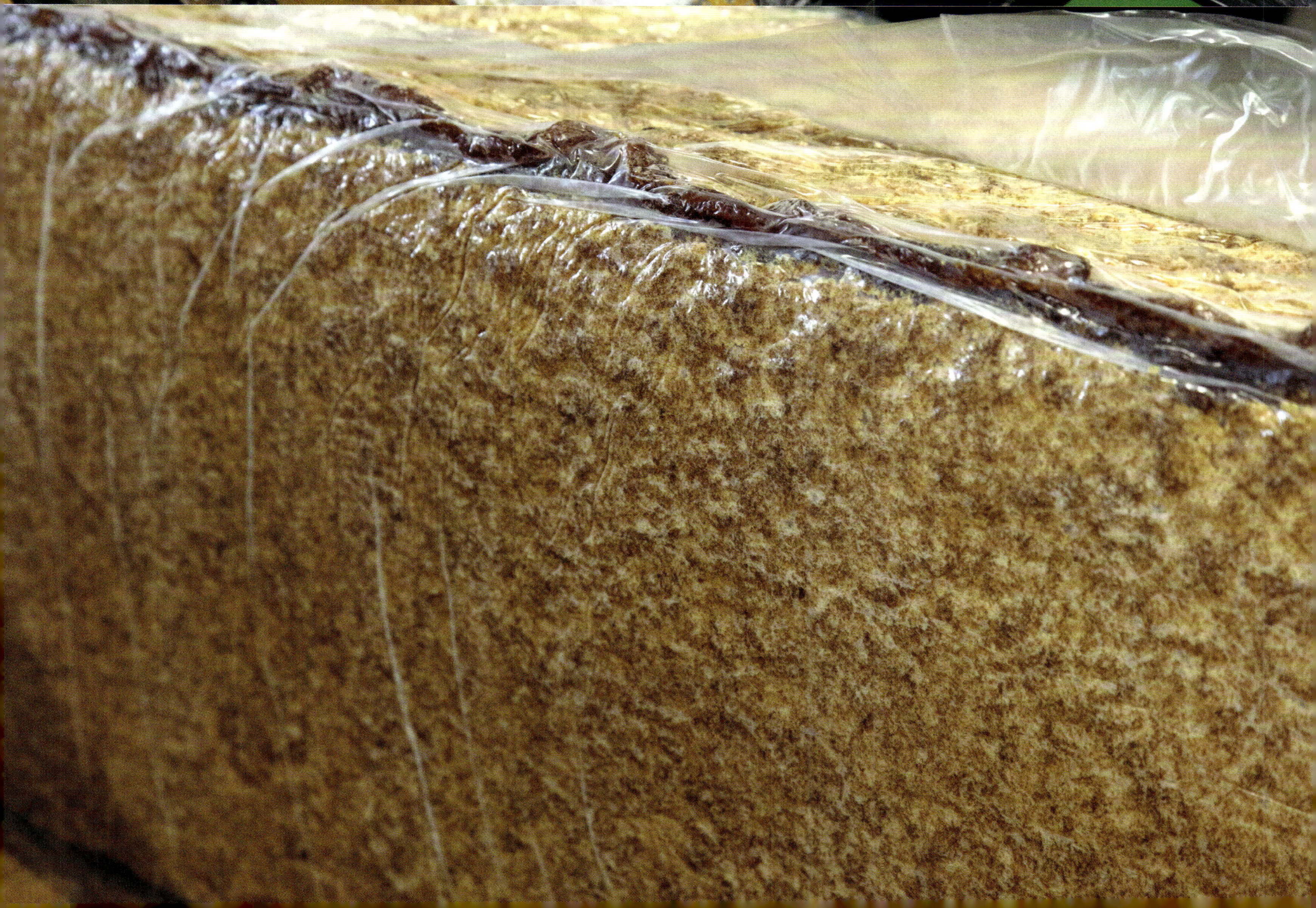

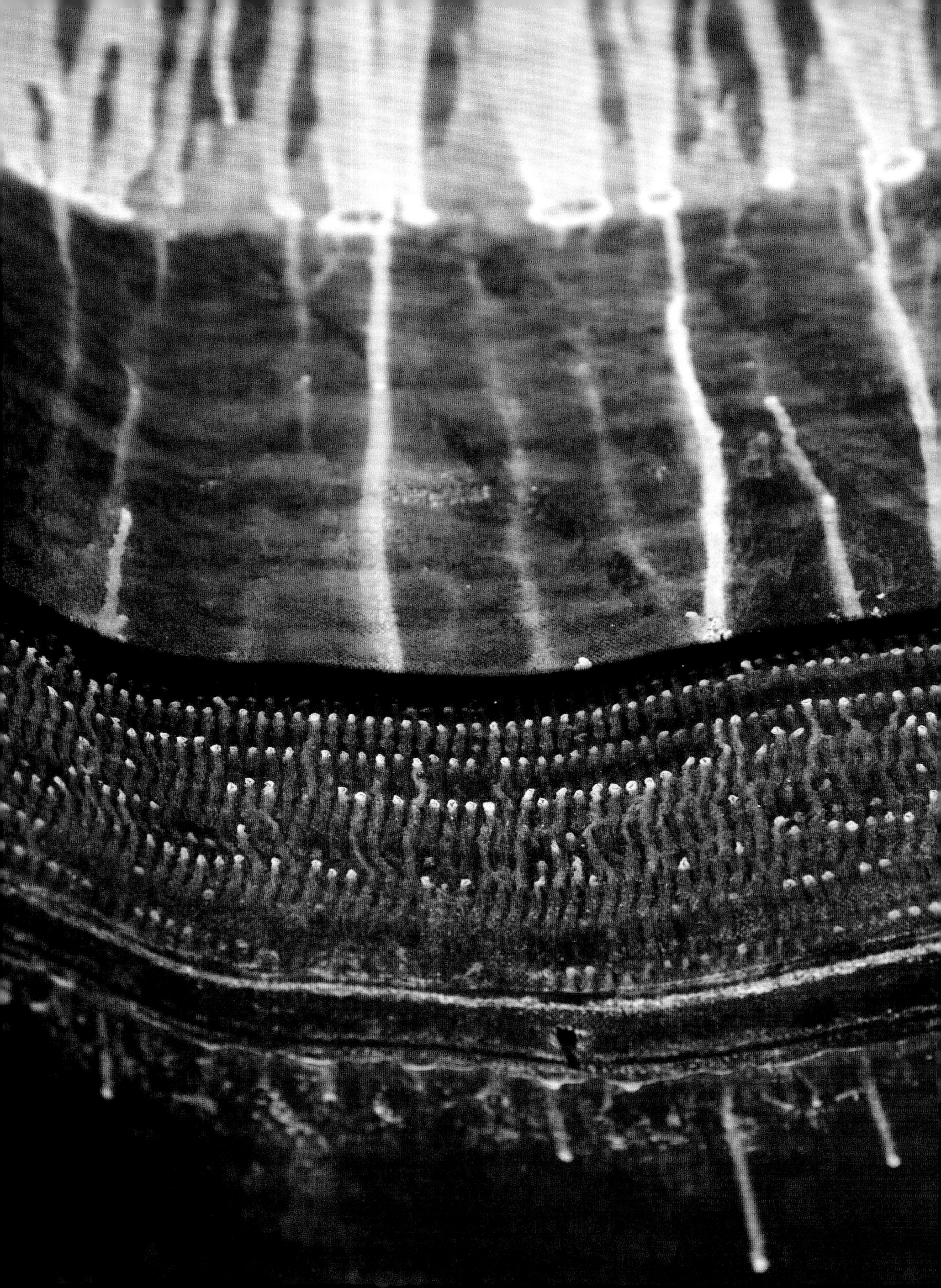

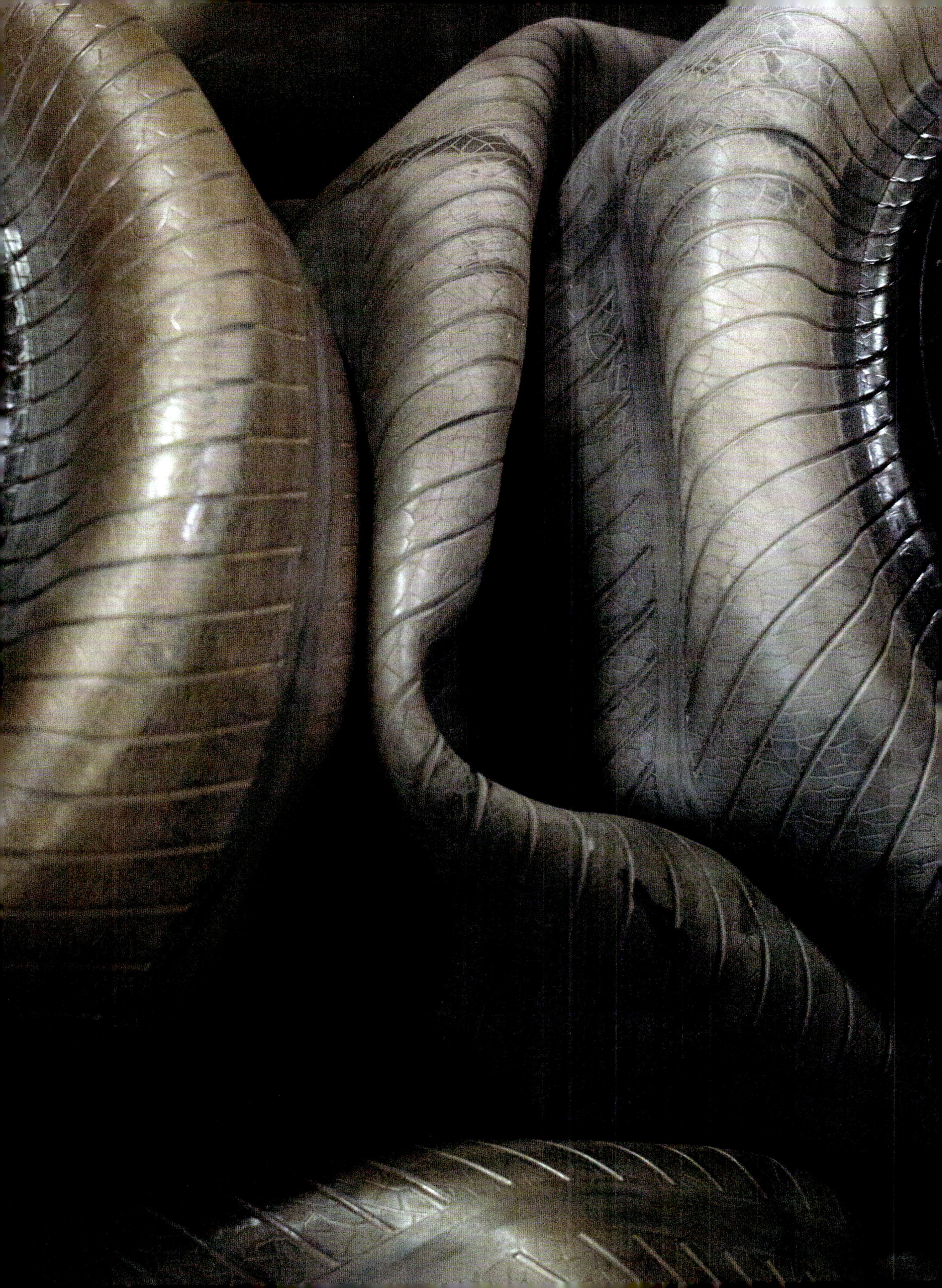

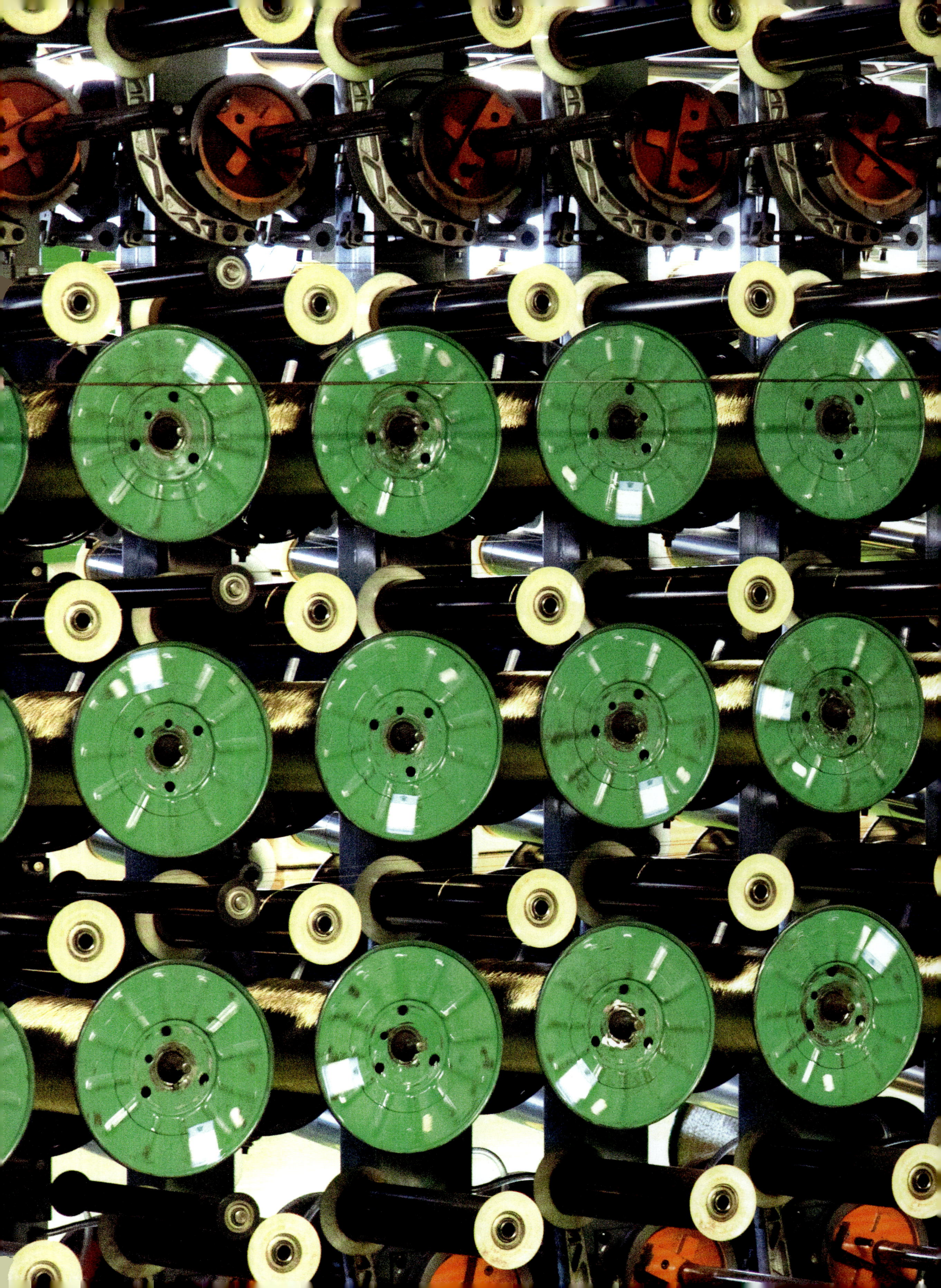

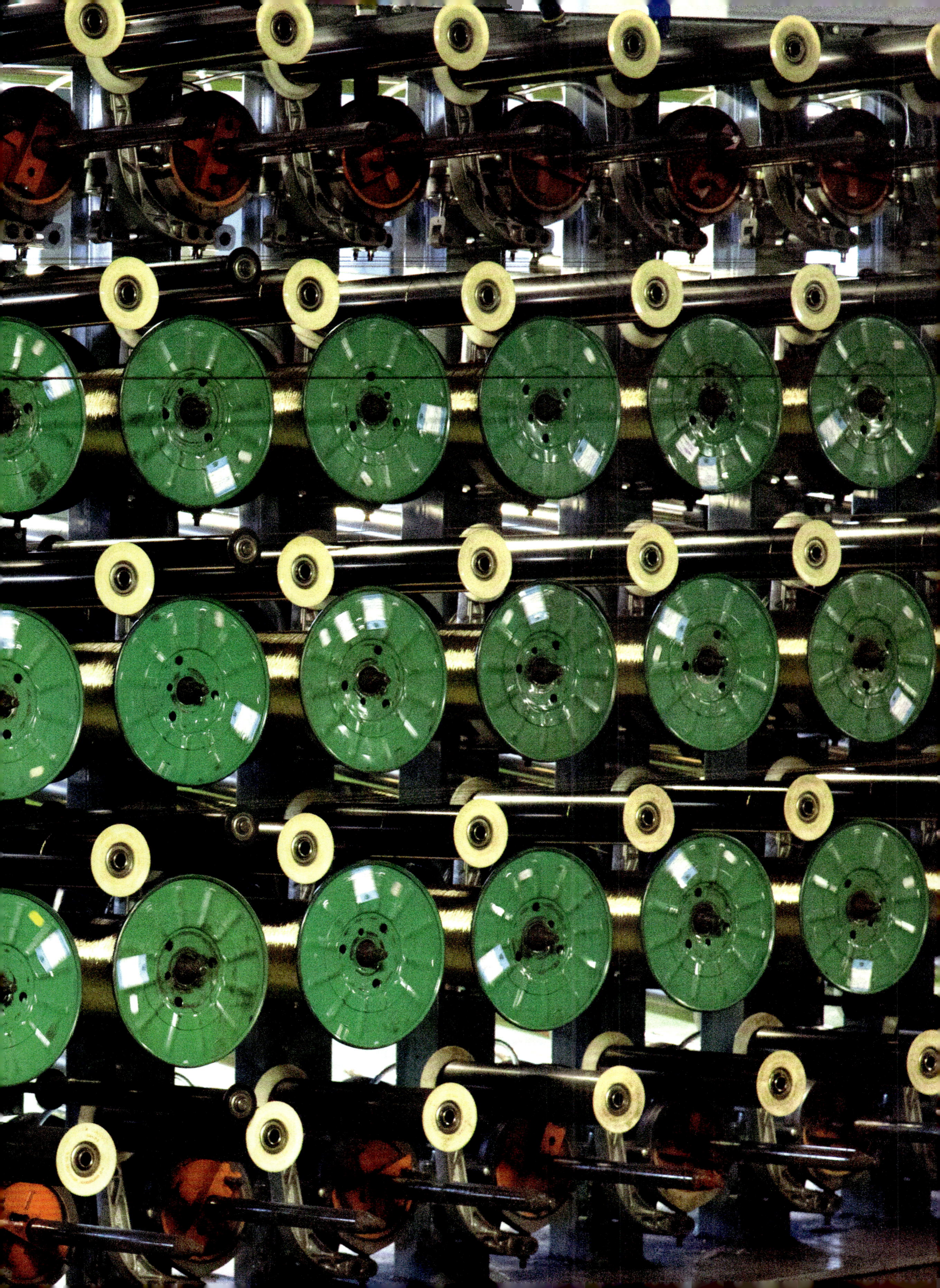

ON FRANCA HELG

We have elected to re-publish here two essays by Antonio Piva—*Yes, A Woman Working as an Architect* and the introduction to the book by Vittorio Prina on the Franca Helg house in Galliate Lombardo—because they seem to shed some light on Franca Helg's abundant personality and at the same time to capture the atmosphere of the Galliate home. Antonio Piva was a student of Helg's at university, and joined the Albini-Helg studio the day after graduating. As he likes to stress, since joining he has never left, underlining just how satisfying both his career and his personal life have been. Helg decided to leave the house in Galliate to him, since she felt that he shared the sensitivity, patience, and stubbornness required to keep the building very much alive. For Piva, keeping a building alive means ensuring continuity, otherwise a large number of the discourses that contain its entire history would be lost. What matters is continuity.

The garden and the house in Galliate live within a continuity that encompasses all of the principles that Helg tried to highlight during her life, but which are fleeting because time has a tendency to change things. Life lies in continuity, and death is always a natural event of which we have to take account. Piva describes how, following the death of a tree in the garden, he had to work out how to replace it, but not with an identical one, since that would be impossible—the aim was, rather, to maintain the equilibrium of the proportions conceived by Helg. It takes a long time, and a lot of sensitivity, to realize that things change, and how they change, because a garden changes over the seasons and over time in a very rapid way, and you need plenty of energy, determination, and passion.

According to Antonio Piva, Leonor Antunes has perfectly encapsulated Franca Helg's approach, and has given it a new interpretation, imbuing it with that continuity that enables it to stay alive. There is a phrase of which Piva is particularly fond, because it embodies his effort to project the house in Galliate into the future: "When Michele cuts the lawn on his tractor, with his two children sitting on his knee, I see Franca's last project being realized."

YES, A WOMAN WORKING AS AN ARCHITECT

Franca Helg was born in Milan in 1920 to a Sicilian father of Swiss origin and a mother from northern Germany. The youngest of four children, with two sisters and a brother, she had a very sheltered upbringing. Her parents' family, who had emigrated to Sicily in the late nineteenth century, had opened a Marsala winery and a furniture factory. The family unit was very close and very much embodied the characteristics of their countries of origin, and had integrated very well into Sicilian culture. The family itself, then, constituted a shining example of the sort of cultural cross-fertilization that Franca was always proud of achieving in her work. Sicilian proverbs, the tales of Sciascia, and the stories of *The Leopard* were often told alongside those of the family.

The Milanese environment in which the family had inserted itself, the aftermath of the crisis of 1929—which had altered their standard of living—and then the war were all factors that contributed to engendering in her a strong desire for independence, causing her to distance herself to a certain extent from the bourgeois attitudes of her family.

In Rossana Rossanda's descriptions (in her autobiography recently published by Einaudi) of the Milanese cultural milieu at the end of the war and during the period following reconstruction, I found numerous analogies with what Franca had told me. I saw the same desperation to participate actively in the construction of the new world, and with the difficulties faced by women in that period as they struggled to assert their financial and intellectual independence. They had both ideologically supported the resistance movement; they had both worked for the journal *Politecnico* founded by Vittorini at the end of the war; and they had both entered the workplace to make a living and to stake their respective claims amongst intellectuals who were certainly enlightened but, all in all, reluctant to acknowledge any woman's intellectual independence.

Very few young women matriculated at the Politecnico, and even fewer of them made it through to graduation. It is worth stressing that Franca—in contrast to her architect colleagues—was one of the very few to have undertaken the profession without abandoning her studies, and returned to the Istituto Universitario di Architettura di Venezia as a voluntary assistant to the Chair of Distributive Characteristics of Buildings, held by Professor Ludovico Belgiojoso. She was one of the few in this sector to be engaged on two fronts: the practical and the theoretical, and vice versa.

With Franco Albini, she shared a large part of her main occupation. She was very much geared towards innovation, and with great intelligence and sensitivity she would take on those roles that, in the practice of architecture, cancel the differentiated authorship of an idea and a result. This victory was an important one in an environment in which, even today, male creativity often triumphs, as if intelligence, imagination, and sensitivity were excluded from the female universe.

Culturally close to the BBPR group and to Giordano De Carlo, with whom she shared her studio on Via Cimarosa for a short period at the start of her career, she threw herself into those cultural activities that put her in contact not just with Italian architects but also with those from other countries who converged on the MSA (Movimento Studi di Architettura) association. The tenacity and seriousness of her commitment were channeled into generations of young people who had the opportunity, in an educational context, to learn from her how to approach design. She mentored many students right up to their graduation. They were captivated by her iron will, by the discipline that marked her out, and by her cultural integrity.

Over the course of her career as an architect and designer, there emerged—at least to me, given that I had a hand in certain projects—a number of precise contributions, such as those of the color of the materials used. In this regard, it is sufficient to cite la Rinascente department store in Rome, the Milan Underground, and Snam in San Donato. It is easy for me to underline the value attributed to light in the landscapes of her residential designs. The little house in Galliate is a testament to her dedication to light. The silverware designed for San Lorenzo, along with her jewelry designs, demonstrate her attention to the smallest and most precious of details.

Franca often travelled to Latin America, where she held courses and participated in conferences and congresses. On numerous occasions she returned from Spain full of enthusiasm and ideas. The emotionally resonant soundtrack to Almodóvar's *Talk to Her* seemed particularly suited to accompanying the images.

Franca was the *grande dame* of twentieth-century Italian architecture, but also, to many, she was a close friend.

ANTONIO PIVA

Extract of the essay originally published in Antonio Piva and Vittorio Prina (eds.), *Franca Helg, "La gran dama dell'architettura italiana"* (Milan: Franco Angeli, 2006), pp. 7–9.

FRANCA HELG, INTRODUCTION

The essay by Vittorio Prina that deals with a small work by Franca Helg, of which she was very fond, is concerned with the architecture that would go on to become the second home to be built in Italy, at the time of greatest economic prosperity, when residential layouts were in the process of being reimagined. I am taking the liberty of introducing myself into this story in order to highlight a number of aspects of this project that involve not only architecture but also very strong feelings, which have guaranteed the continuity over time of its spatial and ideal elements.

With winter now over, we were entering spring, and the witch hamamelis to the side of the garden gate, which wraps its way around the home in Galliate Lombardo, exploded with its intensely fragrant yellow flowers. A large lawn, surrounded by trees and by evergreen shrubs, with the house in the center, gave the impression that it was all of a piece, projecting out towards the Lake of Varese. The lake was only visible through a few gaps created between the trees that had now grown tall and that had originally been planted to transform into a garden what at one time had been a portion of countryside.

I would accompany Franca to her house, which had been built for her parents and where she, after their death, would stay every weekend with one of her two sisters, busying herself with the garden, with a small vegetable patch, and with the farmyard animals that were, for the most part, allowed to run free. The illness that had struck her had progressed so rapidly as to question very bluntly even the fate of the things that had enriched her life. It was at this time that I came on board with her intention to entrust the care of the house to me, counting on our friendship, which had been thoroughly tried and tested.

I had gotten to know Franca at the drawing boards of the Istituto Universitario di Architettura di Venezia in the late 1950s when—while attending the course on the Distributive Characteristics of Buildings held by Professor Lodovico Barbiano di Belgiojoso, of whom she was the assistant—she had taken me under her wing. After graduating, I had joined the Albini-Helg studio, where I began a collaboration that has lasted throughout her life.

The friendship that bound us included the whole family, and above all my son Michele, whom she had always looked after and had helped during the final stages of his time at university, through to graduation. She considered continuity across the generations important, recognizing in the intellectual affinities of those younger than her the forms of moral conduct on which she had built a large part of her certainties.

That visit had marked the start of a laborious path towards ownership of the property, which until then had been in the hands of a small family unit. Slowly but surely, I began taking care of the garden and, later, the house. I was embraced by the understated beauty of the simple spaces, the logic of the layout, and the views outward from the inside, and vice versa. Every space embodied the cultured, civilized spirit of those who had lived there. Even the furniture—all designed by Albini-Helg—and the furnishings occupied spaces that constituted an encapsulation of civility and education.

Over these years, the house has not been subject to alterations; it has absorbed the portraits of my parents and a few pieces such as the tapestry of the Wissa Wassef school, purchased in Cairo following the major exhibition held in Milan in 1974, which was joined by the tapestry that Franca had acquired around the same time.

Internally, the space determines the easy day-to-day movements of the residents, creating habits that are not too different from those previously acquired. The space favors a dialogue between those who live there now and those who created it and lived there initially. The dialogue is based on answers to a series of questions, on the permanent sense of gratitude that regenerates the memory, on the concepts that inspire a simplicity awash with refinements in terms of construction and materials, which are never flaunted, only ever implied. It can be discerned that the house contains a plethora of interests and ideas that are also evident in the volumes found on the bookshelves.

The garden speaks of other things, and its seasonal and annual changes codify other adjustments necessary to combat the damage caused by climate change in recent years. After the felling of the chestnut forest, at the edge of the lake-facing side of the garden, and the construction of a new residential unit, the views from the garden and from the house have been substantially changed. The lake has forced its way into the images that one sees throughout the day, and I have had trouble coming to terms with this new situation, even if the conquest of the other shore of the lake has introduced into those images a perspectival depth that was previously precluded by the woodland.

A perimeter walkway of gneiss paving surrounds the garden, delineating the edges of the wooded area. The crowns of the beech, oak, birch, dogwood, maidenhair, chestnut, and liriodendron tulipifera trees form shaded areas and a sequence of colors, fading to green in spring and in autumn lighting up, taking on strong, contrasting hues. At the foot of the acacia julibrissin (Persian silk tree), a group of azaleas of a different color contrasts with the carpet of grape hyacinth and that of convallaria majalis (lily of the valley), which—in its same season—inundates with its perfume even the laurel, of which it accepts the shade and the humus. The hortensias live isolated in large groups whereas the Indrangee paniculate (panicled hydrangeas) are inserted into contexts in which their rather sparse foliage is enriched by Buxus (boxwood) with its thick, compact leaves. A great Pinus montezumae (Montezuma pine) with reddish branches and bright green needles did not withstand last winter's snowfall and, having removed the broken branches, I had to throw myself into the challenge of coming up with a new shape for what was left.

The design calibrates the wooded areas, pulling together the colors in the various seasons and defining perspectives where nature is present and correct with its fruits and fragrances.

I deal personally with the roses and the irises. The oldest group was planted by Franca's father, who was particularly enamored of roses: every window in the house frames a group of them. The bedrooms, too, offer the opportunity to enjoy the flowers in their long blossoming period, which on occasion extends into December. The dried rosebuds are the final trace of a season that re-starts with the flowers of witch *hamamelis* and camellia, their evergreen bushes announcing the forthcoming flowering.

The path through the garden generates dialogues and reflections: on the changes that nature imposes, through lack of rainfall or an excess of it; on the changes suggested by one's sense of smell, by the color, by the simplicity of the care that each plant requires; and on the rational but also the intuitive reasons that transform a tuft of lavender or heather into a design for the secret perfumes of a garden.

Ever since my childhood, perched on the highest branch of a magnolia, I have carried around olfactory memories and a sense of confident freedom that I found in this garden.

When Michele cuts the lawn on his tractor, with his two children resting on his knee, I see Franca's last project being realized.

I understand the value of the gift and of the friendship, the value of what one can transmit of oneself, almost immortal, in this world that is so difficult to live in, because of the way it is forever putting us to the test.

I consider the home and the garden to be an extraordinary project for everything that they represent, for what has happened and for what will inevitably happen—always, I trust, inspired by their positive force. (August 2005)

ANTONIO PIVA

Originally published in Vittorio Prina, *Franca Helg a Galliate Lombardo* (Florence: Alinea, 2006), pp. 5, 6.

SU FRANCA HELG

È stato scelto di ripubblicare i testi di Antonio Piva che seguono — *Una donna di professione architetto* e l'introduzione al volume di Vittorio Prina sulla casa di Franca Helg a Galliate Lombardo — perché sembrano illuminare la personalità molto ampia di Franca Helg e nello stesso tempo l'atmosfera della casa di Galliate. Antonio Piva è stato allievo di Franca Helg all'università entrando, il giorno dopo la laurea, nello studio Albini-Helg. Come lui ama dire, una volta entrato non ne è più uscito, sottolineando come sia stata una vita professionale e personale di grandi gratificazioni. Franca Helg ha deciso di lasciare ad Antonio Piva la casa di Galliate ritenendo che avesse la sua stessa sensibilità, pazienza e caparbietà, doti che l'avrebbero mantenuta un'architettura viva. Secondo Piva, perché un'architettura resti viva bisogna che ci sia continuità, altrimenti andrebbero persi una grande quantità di discorsi che contengono tutta la storia. Ciò che conta è la continuità.

Il giardino e la casa di Galliate vivono di una continuità che raccoglie tutti i principi che Franca Helg ha cercato di evidenziare durante la sua vita, ma che sono sfuggevoli nel tempo perché il tempo cambia le cose. La vita sta nella continuità e la morte è sempre un fatto naturale di cui bisogna tenere conto. Antonio Piva racconta come dopo la morte di un albero del giardino di Galliate dovesse studiare come sostituirlo, non però con uno identico, perché impossibile, ma in modo da restituirne l'effetto per mantenere l'equilibrio delle proporzioni pensato da Franca Helg. Bisogna avere molto tempo, molta sensibilità per accorgersi che le cose cambiano, e come cambiano, perché un giardino cambia nelle stagioni e nel tempo in una maniera rapidissima e ci vogliono energia, costanza, passione.

Secondo Antonio Piva, Leonor Antunes ha colto perfettamente il pensiero di Franca Helg dandogli un'interpretazione nuova e dunque quella continuità che permette di mantenerlo vivo. C'è una frase che Antonio Piva ama particolarmente perché rende il suo sforzo di proiezione futura della casa di Galliate: "Quando Michele taglia l'erba del prato con il trattore, portando sulle ginocchia i suoi due figli, vedo l'ultimo progetto di Franca realizzato."

UNA DONNA DI PROFESSIONE ARCHITETTO

Franca Helg era nata a Milano nel 1920 da padre siciliano di origine svizzera e madre nata in Germania del nord. Ultima di quattro fratelli, due sorelle ed un fratello, era cresciuta affettivamente molto protetta.

La famiglia dei genitori, emigrati alla fine dell'Ottocento in Sicilia, avevano aperto una industria di marsala ed un mobilificio creando un gruppo familiare molto legato da affetti e da una cultura importata dai paesi di origine che si era molto ben integrata con quella siciliana. Storia esemplare dunque di contaminazione culturale a cui Franca ha sempre fatto riferimento con una punta di orgoglio.

I proverbi siciliani, i racconti di Sciascia come le storie del Gattopardo venivano spesso ad arricchire quelle familiari.

L'ambiente milanese in cui si era inserita, i postumi della crisi del '29 che avevano modificato il tenore di vita e poi la guerra avevano fatto maturare in lei un forte desiderio di indipendenza e prendere, in un certo senso, le distanze dalle abitudini borghesi della famiglia di origine.

Nell'autobiografia di Rossana Rossanda, recentemente pubblicata da Einaudi, nella descrizione dell'ambiente culturale milanese dei periodi finali della guerra e in quelli successivi della ricostruzione, ho trovato molte analogie con quanto Franca mi aveva raccontato. Ho ritrovato l'ansia per la partecipazione attiva alla costruzione del nuovo mondo, le difficoltà della conquista, per una donna di quegli anni, dell'indipendenza economica ed intellettuale. L'una e l'altra avevano affiancato ideologicamente la resistenza, l'una e l'altra si erano ritrovate a lavorare per la rivista "Politecnico" fondata da Vittorini alla fine del conflitto, l'una e l'altra avevano iniziato a lavorare per vivere e per affermare la propria personalità tra intellettuali, certo illuminati, ma tutto sommato poco propensi a riconoscere facilmente l'autonomia intellettuale ad una donna.

Le ragazze che si iscrivevano al Politecnico erano pochissime ed ancora meno quelle che arrivavano al traguardo della laurea. C'è da aggiungere che Franca Helg, a differenza delle colleghe architetto, è tra le pochissime ad aver intrapreso la professione senza abbandonare l'università che riprende all'Istituto Universitario di Architettura di Venezia come assistente volontario presso la cattedra di Caratteri Distributivi degli Edifici tenuta dal professor Ludovico Belgiojoso.

È tra le poche che in questo settore si impegnano su due fronti: quello pratico, quello teorico e viceversa.

Con Franco Albini condivide gran parte della sua attività, quella centrale, assai ricca di fermenti innovativi conquistando con intelligenza e sensibilità quei ruoli che nella pratica della progettazione cancellano le paternità differenziate di un'idea e di un risultato.

Conquista questa assai importante in un ambiente in cui ancora oggi spesso vince la creatività maschile come se intelligenza, fantasia, sensibilità fossero escluse dall'universo femminile.

Vicina culturalmente al gruppo BBPR, a Giordano De Carlo con cui per breve tempo, agli inizi della professione, condivide lo studio di via Cimarosa, si impegna in quelle attività culturali che la mettono in contatto non solo con gli architetti italiani ma anche con quelli di altra nazionalità che convergono nel Movimento Studi di Architettura.

La tenacia e la serietà del suo impegno si riversano sulle generazioni che didatticamente hanno occasione di apprendere da lei il metodo della progettazione. Molti allievi sono seguiti sino alla laurea e vengono catturati dalla volontà di ferro e dalla disciplina che la distingue in modo particolare e dalla sua onestà culturale.

Nell'arco temporale della sua attività di progettista sono evidenti, almeno per me che in alcuni lavori ho partecipato, alcuni apporti precisi, come quelli del colore dei materiali usati. Basterà ricordare la Rinascente di Roma, la Metropolitana Milanese e la Snam di San Donato. Mi è facile sottolineare il valore attribuito alla luce dei paesaggi nello studio delle residenze. La casetta di Galliate ne testimonia la ricerca. Gli argenti disegnati per San Lorenzo come i gioielli evidenziano la cura per il dettaglio minimo e prezioso.

Franca ha viaggiato spesso in America Latina dove ha tenuto corsi e partecipato a convegni e congressi. Molte volte tornava dalla Spagna carica di entusiasmi e di idee. La colonna sonora di *Abla con Ela* [*sic*] di Almodóvar mi è parsa particolarmente adatta ad accompagnare le immagini con la forza anche dei sentimenti.

Franca Helg è stata la grande dama dell'Architettura Italiana del Novecento ma anche, per molti, una grande amica.

ANTONIO PIVA

Estratto del testo originariamente pubblicato in *Franca Helg, "La gran dama dell'architettura italiana"*, a cura di Antonio Piva e Vittorio Prina, Franco Angeli, Milano 2006, pp. 7–9

FRANCA HELG, INTRODUZIONE

Il saggio di Vittorio Prina che si riferisce ad una piccola opera di Franca Helg da lei molto amata affronta il tema dell'architettura destinata alla seconda casa realizzata in Italia nel momento del maggior benessere economico e del rinnovamento dell'organizzazione spaziale della residenza.

Mi inserisco nel racconto per evidenziare alcuni valori di questo intervento che hanno a che fare non solo con l'architettura ma anche con sentimenti molto forti che hanno garantito la continuità nel tempo delle sue componenti spaziali e ideali.

L'inverno si era inoltrato nei mesi del nuovo anno e l'Hamamelis a lato del cancello di ingresso del giardino che avvolge la casa di Galliate Lombardo esplodeva con i suoi fiori gialli dal profumo particolarmente intenso. Un grande prato, contornato da alberi e da cespugli sempre verdi, con la casa nel suo centro facevano intendere come fossero un tutt'uno proiettato verso il lago di Varese.

Il lago era visibile solo attraverso alcuni varchi creati tra gli alberi ormai cresciuti e piantati per trasformare in giardino quello che un tempo era un tratto di campagna.

Accompagnavo Franca nella sua casa costruita per i genitori anziani che lei, dopo la loro morte, abitava tutti i fine settimana con una delle due sorelle occupandosi del giardino, di un piccolo orto e degli animali da cortile lasciati in gran parte liberi.

La malattia che l'aveva colpita non aveva celato le scadenze del suo sviluppo tanto rapido da porre con crudezza i problemi anche del destino delle cose che le avevano arricchito la vita.

In quella occasione mi rese partecipe della sua intenzione di affidarmi la cura di quella casa contando su di una amicizia che aveva attraversato molti collaudi.

Avevo conosciuto Franca Helg sui tavoli da disegno dell'Istituto Universitario di Architettura di Venezia alla fine degli anni '50 quando, frequentando il Corso di Caratteri Distributivi degli Edifici tenuto dal professor Lodovico Barbiano di Belgiojoso di cui era assistente, si era presa cura della mia formazione. Dopo la laurea ero entrato nello studio Albini-Helg dove avevo iniziato una collaborazione che è durata tutta la vita.

L'amicizia che ci ha legati ha compreso tutta la famiglia e soprattutto mio figlio Michele che aveva sempre seguito e che aveva portato alla laurea nelle ultime fasi del suo impegno universitario. Teneva al rapporto di continuità tra generazioni diverse cogliendo nelle affinità intellettuali dei più giovani quei comportamenti morali su cui aveva costruito gran parte delle sue certezze.

Quella visita aveva dato inizio ad un percorso laborioso per la presa di possesso di una proprietà che sino a quel momento era appartenuta a un piccolo nucleo famigliare. Lentamente mi sono occupato del giardino e successivamente della casa. Mi hanno accolto la discreta bellezza degli spazi semplici, le logiche distributive, le viste dall'interno verso l'esterno e viceversa. Ogni ambiente parlava dello spirito colto e civile di chi vi aveva abitato. Anche il mobilio, disegnato tutto da Albini-Helg, come le suppellettili, occupavano spazi che rappresentavano nel loro insieme un documento di civiltà e di educazione.

La casa in questi anni non ha subito alterazioni; ha assorbito i ritratti dei miei genitori e qualche oggetto come l'arazzo della scuola Wissa Wassef comperato al Cairo dopo la grande mostra tenuta a Milano nel 1974 che si è unito a quello di Franca acquisito negli stessi anni.

Lo spazio determina, al suo interno, i movimenti ed un andamento della vita senza forzature, crea abitudini che non si discostano da quelle acquisite in precedenza. Lo spazio favorisce un dialogo tra chi lo vive ora e chi lo ha creato e vissuto. Il dialogo si imposta sulle domande e su risposte ai perché, sul senso di gratitudine permanente che rigenera la memoria, sui concetti ispiratori di una semplicità piena di finezze costruttive e materiche che non ostentano ma suggeriscono.

Si avverte che la casa contiene una vastità di interessi ed idee che trovano ulteriori riscontri nei volumi che riposano nelle librerie.

Il giardino parla di altre cose ed il suo cambiamento stagionale ed annuale codifica altri cambiamenti necessari per far fronte ai danni dei mutamenti di clima degli ultimi anni. Dopo l'abbattimento del bosco di castagni, al confine con il lato del giardino verso il lago, e la costruzione di una nuova unità residenziale, le viste dal giardino e dalla casa sono sostanzialmente cambiate. Il lago è entrato con prepotenza nelle immagini quotidiane ed ho faticato, non poco, ad accettare il cambiamento anche se la conquista dell'altra sponda del lago ha introdotto nelle immagini una profondità prospettica che prima era preclusa dal bosco.

Un camminamento perimetrale lastricato di beola circonda il prato delimitando lungo i confini la zona alberata. Le chiome dei Faggi, delle Querce, delle Betulle, dei Cornus e dei Ginco biloba, dei Castagni, dei Liriodendron tulipifera formano zone d'ombra ed una sequenza di colori, sfumati nel verde in primavera, che in autunno si accendono raggiungendo tonalità forti e contrastate.

Ai piedi dell'Acacia julibrissin un gruppo di Azalee di colore diverso contrasta con il tappeto di Muscari e quello della Convallaria majalis (mughetto) che, nella sua stessa stagione, inonda con il suo profumo anche il Lauro del quale accetta l'ombra e l'humus. Le Ortensie vivono isolate in grandi gruppi mentre le Idrangee paniculate sono inserite in contesti in cui il loro fogliame un po' rado viene arricchito dal Buxus dalla chioma compatta e folta.

Un grande Pinus montezumae dai rami rossicci e dagli aghi verde intenso non ha sopportato la nevicata dell'ultimo inverno ed, eliminati i rami spezzati, ho dovuto impegnarmi con lo studio di una nuova forma da dare a quanto era rimasto.

Il progetto calibra le masse arboree, ne accosta i colori nelle diverse stagioni, definisce prospettive dove la natura è presente con i suoi frutti ed i suoi profumi.

Curo personalmente le Rose e gli Iris. Il nucleo più antico è stato piantato dal padre di Franca che amava particolarmente le Rose: ogni finestra della casa ne incornicia un gruppo. Anche dalle camere da letto si godono i fiori nei lunghi periodi della fioritura che a volte si protrae fino a dicembre. I boccioli di rosa disidratati sono le ultime tracce di una stagione che riprende con i fiori dell'Hamamelis e le Camelie con i loro arbusti sempre verdi che annunciano la prossima fioritura.

Il percorso attraverso il giardino attiva dialoghi e riflessioni sui cambiamenti che impone la natura, con la siccità o l'eccessiva abbondanza di precipitazioni, sui cambiamenti suggeriti dall'olfatto, dal colore, dalla semplicità delle cure che richiede ciascuna pianta, sulle ragioni razionali ma anche dell'intuito che trasformano un ciuffo di Lavanda o di Erica in un disegno dei profumi segreti di un giardino.

Dalla mia infanzia, appollaiato sul ramo più alto di una Magnolia, riporto memorie olfattive ed un senso di libertà fiduciosa che ho trovato in questo giardino.

Quando Michele taglia l'erba del prato con il trattore, portando sulle ginocchia i suoi due figli, vedo l'ultimo progetto di Franca realizzato.

Capisco il valore del dono e dell'amicizia, il valore di quello che di sé si può trasmettere, quasi immortale, in questo mondo difficile da vivere per le continue prove che ci sottopone.

La casa ed il giardino li considero un progetto straordinario per tutto quello che rappresenta, per quello che è accaduto ed inevitabilmente accadrà ispirato sempre, mi auguro, alla forza positiva del bene. (Agosto 2005)

ANTONIO PIVA

Testo originariamente pubblicato in Vittorio Prina, *Franca Helg a Galliate Lombardo*, Alinea, Firenze 2006, pp. 5, 6

BONACINA1889
LURAGO D'ERBA, 2018

PHOTOS BY
HEINZ PETER KNES

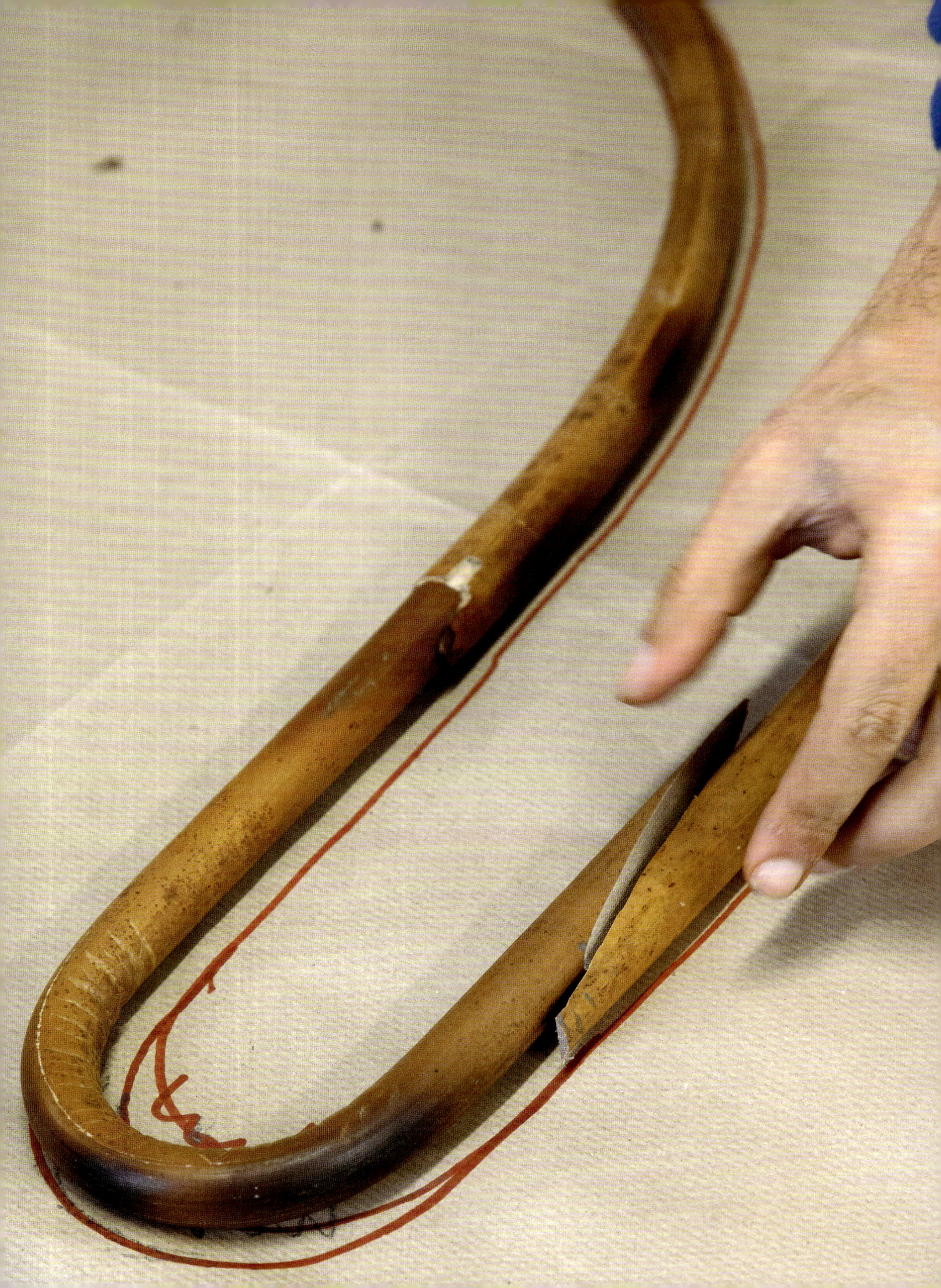

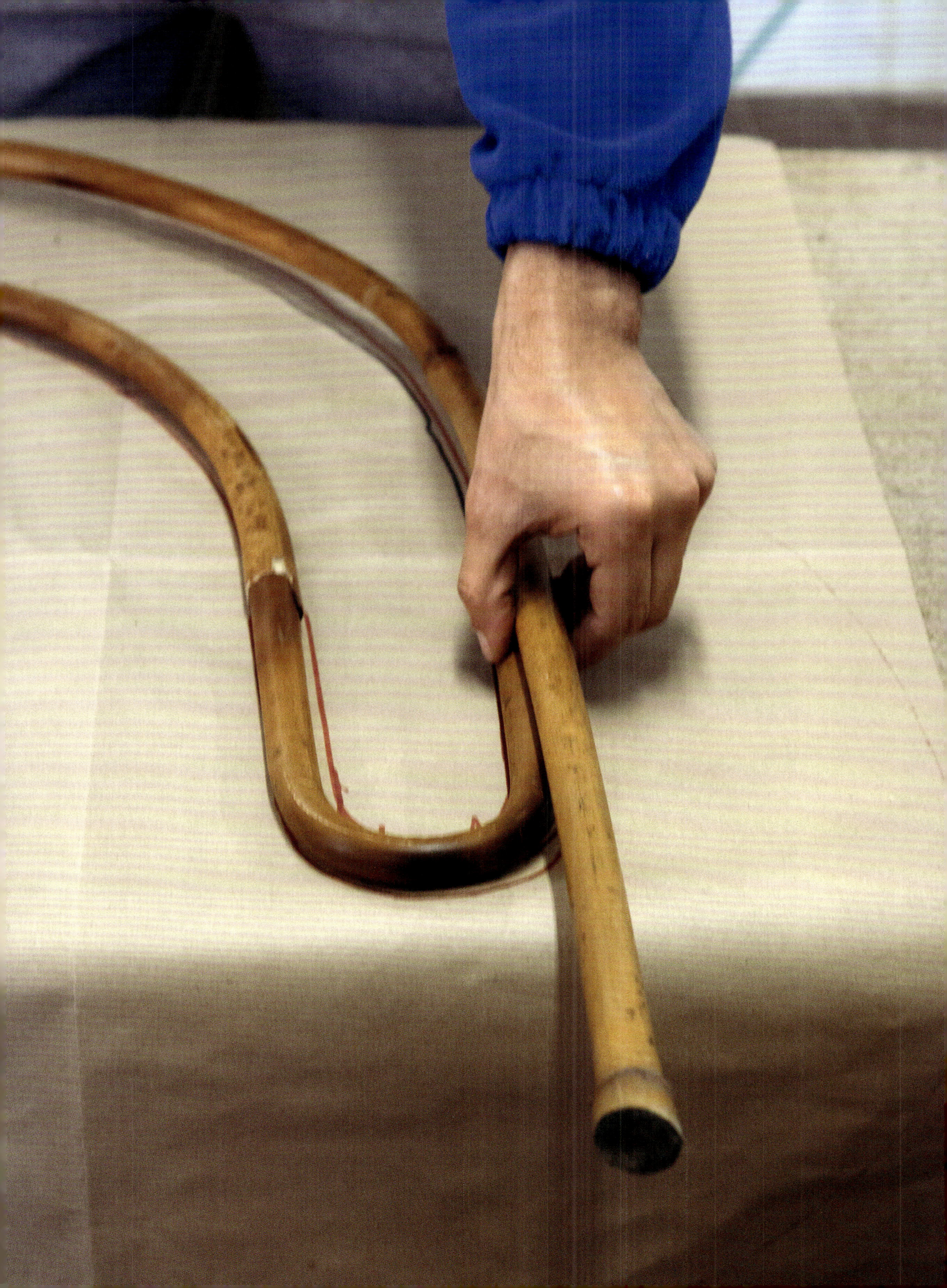

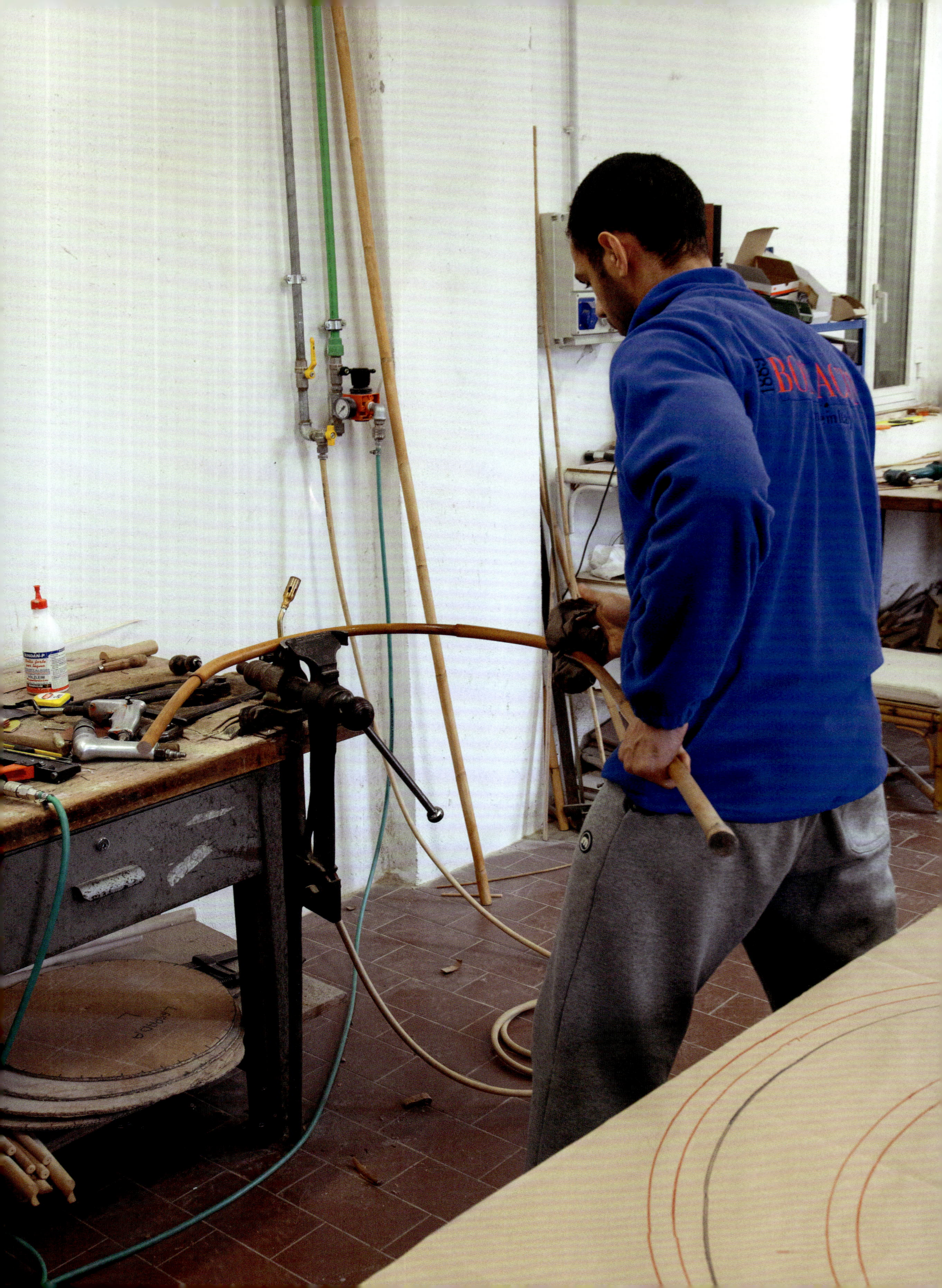

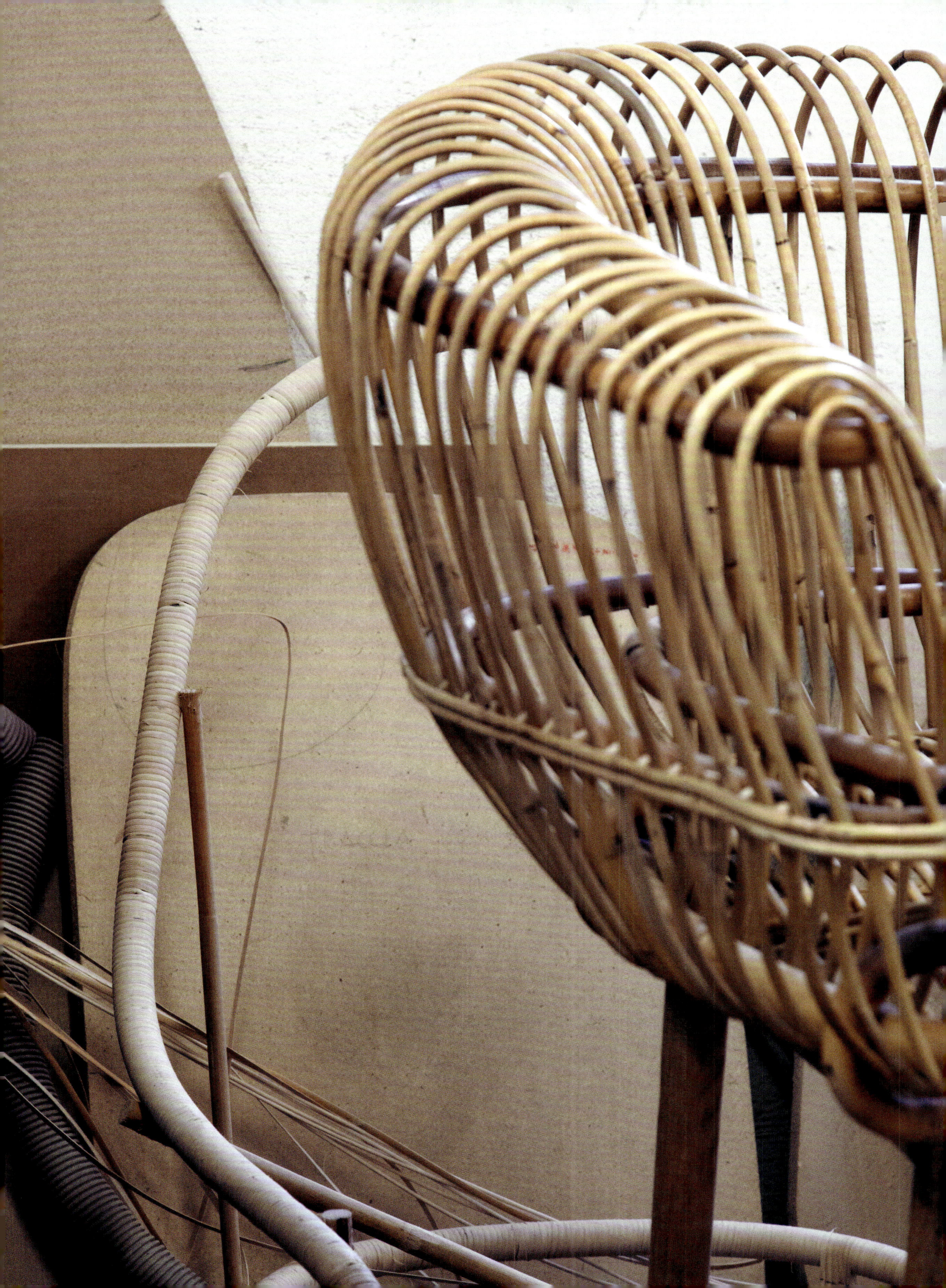

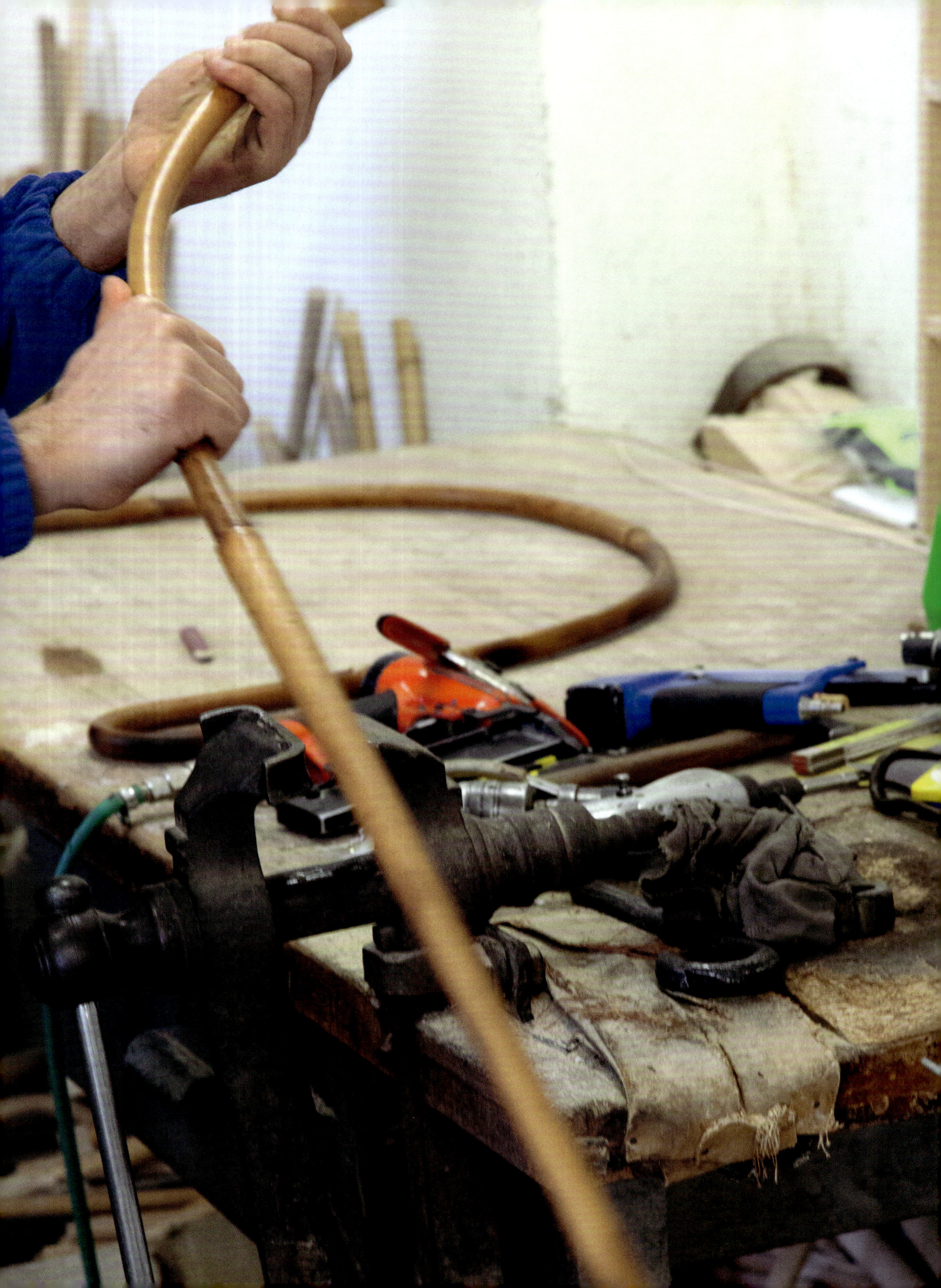

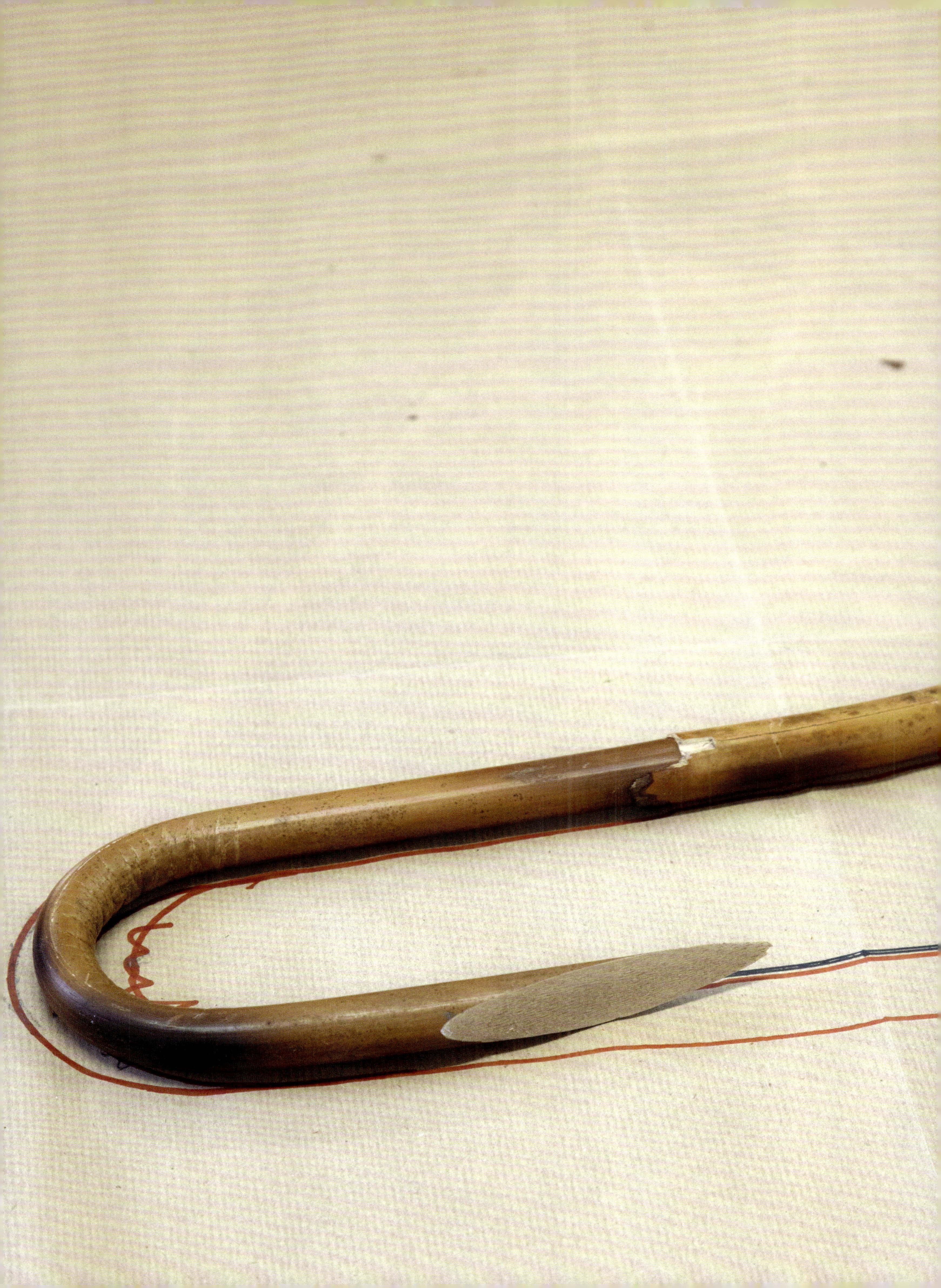

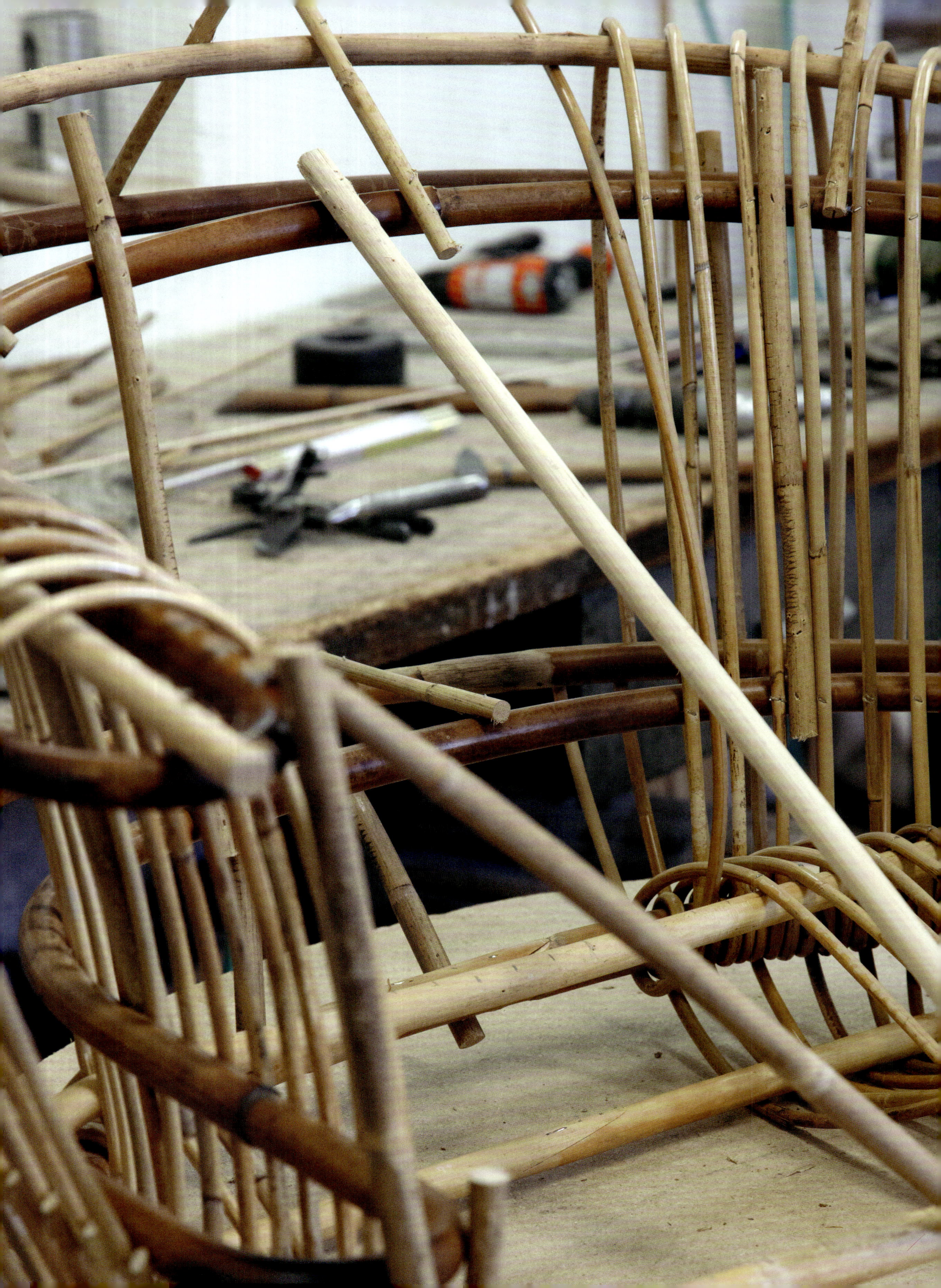

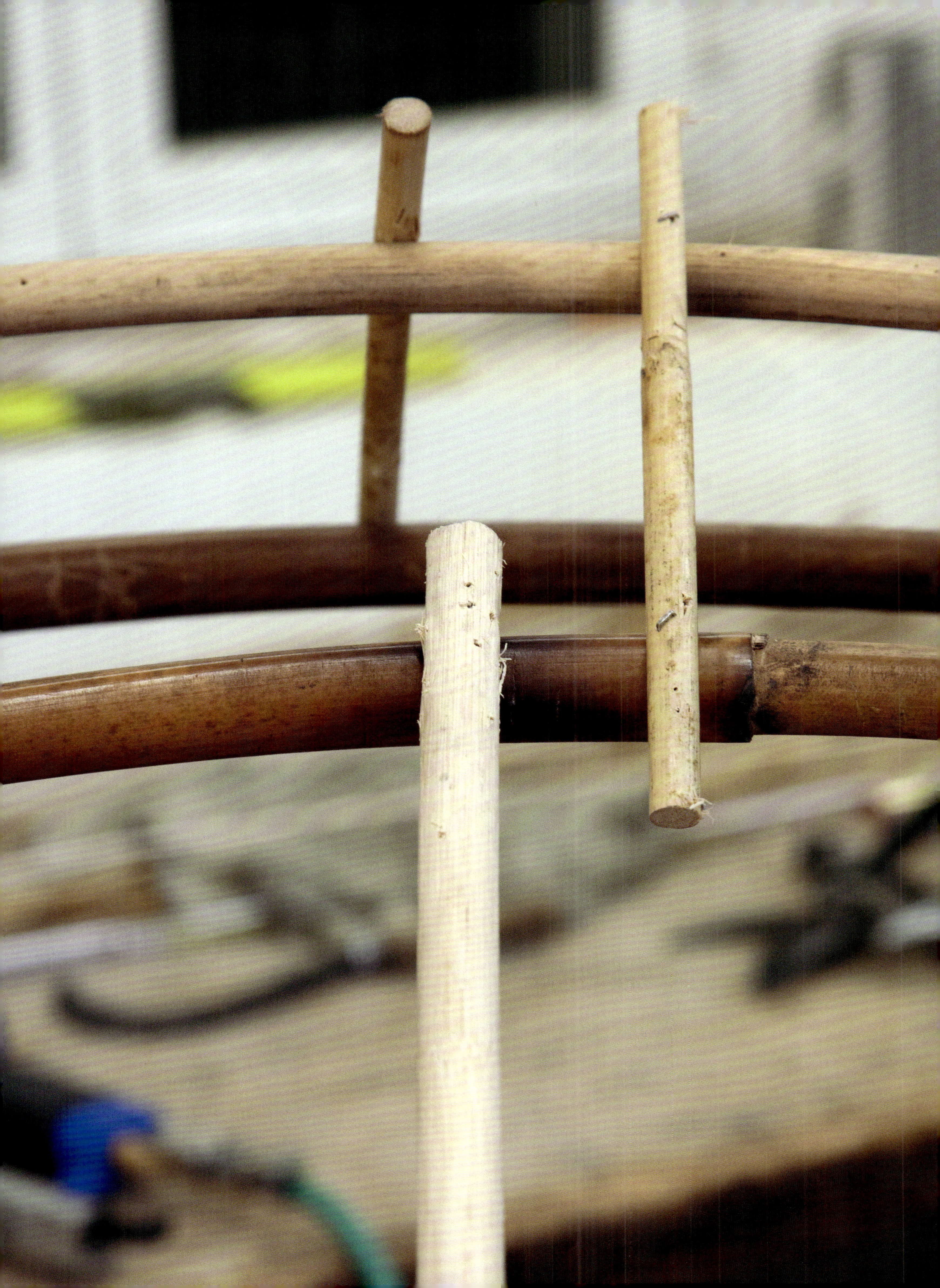

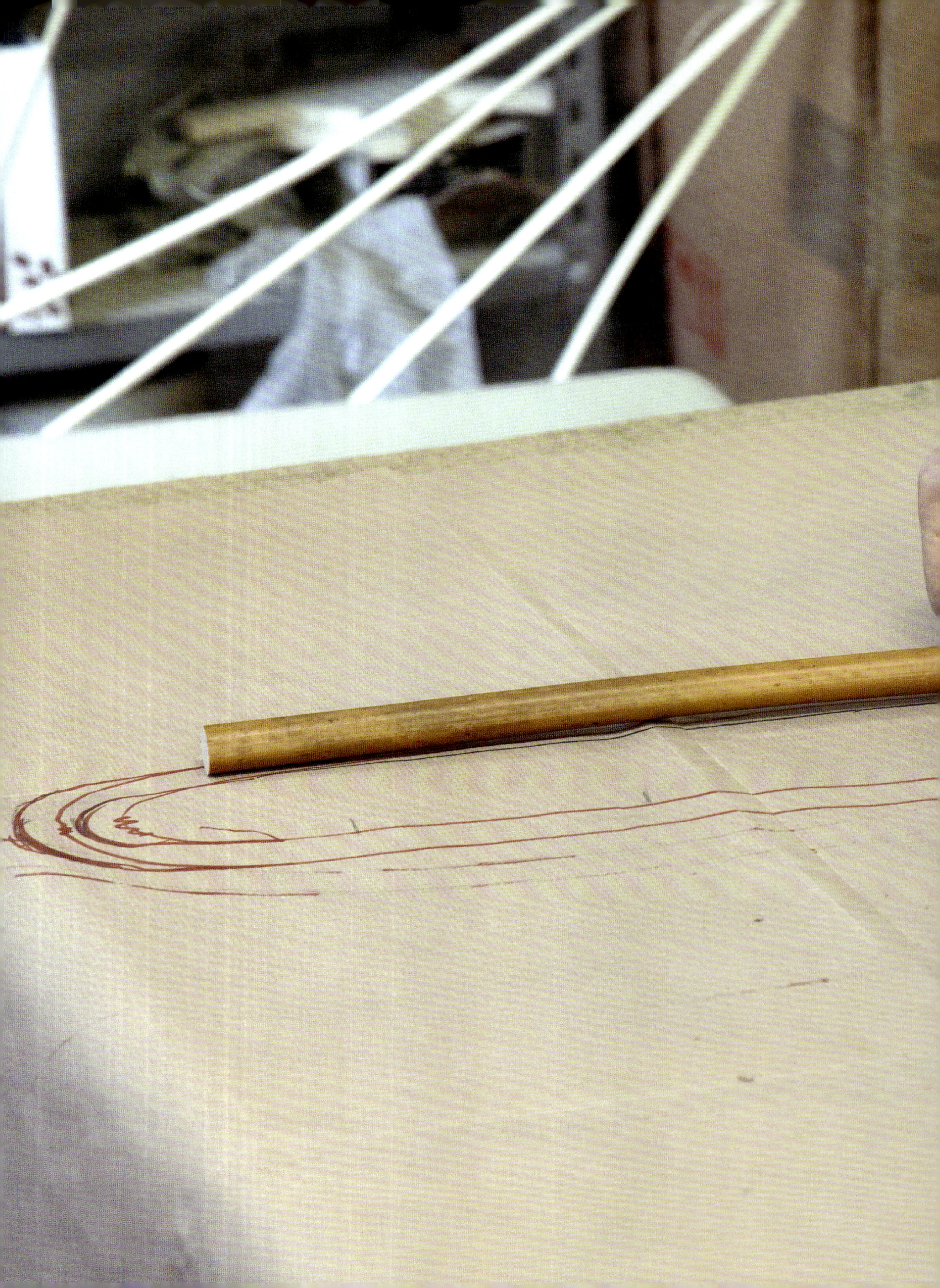

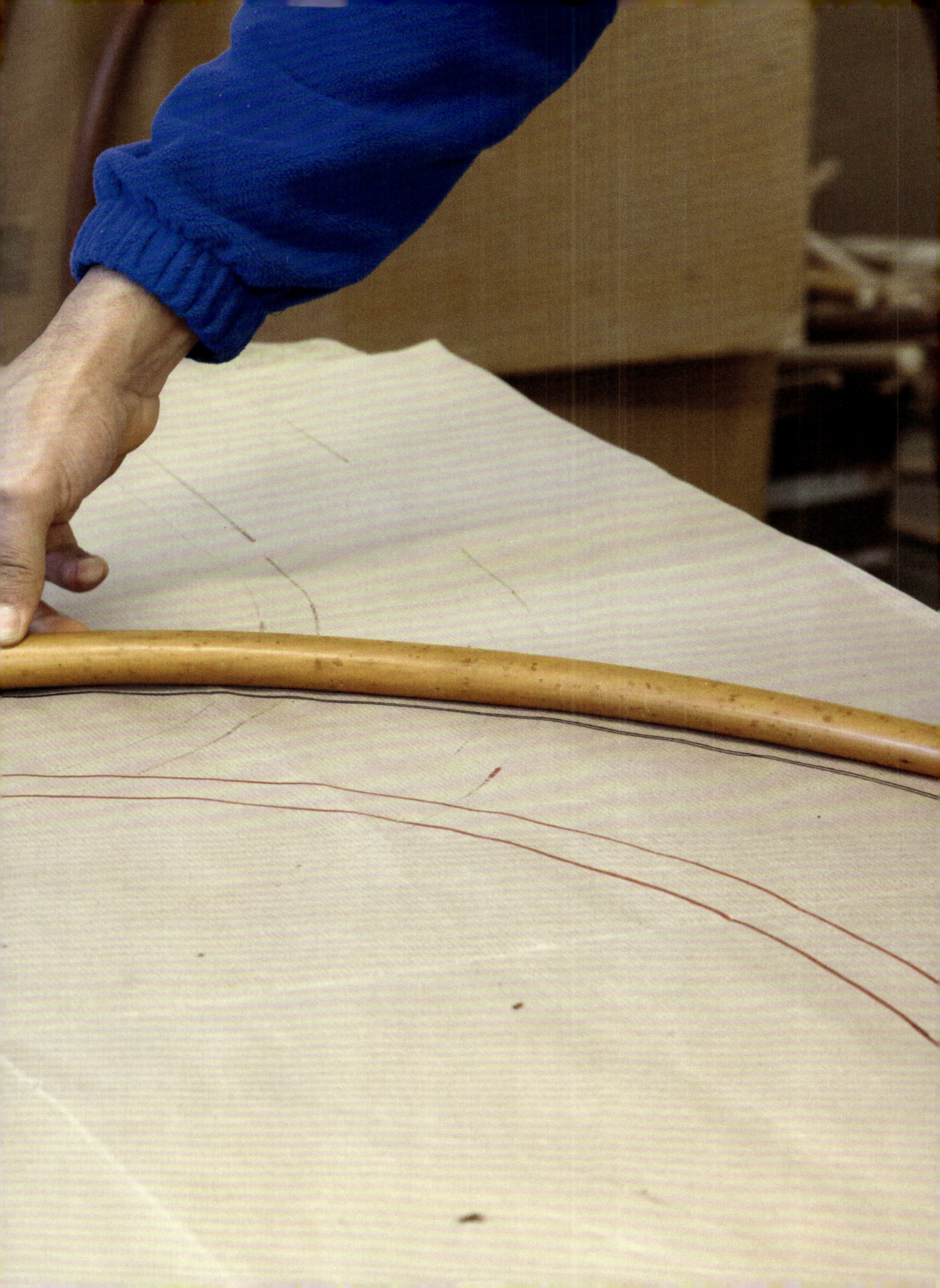

THE LAST DAYS IN GALLIATE
EXHIBITED WORKS

modified double impression, 2018
Linoleum
2800 × 4700 cm
Commissioned and produced by Pirelli HangarBicocca
Courtesy of the artist

alterated climbing form (I, II), 2017
alterated climbing form (III), 2017
alterated climbing form (IV), 2018
Painted brass, steel cable
Various dimensions
Courtesy of the artist and Marian Goodman Gallery

enlarged rods, 2018
Wood, brass, cotton rope
24 elements, 460 × 15 × 15 cm each
Courtesy of the artist

shed, 2018
Powder coated aluminum, brass
32 elements, 460 × 50 × 50 cm each
Courtesy of the artist

alterated knot 4, 2018
alterated knot 5, 2018
alterated knot 6, 2018
alterated knot 7, 2018
Leather, aluminum tube, silicon tube, waxed nylon yarn, hemp rope
Various dimensions
Courtesy of the artist and Marian Goodman Gallery

Clara 2, 2018
Clara 4, 2018
Wood, rope
Various dimensions
Courtesy of the artist and kurimanzutto, Mexico City

discrepancies with F.H. (#1), 2018
discrepancies with F.H. (#2), 2018
discrepancies with F.H. (#3), 2018
discrepancies with F.H. (#4), 2018
discrepancies with F.H. (#5), 2018
discrepancies with F.H. (#6), 2018
discrepancies with F.H. (#7), 2018
discrepancies with F.H. (#8), 2018
Brass, hemp rope
Various dimensions
Courtesy of the artist

Franca (#1), 2018
Franca (#2), 2018
Franca (#3), 2018
Franca (#4), 2018
Franca (#5), 2018
Franca (#6), 2018
Rattan, rattan-core, hemp rope
Various dimensions
Commissioned and produced by Pirelli HangarBicocca
Courtesy of the artist

random intersections #20, 2018
Leather, nylon yarn
430 × 70 × 50 cm
Courtesy of the artist and kurimanzutto, Mexico City

the last days in Galliate, 2018
Leather, aluminum tube, silicon tube, hemp rope
3 elements, 465 × 590 × 260 cm overall
Courtesy of the artist

lamps, 2018
Brass and iron
23 lamps, various dimensions
Courtesy of the artist and kurimanzutto, Mexico City

OPERE IN MOSTRA

modified double impression
[doppia impressione modificata], 2018
Linoleum
2800 × 4700 cm
Commissionato e prodotto da Pirelli HangarBicocca
Courtesy dell'artista

alterated climbing form
[forma rampicante alterata] *(I, II)*, 2017
alterated climbing form (III), 2017
alterated climbing form (IV), 2018
Ottone dipinto, cavo d'acciaio
Dimensioni varie
Courtesy dell'artista e di Marian Goodman Gallery

enlarged rods [aste ingrandite], 2018
Legno, ottone, corda di cotone
24 elementi, 460 × 15 × 15 cm ciascuno
Courtesy dell'artista

shed, 2018
Alluminio verniciato a polvere, ottone
32 elementi, 460 × 50 × 50 cm ciascuno
Courtesy dell'artista

alterated knot [nodo alterato] *4*, 2018
alterated knot 5, 2018
alterated knot 6, 2018
alterated knot 7, 2018
Cuoio, tubo di alluminio, tubo di silicone, filo di nylon cerato, corda di canapa
Dimensioni varie
Courtesy dell'artista e di Marian Goodman Gallery

Clara 2, 2018
Clara 4, 2018
Legno, corda
Dimensioni varie
Courtesy dell'artista e di kurimanzutto, Città del Messico

discrepancies with F.H.
[discrepanze con F.H.] *(#1)*, 2018
discrepancies with F.H. (#2), 2018
discrepancies with F.H. (#3), 2018
discrepancies with F.H. (#4), 2018
discrepancies with F.H. (#5), 2018
discrepancies with F.H. (#6), 2018
discrepancies with F.H. (#7), 2018
discrepancies with F.H. (#8), 2018
Ottone, corda di canapa
Dimensioni varie
Courtesy dell'artista

Franca (#1), 2018
Franca (#2), 2018
Franca (#3), 2018
Franca (#4), 2018
Franca (#5), 2018
Franca (#6), 2018
Giunco, midollino, corda di canapa
Dimensioni varie
Commissionato e prodotto da Pirelli HangarBicocca
Courtesy dell'artista

random intersections [intersezioni casuali] *#20*, 2018
Cuoio, filo di nylon
430 × 70 × 50 cm
Courtesy dell'artista e di kurimanzutto, Città del Messico

the last days in Galliate [gli ultimi giorni a Galliate], 2018
Cuoio, tubo di alluminio, tubo di silicone, corda di canapa
3 elementi, 465 × 590 × 260 cm complessivamente
Courtesy dell'artista

lamps [lampade], 2018
Ottone e ferro
23 lampade, dimensioni varie
Courtesy dell'artista e di kurimanzutto, Città del Messico

Leonor Antunes lives and works in Berlin. She graduated from the Faculty of Art at the University of Lisbon in 1998 with a degree in Visual Arts and Sculpture, and subsequently continued her studies at the Staatliche Akademie der Bildended Künste in Karlsruhe, Germany.

Her work has been exhibited at many internationally renowned institutions, including Pirelli HangarBicocca, Milan (2018–2019); Museo Tamayo, Mexico City (2018); Whitechapel Gallery, London (2017–2018); San Francisco Museum of Modern Art, San Francisco (2016); CAPC musée d'art contemporain de Bordeaux, Bordeaux (2015–2016); New Museum, New York (2015); Kunsthalle Basel, Basel (2013); Fundação de Serralves, Oporto (2011); Museo Experimental El Eco, Mexico City (2011). Her work has also been displayed at important collective exhibitions, such as 12th Gwangju Biennale (2018); 57. Venice Biennale (2017); 12th Sharjah Biennale (2015); 8th Berlin Biennale (2014), and 3rd Singapore Biennale (2011). In 2019, she represented Portugal at the 58. Venice Biennale.

Briony Fer is an art historian who has written extensively on modern and contemporary art. Her research interests have consistently moved between the history of the avant-gardes and the work of contemporary artists, including Gabriel Orozco, Roni Horn, and Tacita Dean. Her books include *Gabriel Orozco: Thinking in Circles* (2013), *Eva Hesse: Studiowork* (2009), *The Infinite Line* (2004), *On Abstract Art* (1997). She co-curated the Anni Albers retrospective at Tate Modern in 2018. She is Professor of History of Art at University College London and a Fellow of the British Academy.

Tom McDonough is a writer and critic based in upstate New York and Toronto. He writes extensively on contemporary art, including recent essays on Leonor Antunes, Theaster Gates, Mario García Torres, Amie Siegel, Christopher Williams, and Haegue Yang. His articles have appeared in journals such as *BOMB*, *Canadian Art*, *Parkett*, *Texte zur Kunst*, and *OSMOS*, where he is a contributing editor. *Boredom*, his anthology in the "Documents in Contemporary Art" series from the Whitechapel, appeared in 2017. He has taught at University of California, Berkeley, and Harvard, and is currently Associate Professor of Art History at Binghamton University, State University of New York.

Antonio Piva graduated in Architecture from the Istituto Universitario di Architettura in Venice. He trained in the studio of Franco Albini and Franca Helg on key themes of architecture, design, and museum studies. In 1975, he was a founding partner of the Franco Albini-Franca Helg-Antonio Piva-Marco Albini studio, which in 2002 became Antonio Piva Michele Piva Architetti Associati. Director of the DIAP design workshop and president of the Architecture and Society study course as well as professor of Architecture Design at the School of Architecture and Society at the Politecnico in Milan, Piva has authored numerous essays and publications on museum studies and architecture criticism.

Roberta Tenconi is Curator at Pirelli HangarBicocca in Milan where she recently curated the solo shows by Giorgio Andreotta Calò (2019), Leonor Antunes, Matt Mullican, Eva Kot'átková (2018), Rosa Barba (2017), Laure Prouvost (2016), Petrit Halilaj (2015), and the group show *Take Me (I'm Yours)* (2017). Part of the curatorial team of the 55. Venice Biennale "The Encyclopedic Palace" (2013) and of the 4th Berlin Biennale (2006), between 2006 and 2015 she worked as Assistant Curator for the Fondazione Nicola Trussardi, Milan.

Leonor Antunes vive e lavora a Berlino. Nel 1998 si laurea in Arti visive e Scultura presso la Facoltà di Arte dell'Universidade de Lisboa, proseguendo poi gli studi presso la Staatliche Akademie der Bildended Künste a Karlsruhe, in Germania.

Il suo lavoro è stato esposto in numerose istituzioni di rilievo internazionale, tra cui Pirelli HangarBicocca, Milano (2018–2019); Museo Tamayo, Città del Messico (2018); Whitechapel Gallery, Londra (2017–2018); San Francisco Museum of Modern Art, San Francisco (2016); CAPC musée d'art contemporain de Bordeaux, Bordeaux (2015–2016); New Museum, New York (2015); Kunsthalle Basel, Basilea (2013); Fundação de Serralves, Porto (2011); Museo Experimental El Eco, Città del Messico (2011). Le sue opere sono inoltre state presentate nell'ambito di importanti rassegne, quali 12ma Biennale di Gwangju (2018); 57ma Biennale di Venezia (2017); 12ma Biennale di Sharjah (2015); 8ª Biennale di Berlino (2014) e 3^{a} Biennale di Singapore (2011). Nel 2019 ha rappresentato il Portogallo alla 58ma Biennale di Venezia.

Briony Fer è storica dell'arte e autrice di molti volumi dedicati all'arte moderna e contemporanea. La sua ricerca si è sempre mossa tra la storia delle avanguardie e la produzione di artisti contemporanei come Gabriel Orozco, Roni Horn e Tacita Dean. Tra i suoi libri si annoverano *Gabriel Orozco: Thinking in Circles* (2013), *Eva Hesse: Studiowork* (2009), *The Infinite Line* (2004), *On Abstract Art* (1997). Co-curatrice della retrospettiva su Anni Albers alla Tate Modern nel 2018, è docente di Storia dell'arte all'University College London e membro della British Academy.

Tom McDonough, scrittore e critico, si divide tra upstate New York e Toronto. È autore di numerosi testi d'arte contemporanea, tra cui alcuni recenti saggi su Leonor Antunes, Theaster Gates, Mario García Torres, Amie Siegel, Christopher Williams e Haegue Yang. I suoi articoli sono comparsi in riviste come "BOMB" "Canadian Art", "Parkett", "Texte zur Kunst" e "OSMOS", con cui collabora regolarmente. *Boredom*, la sua antologia contenuta nella collana "Documents in Contemporary Art" della Whitechapel Gallery, è uscita nel 2017. Ha insegnato sia all'University of California a Berkeley sia a Harvard e attualmente è professore associato di Storia dell'arte alla Binghamton University, State University of New York.

Antonio Piva si laurea in Architettura all'Istituto Universitario di Architettura di Venezia. Si forma presso lo studio di Franco Albini e Franca Helg sui grandi temi del progetto di architettura, del design e della museografia. Nel 1975 aderisce alla formazione dello studio Franco Albini-Franca Helg-Antonio Piva-Marco Albini, che nel 2002 diventa Antonio Piva Michele Piva Architetti Associati. Già professore ordinario di Progettazione architettonica presso la Facoltà di Architettura e Società del Politecnico di Milano, direttore del Laboratorio di Progettazione del DIAP e presidente del Corso di Studi in Architettura e Società, Piva è autore di numerosi saggi e volumi di museografia e di critica architettonica.

Roberta Tenconi è curatore presso Pirelli HangarBicocca, dove ha recentemente curato le personali di Giorgio Andreotta Calò (2019), Leonor Antunes, Matt Mullican, Eva Kot'átková (2018), Rosa Barba (2017), Laure Prouvost (2016), Petrit Halilaj (2015) e la collettiva "Take Me (I'm Yours)" (2017). Parte del team curatoriale della 55ma Biennale di Venezia "Il Palazzo Enciclopedico" (2013) e della 4ª Biennale di Berlino (2006), tra il 2006 e il 2015 ha lavorato come assistente curatore alla Fondazione Nicola Trussardi di Milano.

ACKNOWLEDGMENTS/ RINGRAZIAMENTI

First and foremost we would like to thank
Desideriamo innanzitutto ringraziare:
Leonor Antunes for her invaluable commitment and energy to the exhibition project and to this publication/ per l'inesauribile energia e il costante dialogo profusi nella realizzazione della mostra e di questa pubblicazione

We would like to thank the Lenders
Vorremmo ringraziare i Prestatori:
Marian Goodman Gallery
kurimanzutto, Mexico City
Studio Leonor Antunes

For their precious help
Per il loro prezioso aiuto:
A Practice for Everyday Life, Alessandra Abbate, Air de Paris, Paola Albini, Elena Albricci, Ellen Arkbro, Nick Ash, Malena Bach, Margherita Baetta, Francesco Barcella, Massimo Berardini, Antonia Bonacina, Margherita Bonacina, Mario Bonacina, Florence Bonnefous, Giulia Burgato Negro, Lorenzo Cannavale, Fabio Carboni, Nicole Colombo, Monica del Torchio, Michele De Lucchi, Sophie de Saint Phalle, Roberto Dipasquale, Daniele Fabiani, Attila Faravelli, Briony Fer, Andrea Ferrari, Stefano Gadda, Galeria Luisa Strina, Dimitri Giardino, Francesca Girardi, Chiara Guizzi, Robin Hayward, Andrew Leslie Heyward, Saehee Hwang, Giuseppe Ielasi, Hilary Jeffrey, Elena Kakaliagou, Heinz Peter Knes, Julia Koropoulos, Tilbe Kucukonder, José Kuri, kurimanzutto, Salvatore Licitra, Maddalena Londero, Alessandro Longoni, Michele Maddalo, Maria Isabel Malo, Mónica Manzutto, Marian Goodman Gallery, Carlo Martini, Vittoria Martini, Tom McDonough, Edouard Merino, Luigi Meroni, Dario Moalli, Cristina Moro, Nikita Mosca, Paola Nicolin, Matteo Nobile, Margot O'Sullivan, Lorenza Pambianco, Antonio Piva, Michele Piva, Maria Quiroga, Éliane Radigue, Iolanda Ratti, Laura Riboldi, Hong Sang Hee, Marco Secondin, Luisa Strina, Simone Trabucchi, Francesca Vaccaro, Laura Voghera, Nina Yashar

We also thank
Ringraziamo inoltre:
Editore FrancoAngeli for the kind concession for the republication of the text by/per la gentile concessione per la ripubblicazione del testo di Antonio Piva

The artist wishes to personally thank
L'artista vorrebbe ringraziare personalmente:
Sergio and/e Olga Taborda for their daily confidence and support/per la fiducia e il supporto quotidiano, Franca Helg, Franco Albini, Marta Luzena, Heinz Peter Knes, Nick Ash, Julian Schulz, Mario Bonacina, kurimanzutto, Marian Goodman Gallery, Galeria Luisa Strina, Air de Paris Gallery, Briony Fer, Tom McDonough, Franco Albini Foundation, Antonio Piva, Saehee Hwang, Andrew Leslie Heyward, Margot O'Sullivan, Mónica Manzutto, José Kuri, Malena Bach, Luisa Strina, Maria Quiroga

PHOTO CREDITS/ CREDITI FOTOGRAFICI

Photos by
Foto di:
Heinz Peter Knes (pp. 3–15, 35–51, 144–155, 168–177, and/e back cover/quarta di copertina), N ck Ash (pp. 63–131)

All images
Tutte le immagini:
Courtesy Pirelli HangarBicccca and/e Leonor Antunes

Chairman
Presidente
Marco Tronchetti Provera
Board of Directors
Consiglio di Amministrazione
Maurizio Abet
Nina Bassoli
Gustavo Bracco
Elena Pontiggia
Ilaria Tronchetti Provera
General Manager
Marco Lanata
Operations Manager
Paolo Bruno Malaspina

Artistic Director
Direttore Artistico
Vicente Todolí

Curator
Curatore
Roberta Tenconi
Assistant Curator
Assistente Curatore
Lucia Aspesi
Assistant Curator
Assistente Curatore
Fiammetta Griccioli
Research and Editorial Assistant
Assistente alla Ricerca e Pubblicazioni
Mariagiulia Leuzzi

Head of Cultural and Institutional Programs
Responsabile Programmi Culturali e Istituzionali
Giovanna Amadasi
Educational
Progetti Educativi
Laura Zocco
Music and Sound Performance Curator
Pedro Rocha

Head of Communication and Press Office
Responsabile Comunicazione e Ufficio Stampa
Angiola Maria Gili
Press Office and Digital Communication
Ufficio Stampa e Comunicazione digitale
Alessandro Cane
Communication
Comunicazione
Francesca Trovalusci

Partnership Development
Sviluppo Partnership
Fabienne Binoche

Event Organization and Bookshop
Organizzazione Eventi e Bookshop
Valentina Piccioni

Head of Production
Responsabile di Produzione
Valentina Fossati
Installation
Allestimenti
Matteo De Vittor
Installation
Allestimenti
Cesare Rossi

Registrar
Dario Leone

Leonor Antunes
the last days in Galliate
Pirelli HangarBicocca
14.09.2018–13.01.2019

Exhibition curated by
Mostra a cura di
Roberta Tenconi

Assistant Curator
Assistente Curatore
Lucia Aspesi

Installation
Allestimenti
Valentina Fossati with/con Matteo De Vittor

Lenders
Prestatori
Marian Goodman Gallery
kurimanzutto, Mexico City
Studio Leonor Antunes

Public Program
Curated by/A cura di Giovanna Amadasi

Lecture with/Incontro con Briony Fer, Leonor Antunes, Roberta Tenconi
21.11.2018

Sound performance by/di Zinc & Copper
Program/Programma:
Ellen Arkbro – *THREE*
Zinc & Copper with/con Leonor Antunes – new composition/nuova composizione
Éliane Radigue – *OCCAM OCEAN – DELTA X* for/per Zinc & Copper
Curated by/A cura di Pedro Rocha
18.12.2018

Is architecture a craftsmanship?
L'architettura è artigianato?
Lecture with/Incontro con Michele De Lucchi
10.01.2019

Art Handling
Allestimento Opere
Attitudine Forma
Engie
Tarkett
Way

Technical Support
Supporto e Assistenza Tecnica
Massimo Berardini
Alessandro Longoni

Executive Project, Safety, and Permits
Progetto Esecutivo e Sicurezza
Francesco Barcella
Studio Mosae

Technical and Structural Project
Progetto Tecnico-Strutturale
Luisa Basiricò
Studio Mosae

Conservation and Registrar
Conservazione e Registrar
Yulia Kalinichenko
Dario Leone

Graphic Design
Leftloft

Photographs
Fotografia
Nick Ash

Video
Documentazione Video
Francesco Margaroli

Insurance
Assicurazione
Lloyd's

Transports
Trasporti
Cordova Plaza
Crown Fine Art
HT Transport

Sponsor

PIRELLI

The catalogue is published on the occasion of the exhibition
Il catalogo è pubblicato in occasione della mostra

Leonor Antunes
the last days in Galliate
Pirelli HangarBicocca
14.09.2018-13.01.2019
pirellihangarbicocca.org

Catalogue edited by
Catalogo a cura di
Roberta Tenconi

Managing Editor
Lucia Aspesi with/con Teodora di Robilant

Texts by
Testi di
Briony Fer
Tom McDonough
Antonio Piva
Roberta Tenconi

Design
A Practice for Everyday Life

Editorial Coordination
Coordinamento Editoriale
Vincenza Russo

Editing
Redazione
Emily Ligniti
Alessandro Prandoni

Translations
Traduzione
Gordon Fisher, Traduzioni Liquide
Roberta Zuppet

Printing
Stampa
Gianotten printed media, Tilburg

First published in Italy in 2019 by
Skira Editore S.p.A.
Palazzo Casati Stampa
via Torino 61
20123 Milano
Italy
www.skira.net

Printed and bound in the Netherlands. First edition

ISBN: 978-88-572-4102-9

Distributed in USA, Canada, Central & South America by
ARTBOOK | D.A.P. 75 Broad Street Suite 630
New York, NY 10004, USA.

Distributed elsewhere in the world by
Thames and Hudson Ltd., 181A High Holborn,
London WC1V 7QX, United Kingdom.

Finito di stampare nel mese di agosto 2019
a cura di Skira, Milano
Printed in the Netherlands

This publication has received additional support from/
La pubblicazione ha ricevuto supporto aggiuntivo da:
Air de Paris; Galeria Luisa Strina, São Paulo; kurimanzutto, Mexico City; Marian Goodman Gallery